KU-257-194

Nuno Severiano Teixeira
and António Costa Pinto
Edited by

The Europeanization of Portuguese Democracy

SOCIAL SCIENCE MONOGRAPHS, BOULDER

DISTRIBUTED BY COLUMBIA UNIVERSITY PRESS, NEW YORK

2012

© 2012 Nuno Severiano Teixeira and António Costa Pinto

ISBN 978-0-88033-946-9

Library of Congress Control Number: 2012931142

Printed in the United States of America

Contents

List of Tables

List of Figures

Preface and Acknowledgements

Driven primarily by political concerns to secure democracy, Portugal's accession to the EU in 1986 also served as a catalyst for dynamic economic development following a complex process of democratization as well as the decolonization of Europe's last empire. This book looks at how the European Union (EU) helped shape the political process in Portugal on such matters as key institutions, elites and citizen attitude.

The introduction by Nuno Severiano Teixeira, entitled "Portugal and European Integration, 1974–2010", frames Portugal's participation in the process of European integration in historical perspective. The text encompasses the period of the democratic regime (1974–to date), characterizing the various steps of Portugal's position towards the evolution of the European project, while also evaluating the cost/benefit of Portugal's Europeanization.

In Chapter 2, "The Portuguese Political Elites and the European Union", João Pedro Ruivo, Diogo Moreira, António Costa Pinto and Pedro Tavares de Almeida, analyze the attitude of the Portuguese national political elites towards the European polity, their evaluation of the political institutions of the European Union and which kinds of policies should, in their opinion, be delegated by the member states to the European supranational level of government.

In Chapter 3, "Governing from Lisbon or Governing from Brussels? Models and Tendencies of the Europeanization of the Portuguese government", Carlos Jalali evaluates both the extent and process of the Europeanization of executive power in Portugal, with particular emphasis on the period subsequent to the country's accession in 1986. The Portuguese experience tends to confirm the notion that European integration processes generate an adaptation by national institutions to European demands, rather than fundamental transformations. At the same time, the Portuguese adaptation process appears to contradict the theoretical prediction that centralized and unitary states will experience a more difficult process of adaptation.

In Chapter 4, "Implementing the Treaty of Lisbon: The Portuguese Parliament as an Actor in the European Legislative Arena", Madalena Meyer Resende and Maria Teresa Paulo consider the response of the Portuguese parliament to the Treaty of Lisbon's (2009) provisions for the involvement of national parliaments in the European legislative process, by providing a quantitative and qualitative assessment of the parliament's work in the scrutiny of European legislation since 2006.

Chapter 5, "Europeanization of the Portuguese Courts", by Nuno Piçarra and Francisco Pereira Coutinho, deals with the Portuguese courts' assimilation of the European Union legal order since the accession of Portugal in 1986 and reviews "European duties" entrusted to the courts in the member states, as made explicit by the European Court of Justice in the framework of the preliminary ruling procedure, and the way Portuguese courts have implemented such duties during the last two decades.

Chapter 6, "The Europeanization of Portuguese Interest Groups? Trade Unions and Employers' Organizations", by Sebastián Royo, looks at the impact of the European integration process on Portugal's industrial relations. European integration has led to the transformation of the Portuguese economy and influenced the strategies and actions of social actors, namely, the transformation of Portuguese trade unions and employer associations, and outlines the main features of the country's industrial relations framework.

In Chapter 7, "European Integration and Party Attachments: The Portuguese Case as an Example for New Democracies", André Freire analyzes the impact of voting behaviour in elections to the European Parliament on the anchors of partisanship in Portugal (as an example of a new democracy). Concluding that, as a consequence of their second-order nature, elections to the European Parliament are usually contested by the same actors, emphasizing mainly the same (national) issues and de-emphasizing European issues.

Chapter 8, "The Support in Portugal for European Integration: Dimensions and Tendencies", by Pedro Magalhães, notes that the indicators of instrumental support for European integration have exhibited a tendency to decline since 1992. Furthermore, it argues there is also an apparent increase of another form of support for integration: accepting the sharing of power between member states and the EU's institutions in the definition of public policies. It suggests the nature of the reservoir of support for integration is changing in Portugal, from one based in the perception of benefits accruing to the nation state, towards support based in the acceptance of the EU as a political community and political system.

The conclusion, "Europeanization and Democratization in Portugal: Brothers-in-Arms or *Frères Ennemis?*", by Maarten Vink, returns to the central theme of the book and discusses the broader implications of European integration for Portuguese democracy, using the findings from the preceding chapters to discuss to what extent European integration has strengthened or undermined democracy in Portugal.

* * *

This book succeeds an earlier edition, also published by this press, titled *Southern Europe and the making of the European Union* (2003), which focused primarily on a comparative analysis of the pre-accession period in Southern Europe. The focus of this text is on the Portuguese case alone during the period following accession, i.e. an investigation of 25 years of Europeanization.

This book is the result of a revised and updated edition of a selection of papers presented at the Portuguese Institute of International Relations, Universidade Nova de Lisboa's (IPRI-UNL) summer school in June 2006, which was organized by the editors, IPRI-UNL, the European Commission in Lisbon and the Municipality of Óbidos.

The authors would like to express their sincere thanks to all of those who provided the institutional and financial support that has made it possible to produce this volume. We would especially like to thank the *Diário de Notícias* and LUSA-Agência de Notícias de Portugal, for their support for the IPRI-UNL summer school, and the Luso American Development Foundation (FLAD) and Instituto Português de Relações Internacionais-Universidade Nova de Lisboa (IPRI-UNL) and the Institute of Social Science, University of Lisbon (ICS-UL) for editing support.

We would also like to thank all those who attended the IPRI-UNL summer school conferences and debates, including those who did not publish their contribution, especially António Vitorino, a former EU commissioner who at the time was president of the European Affairs Parliamentary Commission, and who presided over the summer school's closing session.

We extend our special gratitude to Stewart Lloyd-Jones of CPHRC Editorial Services, who translated and edited many of the contributions to this volume, typeset the book and composed the index, to Alexandra Abreu Loureiro for her assistance in preparing this volume, and Isabel Alcario for organizing and providing the project with constant support.

The editors, Nuno Severiano Teixeira and António Costa Pinto, would like to thank their academic institutions—FCSH-UNL and ICS-UL, respectively—for having provided them with the conditions which made it possible to work on this volume.

A final word of thanks must go to Nancy Tyson for including this volume in this series.

1 | Introduction: Portugal and European Integration, 1974–2010

Nuno Severiano Teixeira

Introduction

Two political factors conditioned Portugal's integration into the process of European unification between 1945 and 1974: the dictatorial nature of Salazar's regime and its tenacious resistance to decolonization.[1] It was only following the institutionalization of democracy and the process of decolonization during 1974–75 that the first serious steps were taken to follow a strategy of integrating Portugal into what was then the European Economic Community (EEC).

Portugal did not experience the same levels of international isolation as neighbouring Spain following the Second World War. Its status as a founding member of the North Atlantic Treaty Organization (NATO) and as a participant within other international organizations such as the Organization for European Economic Cooperation (OEEC) and the European Payments Union (EPU), and the fact it received funds from the Marshall Plan—albeit on a relatively small scale—are all examples of the country's international acceptance.

1 N. S. Teixeira, "Between Africa and Europe: Portuguese foreign policy, 1890-1986", in A.C. Pinto (ed.) *Modern Portugal* (Palo Alto, CA: SPOSS, 1998), pp. 60–87; A. C. Pinto, *O fim do Império português: A cena internacional, a guerra colonial e a descolonização, 1961–1975* (Lisbon: Horizonte, 2000).

Excluded from and mistrustful of the Treaty of Rome, which paved the way to the EEC, and following positions adopted by the United Kingdom, Portugal's membership of the European Free Trade Association (EFTA) was an important economic aim for the dictatorship throughout the 1960s.[2] Negotiated on favourable terms for Portugal, which saw most of its economic activities largely protected, the EFTA agreement laid the ground for the economic growth of the 1960s and the significant increase in commercial relations with Europe. It also boosted the emergence of interest groups less involved with the colonies. However, the development of a pro-European outlook was essentially a consequence of the decolonization process and the institutionalization of democracy.

Following a complex transition process, the Portugal's integration into the EEC became a strategic objective, with simultaneous political and economic overtones. Democratic consolidation and European integration in were to become inseparable.

Democracy and European Integration (1974–1986)

The military coup of 25 April 1974, paved the way for the institutionalization of Portuguese democracy. Portugal's transition occurred at the height of the Cold War, a time when there were few international pressures for democratization. The rupture provoked by the military coup accentuated the crisis of the state, fuelled by the simultaneous process of democratization and decolonization of the last European colonial empire.[3] Powerful tensions, which incorporated revolutionary elements, were

2   N. Andresen Leitão, "Portugal's European integration policy, 1947–1972", *Journal of European Integration History* 7 (2001), pp. 25–35.

3   K. Maxwell, *The making of Portuguese democracy* (Cambridge: Cambridge University Press, 1997).

concentrated into the first two years of Portugal's democracy. During 1974–75, Portugal also experienced a high level of foreign intervention, ranging from diplomatic pressure to the creation of political parties and social organizations (such as trade unions and interest groups), as well as the anti-left strategies of the so-called 1975 "hot summer". As a result, Portugal was a constant topic of discussion at international forums from NATO to the EEC, and within the institutions of the Soviet bloc.

The military coup took the international community, particularly the United States, by surprise.[4] Faced with the intense social and political mobilization of the left, and concerned with the flight of the country's capital and its economic elite, the moderate parties only had limited success in establishing themselves and were only able to function during the crisis due to financial and technical support from leading figures in the US administration and from other European 'political families', mainly the German Social Democrats, which often served as guarantors.

Transition to Democracy and Decolonization

The EEC observed Portugal's transition with discretion, although it gave ambiguous signals. It favoured the emergence of a pluralist democratic system, whilst simultaneously granting some limited economic assistance. In 1975, soon after the first democratic elections, the European Council announced it was prepared to begin economic and financial negotiations with Portugal, although it stressed that, "in accordance with its historical and political traditions, the European Community can only support a pluralist democracy".[5]

4   M. del Pero, "Kissinger e la politica estera americana nel Mediterraneo: Il caso portoghese", *Studi Storici* 4 (2001), pp. 973–88.

5   See J. Magone, "A integração europeia e a construção da democracia portu-

The first significant international challenge for Portuguese democracy was the disposal of its colonial empire. The second was to open the country to the world and re-establish diplomatic relations with all countries, bringing an end to the international isolation suffered by the deposed regime.[6] Decolonization and the re-establishment of diplomatic relations did not constitute a new strategic direction for Portugal's foreign policy; rather, in the midst of the strenuous conflicts during the process of democratization, there was another silent battle taking place, one concerned with the international strategic choices to be made by the new democracy.

The transition period was characterized by a political and ideological conflict centred on the country's foreign policy goals and which was translated into the practice of parallel diplomatic actions led through various institutional agents, and which was consequently reflected in the absence of a clear foreign policy.

Despite the conflicts, hesitations and indecision, the provisional governments, particularly those with a preponderance of military ministers, tended to favour adopting a Third-World approach to foreign policy and promoted the formation of special relations with the former colonies. This was the final manifestation, albeit in a pro-socialist form, of the thesis that was so close to Salazar's heart—Portugal's "African vocation".

guesa", in A. C. Pinto and N. S. Teixeira (eds), *Penélope: Portugal e a unificação europeia*, 18 (1998), p. 137. See also J. Magone, *European Portugal: The difficult road to sustainable democracy* (London: Macmillan, 1997).

6   S. MacDonald, *European destiny, Atlantic transformations: Portuguese foreign policy under the Second Republic* (New Brunswick, NJ: Transaction, 1993); J. M. Ferreira, "Political costs and benefits for Portugal arising from membership of the European Community", in J. da S. Lopes (ed.), *Portugal and EC membership evaluated* (London: Pinter, 1993); J. Gama, "A adesão de Portugal às Comunidades Europeias", *Política Internacional* 10, (1994-95), pp. 5–19.

The consolidation of democracy, which began with the election of the first constitutional government in 1976, can be characterized by a clear choice of Portuguese foreign policy as a Western country, simultaneously Atlanticist and European.

These were to become the basic strategic foreign policy vectors for the recent democracy. The Atlanticist outlook was predicated on the permanence of Portuguese foreign policy's historical characteristics, and played an important role both in directing Portugal externally and in stabilizing it domestically. The establishment of bilateral relations with the United States, and the strengthening of its multilateral participation within NATO, was the clearest expressions of the new democracy's international position.

Having finally overcome the Third World temptations of the revolutionary period, Portugal unreservedly adopted the "European option" from 1976 onwards. Now, however, this choice was a strategic decision and a political project, rather than the merely pragmatic, economic stance it had been under the authoritarian regime.

Democratic Consolidation, European Option and Adhesion to the EEC

Contacts between Lisbon and European institutions were initiated as early as 1974. The European Commission granted Portugal economic assistance while the European Council made its political position clear: it was ready to begin negotiations on the condition that pluralist democracy was established. Nevertheless, the country's economic situation, the political instability and continuing uncertainty during the transitional period ruled out any advance on the European front.

The first constitutional government, led by Mário Soares, adopted the "European option". The first step in this process took place in August 1976, when the Portuguese government successfully applied for membership at the Council of Europe. Once a member of this organization, which also consolidated the international community's recognition of the new democratic regime, Lisbon began to outline its next decisive step: its accession application to the EEC.

Following a series of successful negotiations in a number of European capitals between September 1976 and February 1977, the government made its formal application for EEC membership in March 1977. The European Council accepted Portugal's application the following month and initiated the formal accession process according to the treaties, including the mandatory consultation of the European Commission. In May 1978 the commission presented a favourable report, clearing the way for formal negotiations to begin in Luxembourg the following October.[7] With the formal application made, and accession negotiations under way, the hesitations and polemics over the nature of Portugal's integration had finally been superseded, placing Portugal firmly on the European path.

The government was motivated by, and based its decision to follow this strategic option on, two principal goals. First, EEC membership would consolidate Portuguese democracy; second, EEC assistance would guarantee the modernization of the country and its economic development. Several Portuguese economists remained fearful, with the majority expressing grave reservations

    7   J. M. Ferreira, "Os regimes políticos em Portugal e a organização internacional da Europa", *Política Internacional* 11 (1995), pp. 5–39.

regarding the impact EEC membership would have on some sectors of the Portuguese economy.[8]

There then followed a complex series of negotiations over the ensuing seven years. A first step had been taken in September 1976, prior to the country's formal application, with the revision of the 1972 EEC trade agreement through the conclusion of the Additional and Financial Protocols, which Portugal interpreted as representing a form of pre-membership agreement.[9] Despite these prior agreements, formal negotiations on Portugal's membership continued from October 1978 until June 1985.[10]

There were two important domestic factors explaining why the accession negotiations for such a small country with a relatively weak economy were so complex and drawn out. First, Portugal's economic situation immediately prior to transition and, more importantly, the economic measures taken during the revolutionary period—in particular, the nationalization of important economic sectors.

Second, the continuous governmental instability and the nature of the country's political and constitutional regime. After 1976 the democratic regime was undeniably pluralist and was generally considered as such; however, the 1976 constitution was a product of the revolutionary period, and consecrated within it the Council of the Revolution. It was a democracy, but a democracy under the tutelage of an undemocratic military institution. These factors weighed heavily in the negotiations, delaying their conclusion.

8   J. Cravinho, "Characteristics and motives for entry", in J. L. Sampedro and J. A. Payno (eds), *The enlargement of the European Community: Case studies of Greece, Portugal and Spain* (London: Macmillan, 1983), pp. 131–48. See also A. Tovias, *Foreign economic relations of the European Community: the impact of Spain and Portugal* (Boulder, CO, and London: Lynne Rienner, 1990).

9   Ferreira (note 7), p. 28.

10   P. Alvares and C. R. Fernandes (eds), *Portugal e o Mercado Comum: Dos Acordos de 1972 às negociações de adesão*, vol. 2 (Lisbon: Pórtico, 1980).

During the early 1980s, Portuguese democracy overcame all of these objections. The constitution was revised in 1982 and the Council was abolished. The new national defence law finally established the subordination of the armed forces to the civilian political authorities. By 1983, democracy in Portugal had been consolidated, clearing the domestic obstacles to the successful conclusion of the accession negotiations.

One external hurdle remained. In the framework of Europe's southern enlargement, the EEC was also conducting accession negotiations with neighbouring Spain, a much larger economy than Portugal, and a country that did not share its history of close relations with European economic institutions. Portugal's diplomatic strategy was to keep its negotiations separate from Spain, thus hoping to secure a fast track to accession, in order to guarantee the status of member state before Spain. This tactic unsuccessful, however, as the community's policy was to negotiate with both Iberian nations simultaneously. This resulted in Portugal's accession being delayed by two years, until negotiations with Spain had been concluded.

The accession process culminated in the signing of the Treaty of Accession by the new government led by Mário Soares in June 1985. Portugal became a full member of the EEC on 1 January 1986.

The Europeanization of Portugal (1986–2010)

Portugal's membership of EEC paved the way to a period of Europeanization of the Portuguese society, registering profound domestic and foreign policy changes. These changes followed the deepening and enlargement process of European integration.

Since the democratic constitution of 1976 came into force, Portugal has known a wide political consensus on foreign policy, particularly regarding European integration. Apart for cyclical moments of greater ideological cleavage, there has always been agreement in this matter between the main Portuguese political parties: the centre-left Socialist Party (PS), the centre-right Social Democratic Party (PSD) and the right wing Democratic and Social Centre (CDS).

Such an agreement is based upon the "perception of Portugal as a nation, simultaneously Atlantic and European", with the latter dimension being more important in recent decades.[11]

Faithful to its Atlantic roots, from 1986 Portugal's foreign policy strengthened its European focus. The "European option" played a fundamental role in the consolidation of democracy and in the country's modernization. Therefore, it can be said democratization and modernization were the main domestic echoes of Portugal's European integration during the last quarter of the 20th century.

Generally speaking, Portugal supported the 1986 Single European Act, the 1992 Maastricht Treaty and the ensuing treaties that deepened the process of European political and economic integration. The various governments viewed Portugal's presence in the European Union (EU) as a commission and council support guarantee for Portuguese economic and structural development plans, despite realizing these alterations implied changes at the domestic and foreign policy levels.[12]

This process was not linear. Three core moments highlight Portugal's participation in the European integration process after 1986.

11 S. Royo (ed.), *Portugal, Espanha e a integração Europeia: Um balanço* (Lisbon: Imprensa de Ciências Sociais, 2005), p. 36.

12 Royo (note 11).

First, between 1986 and 1992, which was characterized by a position of pragmatism and moderation towards the European integration process, as the country sought to adjust to the challenge of Europe.

Second, from 1992 to 2000, when Portugal's participation in the European project reached its peak with successive Portuguese governments placing the country at the forefront of the European integration process.

Finally, from 2000 onwards, which has seen a return to pragmatism, Portugal has used European integration tools to maximize its external role, balancing the costs and benefits of the country's presence at the heart of the EU.

Prudence and Pragmatism: The First Years of Membership

Portugal joined the EEC at the same time as the European integration process was getting under way. By 1986, the EEC was undergoing a period of institutional relaunch through the signing of the Single European Act (SEA), the first revision of the Treaty of Rome in about 30 years. This change received a cautious welcome in Portugal, as the political intensification brought about by the SEA led the political elite to doubt Portugal's ability to meet the new demands. The opening of the Portugal's economy, which was backward compared to most of its European partners meant the country's accession had to be followed by compensatory economic measures.[13]

In terms of the political goals, the Portuguese government, led since 1985 by Aníbal Cavaco Silva, followed a strategy that

---

13 P. Lains, "Os caminhos da integração: Da autarcia à Europa do Euro", in M. C. Lobo and P. Lains (eds), *Em nome da Europa: Portugal em mudança (1986–2006)* (Cascais: Princípia, 2007), pp. 14–40.

focused on the credibility of full Portuguese membership, while at the same time seeking to profit from the economic and social advantages arising from EEC participation.[14]

Despite the moderation and pragmatism of the Portuguese position, the first phase of the country's EEC membership was nevertheless marked by one of the base principles of the SEA: the decision to create a single market was intimately connected with the need to promote economic and social cohesion within the community. As a consequence, with the approval of the Delors I plan, Ireland and the countries of southern Europe received considerable levels of financial compensation to help them meet the challenges of an increasingly liberalised European market. This was decisive for Portugal. The Lisbon government was one of the main beneficiaries of these measures, with strong consequences in the structural transformations performed in Portugal. Such transformations also helped change the Portuguese public's perception of Europe and the benefits of the country's European integration.

If in the early years of membership the dominant perception was of one of concern, regarding the country's ability to meet the challenges of accessing the EEC. The massive financial transfers rendered clear and visible the advantages of integration, hence radically changing Portugal's perception of Europe.[15]

From the political perspective, European integration forced the Portuguese government to rethink its alliances within Europe. During the early years of membership, Portuguese prudence and the pragmatism of Cavaco Silva's governments, ensured Portugal retained its Atlanticist position, aligning with its former EFTA

14 V. Martins, "Os primeiros anos' in N. Andresen Leitão (ed.), *20 anos de integração Europeia (1986–2006): O testemunho português* (Lisbon: Cosmos, 2007).

15 A. G. Soares, "Portugal e a adesão às Comunidades Europeias: 20 anos de integração europeia", in R. G. Perez and L. Lobo-Fernandes (eds), *España y Portugal: Veinte años de integración europea* (Salamanca: Tórculo Ediciós, 2007), p. 69.

partners. Following its traditional foreign policy line, at least as far as the European integration process was concerned, Portugal remained aligned with the United Kingdom, believing Margaret Thatcher's government were safe and prudent allies with which to face the growing supranational trends within Europe.

In the autumn of 1989, when the Berlin Wall fell and the communist regimes in central and Eastern Europe collapsed, Portuguese foreign policy still followed the traditional Atlanticist line. However, after the collapse of the Soviet Union, German reunification, and European enlargement and deepening that was the result of the Maastricht Treaty, Lisbon's position evolved into a more flexible Euro-Atlantic position. This new position became evident during the first half of 1992, when for the first time Portugal assumed the presidency of the EU. At the time, the European question was posed as new national goal, with the country truly committed to the EU's new institutional form: Political Union.[16]

Euro-Enthusiasm:
A Decade of Convergence

Portugal's 1992 EU presidency marked a change in the process of Portugal's integration. The Portuguese success in ensuring reform of the Common Agricultural Policy (CAP), contributed to changes in the position of Cavaco Silva's governments from the conservative of the early years, initiating a period of enthusiasm towards more active participation in the European project. While the EU entered a new stage following the signing of the Maastricht Treaty, Portugal revealed itself to be a *good student*; moreover, one that was truly committed to the European process. [17]

16 C. Gaspar, "Portugal e o alargamento da EU", *Análise Social* XXXV, 154–155 (2000), pp. 327–72.

17 Soares (note 15), p. 72.

Left behind was the conservative, traditionally Atlanticist and, until then, dominant trend in strategic and diplomatic culture, which saw the Atlantic focus and the special relationship with the US and the Portuguese-speaking world as the Portugal's foreign policy priority. With the end of the Cold War, Portugal's international position became increasingly Euro-Atlantic, reflecting the Europeanization of Portugal's strategic orientation.

This was particularly so from 1995, with the European outlook being strengthened during the remainder of the decade. The country's participation in peace missions in the Balkans clearly reflected the change in Portuguese foreign policy. Portugal had fully assumed its European status both in foreign and defence policy, and for the first time since the First World War, Portuguese armed forces took part in military operations on the European continent.[18]

Clearly taking on an Europeanist tone, which had been the political line of the PS since 1976, the socialist government led by António Guterres, adopted the European monetary union project as its main goal in the European integration process.[19] The Lisbon government asssumed the goal of placing Portugal at the head of the integration process as the only way to keep a peripheral country at the heart of the EU's decision-making process.[20] This strategy involved the immediate Europeanization of Portuguese public policies in all fields, which was reflected in the swift adoption of legislative changes outlined in the EU treaties, particularly in the 1997 Amsterdam Treaty. In this sense, one could observe

18 N. S. Teixeira, "A democracia, a defesa e as missões internacionais das forças armadas', in N. S. Teixeira (ed.), *Os militares e a democracia*, (Lisbon: Colibri, 2006), pp. 71–89.

19 M. C. Lobo, "A atitude dos portugueses perante a UE: Perspectivas sociais e políticas", in S. Royo (note 11), pp. 150–51.

20 Gaspar (note 16).

the incorporation of the EU's political values at all the levels of Portuguese policy.

The zenith of this strategy was reached in 1998. Despite the atavistic financial indiscipline of southern European countries, Portugal met all the conditions and was accepted into the select club of European states admitted to the single European currency, the euro.

Portugal achieved this aim just as Portuguese diplomacy achieved one of its flagship successes of the democratic regime with the resolution of the East Timor issue.

Not even a UN Security Council condemnation could force Indonesia into ending its occupation of the former Portuguese territory, which it seized in 1975. During the 1990s, the diplomatic persistence of the Portuguese government kept East Timor on the international agenda. In this context, the sense of belonging to the EU was without doubt a decisive factor in this, as it gave Lisbon an increasing international role enabling the people of East Timor to exert their right to self-determination through a UN supervised political transition.[21]

Portugal entered its second presidency of the EU in the first half of 2000 with Europe as the priority of its national interests.. Unlike in 1992, during this presidency the Portuguese government transmitted the image of a country that was comfortably integrated into the European project, and able to mobilize its peers to ensure the development and improvement of the union.

In the European Council of March 2000, the Portuguese presidency obtained approval for the Lisbon Strategy, a declaration of principles that sought to place the EU as the world's leading economy within a decade. Through the promotion of social,

21 J. J. P. Gomes, "A internacionalização da questão de Timor", *Relações Internacionais* 25 (2010), pp. 67–89.

educational and environmental policies, the Lisbon Strategy sought to make the European economy more competitive and better prepared for the challenges of globalization.

Although bearing important fruit for the affirmation of Europe at the start of the 21st century, Lisbon's aims were not entirely achieved, partly because the implementation method allowed the move away from traditional communitarian integration formulae by introducing non-binding obligations.

In fact, in 2000 most European countries were far more interested in improving the EU institutions in order to prepare Brussels for the Eastern enlargement. The 2000 intergovernmental conference in Nice, which sought to solve the questions left over by the Amsterdam Treaty, was also the moment the larger member states began to the diplomatic pressure in order to have their political weight acknowledged and enhanced within the European decision-making process. This period culminate in a moment of Europeanist euphoria: the Nice intergovernmental summit gave Portugal a platform upon which it was able to fulfil a leadership role in respect of the medium and smaller European states, defending their interests from the demands of the larger states. This role was paramount during the negotiations over institutional reform, at a time that was without doubt one of the most active moments of Portugal's participation in the process of European integration.[22]

At the external level, the Portuguese presidency sought to strengthen the EU's international presence, benefiting from Portugal's historical relations with regional areas traditionally linked to its national interest.

Successes included the approval of the Common Strategy for the Mediterranean and the launch of the EU-India

22 Soares (note 15), p. 77.

strategy following the Lisbon Summit. The Portuguese presidency's two main goals in relation to Africa were also achieved: the EU–ACP Cotonu partnership agreement, which replaced the Lomé Convention,and the first EU-Africa Summit, which took place in Cairo.

Return to Pragmatism:
A Decade of Divergence

The conclusions of the 2001 Nice Treaty, coupled with the eastern enlargement of the EU, signalled the beginning of the end of Portuguese enthusiasm for European integration.

At this point, internal and external factors contributed towards the Portuguese gaining a more realistic perception of their belonging to the European Union. In 2001, with the resignation of Prime Minister António Guterres and the call for early elections, Portugal returned to internal political instability. The total commitment to the EU presidency and its leadership of the medium and smaller member states during the negotiations over the Nice Treaty contributed to the socialist government neglecting domestic policy. The new political instability was accompanied by an economic and financial downturn that came about partially as a result of a fall in domestic consumption and the loss of national export competitiveness.[23]

Major political and strategic changes in the international arena took place in the aftermath of 9 September 2001, particularly the transatlantic crisis and divisions within Europe caused by the US-led intervention in Iraq in 2003. For Portugal, however, it was EU enlargement to countries of the former Soviet bloc that had the most impact on its perception of the integration process.

23 Soares (note 15), pp. 82–3.

At this time there were no alterations registered in either the course of these EU trends or in Durão Barroso's government's European policies between 2002 and 2005.

From a geopolitical perspective this enlargement contributed towards moving Europe's centre of gravity to the East, thereby accentuating Portugal's peripheral condition in the European context.

Economically, the new member states were more attractive to multinational corporations seeking to benefit from the lower wages and skilled labour available in central and eastern Europe. Portugal was unquestionably one of the countries most affected by the relocation of companies to the east. To this situation another element was added—competition for structural funds—and again, Portugal was left behind.[24]

At this point, it should be noted the financial constraints deriving from economic and monetary union and adhesion to the euro, as well as the ongoing economic issues affecting Portugal, were aggravated from 2008 by the global financial crisis.

During the first decade of the 21st century, Portugal's GDP diverged from the EU average and from those of its cohesion partners. In 1999 Portugal's GDP per capita was 68 per cent of EU GDP per capita: by 2008 it had fallen to 64 per cent.

Despite these various difficulties at this time Portugal did not go back to the scepticism that was characteristic of Cavaco Silva's early years in government. With the Socialist Party returning to power in 2005, and the European crisis and French and Dutch vetoes of the European constitution notwithstanding, Portugal's attitude was one of responsible realism. Portugal's 2007 EU presidency offered proof of the country's political maturity in the

24 Soares (note 15), p. 83.

European integration project. This was felt both at the EU's internal level and through its international presence.

Domestically, the priority of the governments led by José Sócrates was to ensure the conclusion of the political process for EU reform, which was achieved with the signing of the Lisbon Treaty on 13 December 2007.

Internationally, the priorities of Portugal's presidency focused on strengthening and diversifying the EU as a global actor. This was achieved through a series of successful international summits, including the EU-Russia summit, the second EU-Africa dummit and the first EU-Brazil summit, which resulted in the celebration of a new strategic partnership.

While these summits contributed towards strengthening the EU's international presence, they also favoured Portugal's national interest by extending the EU's strategic partnerships into areas of its traditional strategic interest: Africa and Brazil.[25]

Conclusion

Portuguese participation in the process of European integration had political, economic and social costs and benefits for the country.

From the global standpoint, Portugal's accession to the EEC was important both for the domestic consolidation of democracy and the external definition of a new model for international insertion. Although Portugal was already part of the international post-Second World War system, as member of the UN, NATO, OECD and EFTA, integration into the EEC closed the cycle of normalization of the country's presence in the international

---

25 L. Ferreira-Pereira, "Portugal e a presidência da União Europeia (1992–2007)", *Relações Internacionais* 20 (2008), pp. 131–43.

system, thus placing it in the select club of politically stable and economically developed Western democracies.

Economically and socially, a profound change occurred during the two decades of Portugal's European integration. The country's economy experienced accelerated modernization, which had a clear impact at the productive structure level, as well on external commerce and social cohesion. Portugal's accession to the EEC took place at precisely the moment Europe was seeking to strengthen and intensify its integration through the SEA.

Through the provision of European structural funds and the introduction of cohesion policies, Portugal's economy and society set out on a process of structural reformulation, with the goal of achieving macroeconomic stability and increased competitiveness, which became one of the key-consequences of accession. Yet despite its difficulties and limitations, Portuguese participation in the integration process was translated at the economic and social level. During the first decade it resulted in its convergence with its European partners, and its growing divergence since the end of that first decade.[26]

Politically there was a process of Europeanization of Portuguese institutions and public policies. The transposition of European legislation resulted in significant changes that shaped public institutions and policies to the practices of European institutions and their decision-making processes. During the course of this process, the costs in terms of sovereignty transfer within the various affected sectors seem to have been widely compensated by the economic benefits obtained, which was reflected in the

---

26 S. Royo, "O alargamento de 2004: Lições ibéricas para a Europa pós-comunista", in Royo (note 11).

Portuguese public's support for European integration and Portugal's participation in the European project.[27]

As far as Portugal's foreign policy is concerned the impact of European integration was tremendous, even determining the emergence of a new model for the country's international insertion. First, it changed the contradictory perception between Europe and the Atlantic to one of complementarity. For Portuguese foreign policy, the European Atlanticist outlook may bring added value in the Atlantic and in post-colonial relations. Second, while the Europe/Atlantic equation remained, priorities were inverted: traditionally Portugal had prioritised the Atlantic and the colonies while looking for European compensations; now Portugal's priority is Europe and the European Union, and to obtain added value at the international level it seeks to take advantage of its Atlanticist position and post-colonial relations.

27 Lobo (note 19), pp. 158–59.

2 | Portuguese Political Elites and the European Union

João Pedro Ruivo, Diogo Moreira,
António Costa Pinto and
Pedro Tavares de Almeida

Do the Portuguese national political elites feel they belong to the European polity? How do they evaluate the political institutions of the European Union (EU)? And what kind of policies should be delegated by the member-states to the supranational European level of government?

Through the analysis of data collected in the 2007 and 2009 IntUne project elite surveys,[1] this chapter addresses these questions in order to assess how the three main dimensions of European citizenship—identity, representation and scope of governance—feature among deputies to the Portuguese parliament. In doing so, our main goal here is to describe the attitudes of those national representatives within a set of comparative perspectives. First, vis-à-vis the attitudes of Portuguese parties, in order to assess the coherence of the deputies' attitudes with the official positions of their parties; second, with public opinion, in order to explore convergent and divergent attitudes between the elite and citizens; and, finally, with the attitudes of two groups of

---

1 For a theoretical introduction of the IntUne project, see M. Cotta and P. Isernia, *Citizenship in the European polity: questions and explorations, report on IntUne theoretical framework* (2007), www.intune.it/research-materials/theoretical-framework [accessed 20 April 2009]. For a brief methodological introduction to the project, see G. Ilonski, "Introduction: A Europe integrated and united—but still diverse?" *Europe-Asia Studies* 6 (2009), pp. 913–15.

national parliaments to which Portugal belongs—southern European member-states and the more diverse group of 17 European countries in which the IntUne elite surveys were conducted—thereby mapping the attitudes of Portuguese representatives within the broader European context.

A Europe of Elites and of Executive Elitism

European integration has been described as a matter of elites, with limited space for the voice of the citizens. Indeed, the major processes of European integration have been driven by top political leaders who have played a central role in both the founding steps of the European Communities in the 1950s and in the ensuing stages of enlargement (from the accession of several northern European countries in 1973 to that of eastern European countries in 2004 and 2007), and in the institutional deepening of the EU (i.e. the Single European Act and the Maastricht, Amsterdam, Nice and Lisbon treaties).

During the periods between these major processes, smaller steps of functional integration within the bounds defined by the treaties have been advanced largely on the initiative of bureaucratic elites from the European Commission.[2]

Broadly speaking, the territorial, institutional and functional advancements of the EU have been developed with a timing that is not coincidental with that of most national political agendas. The top-down approach of EU decision-making, which has resulted in ever greater impacts and constraints on national political decision-making,[3] has no proportional bottom-up counterweight.

2   M. Haller, *Elite integration as an elite process: The failure of a dream?* (London, New York, NY: Routledge, 2003).

3   Jalali, chapter 3.

The most directly representative of the European institutions—the European Parliament—lacks the legislative initiative, a core competence of democratic chambers, and its power to decide upon legislative proposals from the commission is shared with the European Council.

Furthermore, elections to the European Parliament traditionally have been regarded as second-order electoral disputes, the agenda of which are dominated by national issues,[4] and the turnout at which are consistently lower than the declining turnout rates for domestic general elections, which tends to undermine the legitimacy of the European Parliament within the European polity.

Nevertheless, a large and growing number of policies are dealt with at the European level and impact on the everyday lives of millions of citizens across Europe. This has made clear the imbalance between the beginning and the end of the chain of delegation and accountability in the European political system. The beginning of the chain is characterized by feeble links among electors (and their preferences expressed through votes), parties (and their preferences expressed through manifestos) and parliament (and their preferences expressed through full legislative capacity, which is absent in the case of the European Parliament).

Conversely, the major flows of delegation and accountability in European policy-making seem to take place at the very end of a highly complicated and blurred chain, mostly between institutions of executive nature (the European Commission, the European Council and national governments) that, while having a very indirect mandate from their citizens, are designed to propose, negotiate and decide upon policies that are very important both in nature and in scope.

4   Freire, chapter 7.

At the national level, the mainstream political parties that are the usual winners of national legislative (and European) elections, and which hold the bulk of public offices, have supporting discourses towards the EU, but they are often vague and lack coherent positions on a number of important issues for ordinary citizens.[5]

In this context, national parliaments seem not to play a leading role as political decision-makers, since their main decisional competences are, to a certain extent, confined to those of ex-post ratifiers and transposers of European legal instruments (and only when national constitutions so demand).

What European integration has provoked across Europe, or at least has reinforced, is a trend towards executive decision-making at the national level. True, there have been efforts to enhance parliamentary oversight over governments on European issues (through the setting up of European Affairs Committees, the use of parliamentary questions, etc.).[6] There have also been some institutional innovations at the European level that directly link national legislatures to the European Commission (the core legislative entrepreneur) within the framework of the European legislative process.[7]

But it is still national governments that meet at the European Council to decide upon the direction of European policy-making

5   N. Conti, "European citizenship in party Euromanifestos: Southern Europe in comparative perspective (1994–2004)", in N. Conti, M. Cotta and P. T. Almeida (eds), *Perspectives of national elites on European citizenship: A south European view* (New York, NY: Routledge, 2012), pp. 97–117.

6   E. Damgaard, "Conclusion: The impact of European integration on Nordic parliamentary democracies", *The Journal of Legislative Studies* 6 (2000), pp. 151–69.

7   See Resende and Paulo, chapter 4, on recent developments in the *ex-ante* dissemination of information from the European Commission to national legislatures and in the scrutiny by national parliaments. The option for these mechanisms does not preclude (rather, it strengthens) the idea that parliaments have not played their main role as policy initiators in important issues for their constituents.

(in some matters together with the European Parliament), which are then specified and adopted by national parliaments when major issues of their competence are at stake.

This process seems to contradict the traditional view of parliamentary democracy, according to which the government should specify and execute legislation passed by parliament (even if in practice sometimes the government is able to control the legislative process through imposing party discipline upon parliamentary majorities). The inversion of roles between legislatures and executives in the approval and specification of legislation is quite similar to that which occurs in respect of government approval of international treaties followed by parliamentary ratification. What is new in European politics, however, is that these role shifts are no longer exceptional (as they are in traditional international relations), they have become systematic, a common practice of the European political system that might have significant constitutional implications, both in the theory and in the practice of European parliamentary democracies.[8]

While strengthening the national parliaments' control mechanisms, some member states have also sought legitimacy through the means of referendum. Nevertheless, of the 35 referenda to have taken place from 1973 to 2009, more than half (18) were related to the accession of new member-states and only 17 took place within the framework of major treaties.

Apart from Ireland (seven) and Denmark (six), referenda have not been systematically used by member-states to legitimate major institutional advancements. This suggests that in relation to the European polity most national elites have used the referendum as an eternally valid blank cheque signed by their constituents.

8 For a more profound discussion of the impact of Europe integration on the national chains of delegation and accountability, see Damgaard (note 6).

The Portuguese Contribution to European Executive Elitism

Portugal has played its part in the construction of European executive elitism, from the long road to accession (1976–86) right up until late into the first decade of the 21st century. In the context of the polarized Portuguese transition to democracy in 1974–76, when the crucial political divisions corresponded to a conflict "between democrats and revolutionaries [rather] than between democrats and 'involutionaries'",[9] the European option was an important factor in the break from a dictatorial, isolationist and colonialist past that also assumed an anti-communist and anti-revolutionary orientation.[10] As in other southern European transitions to democracy—particularly in Spain—"the idea that accession to the European Community would help guarantee liberal democracy was more overtly voiced",[11] and was central to the strategy of the political elites during this period.

The governing elites successfully sought to legitimate the new democratic order using the arguments of Europe and of membership of the European Economic Community (EEC) as crucial means for reform towards democratic consolidation. The swift Europeanization of the newly founded political parties was also stimulated by their merging in the transnational networks of the European political families. The theme of EEC membership soon emerged in the programmes of the right- and centre-right parties, with the Social and Democratic Centre (CDS—Centro

9   B. Alvarez-Miranda, *Sur de Europa y la adhesión a la Comunidad: los debates políticos* (Madrid: CIS/Siglo XXI de España, 1996), p. 202.

10   A. C. Pinto and N. Teixeira, "From Africa to Europe: Portugal and European integration," in A. C. Pinto and N. Teixeira (eds), *Southern Europe and the making of the European Union* (New York, NY: SSM-Columbia University Press, 2003).

11   Alvarez-Miranda (note 9), p. 202.

Democrático e Social) proclaiming itself fully pro-European, and the Social Democratic Party (PSD—Partido Social Democrata) adopting a more cautious approach.[12] The CDS, which was affiliated to the European Christian Democratic family, adopted a strongly pro-European strategy right up until accession. The PSD, which was formed by the reformers and "liberals" of the dictatorship's final years, first inserted itself into the European "liberal" family (although it would defect to the European People's Party in 1996). In 1976 the main slogan of the Socialist Party's (PS—Partido Socialista) electoral campaign was "Europe with us", and the proposal of EEC accession was incorporated in the party's programme.

Only the Communist Party (PCP—Partido Comunista Português) remained consistently opposed to EEC membership and rejected the prospect of accession. This opposition was an important element in its political campaigns between 1977 and 1986. After the accession of Portugal in 1986, the PCP adopted a more moderate position: instead of calling for Portugal's withdrawal from the community, it started advocating the construction of "another Europe". In recent years, the Left Bloc (BE—Bloco de Esquerda) has proposed a similar position.

Civil society and the interest groups representing those who would be most affected by EU membership had practically no role to play at any stage of the accession negotiations. The governing elites dominated the negotiating process, with only limited involvement from the business associations or the organized agricultural interests. Both the Confederation of Portuguese Industry (CIP—Confederação da Industrial Portuguesa) and the

---

12 J. M. Barroso, *Le système politique portugais face à l'integration européenne: partis politiques et opinion publique* (Lisbon: Associação Portuguesa para o Estudo das Relações Internacionais, 1983).

Portuguese Industrial Association (AIP—Associação Industrial Portuguesa) supported accession, although to different extents. The CIP wavered between domestic liberalization and protectionism towards the EEC, initially demanding more pre-entry economic aid and later demonstrating its opposition to the final agreements, while the AIP adopted a more pragmatic "join and see" position.[13] Nevertheless, despite the CIP's occasional attacks, the hypothesis that the attitudes of these two organizations reflected an attempt to make the government adopt an aggressive negotiating stance rather than any principled opposition appears plausible, especially since these attitudes did not enjoy much support among their affiliates. Several interviews with leading figures within the employers' organizations reveal their attitudes towards accession were driven by political considerations, with the EEC being presented as the "guarantor for greater political security that will encourage investment in and modernization of the productive structures in the country".

The very perception of EEC membership as a positive goal was initially restricted to the political elite. In 1978, shortly after the formal membership application had been submitted, most Portuguese had no opinion on Europe, with more than 60 per cent of the population stating they did not know if EEC membership was essential for the future of Portugal's economy.[14] It was not until the early 1980s that the Portuguese had become better informed and thus better able to express a clear view on the matter.

The increasing importance of the European issue, together with the broad party consensus, eventually had a favourable

13 M. Lucena and C. Gaspar, "Metamorfoses corporativas? Associações de interesses económicos e institucionalização da democracia em Portugal (I)", *Análise Social* XXVI, 114 (1991), p. 899.

14 M. Bacalhau, *Atitudes, opiniões e comportamentos políticos dos portugueses, 1973–1993* (Lisbon: Bacalhau e Bruneau, 1994).

impact on public opinion. The Eurobarometer survey has regularly recorded Portuguese public opinion since 1980, and its reports have revealed a clear upward trend in support of EEC membership, with a large increase in the year Portugal joined (1986).

Still, rather than "a response to popular demand", accession persisted as a path désigned, negotiated and approved by the top political elite alone,[15] mainly backed by a large degree of political consensus among the governing parties between 1976 and 1985 (PS, PSD and CDS). The Portuguese elitist approach to the EU was eventually sharpened by the absence of a referendum, which had been held during the previous accession processes of Ireland, Denmark and the UK in 1973—but which was also absent in the processes of Greece and Spain, Portugal's southern European peers in the third wave of democratization.

The first ten years of Portugal's membership in the EEC are usually regarded as a "golden era". It was a time of economic growth, rising incomes and social change in an optimistic atmosphere of modernization that culminated with the country meeting the convergence criteria for membership of the single currency, the euro, and then joining the single currency in 1999. Portuguese foreign affairs also benefited from the country's status as a member of the EU—for example, it helped relieve the tensions that existed between it and its former colonies in Africa.

In the internal political sphere, a large degree of pro-European consensus persisted among parties that had held government positions. The only exception to the consensual support of governing parties was the shift of the right-wing CDS (when it was in opposition) towards an anti-Maastricht Europe, which was the policy followed by a new generation of party leaders in 1992. The

15 N. Bermeo, "Regime change and its impact on foreign policy: The Portuguese case", *Journal of Modern Greek Studies* 6 (1988), p. 14.

party maintained this position until 2002, when it was compelled to become more pro-Europe as a condition of forming a government coalition with the PSD.

The mainstream centre-left PS and centre-right PSD, which for many years shared around 80 per cent of the electorate, have remained largely supportive of European integration, which is consistent with the trend across European member states in which the mainstream parties constitute the bulk of political support for the EU.

It should be noted, however, that in the Portuguese case, Sanches and Pereira (2010) found a variation within parties according to their government/opposition status in respect of specific issues of European integration. When in government, parties tend to be strongly in favour of European integration on all issues, while when in opposition they tend to be more critical. This government/opposition status-based variation differentiates Portugal from the wider spectrum of southern European member states, where similar variations were found to be rather limited.[16]

It was in such an environment of economic and social modernization and overall political consensus on European integration that the proportion of the population believing EEC membership a good thing rose from 24.4 per cent in 1980–82 to 64.5 per cent in 1986–90 and finally to more than 70 per cent during the early 1990s.[17] In 1993, 65 per cent believed Portuguese economic

---

16 Conti (note 5).

17 As appears to be the case in other southern European countries, there seems to be a strong suggestion the urban middle classes generally tend towards being pro-European and have a weaker sense of "national pride", while the less educated and the rural lower classes generally have weak pro-European sentiments and a strong sense of "national pride". See Bacalhau (note 14), p. 269.

development had been greatly boosted as a result of EEC membership.[18]

This momentum of the 1990s can be contrasted with the situation found during the first decade of the 21st century. The EU's movement towards institutional reform and enlargement, as well as the eventual reduction of EU financial support, has resulted in Portuguese public opinion displaying slightly but consistently declining levels of Euro-optimism.[19]

On the whole, the attitude of Portuguese citizens towards the EU has been positive, both in terms of affective and instrumental views. However, it is important to note that the consensus has been mainly based on a narrow instrumental view of the benefits of membership for Portugal rather than on wider perceptions of the EU as "a good thing".

With respect to attitudes towards the EU as a political system, the evidence is somewhat paradoxical: while the Portuguese tend not to participate in elections to the European Parliament and feel dissatisfied with the way democracy works in the EU, they have increasingly defended the transfer to the European level of key sovereign public policies, such as foreign and currency affairs,[20] and increasingly of welfare policies such as education, health and social security.[21] This suggests that towards the end of the first decade of the 21st century, the attitudes of Portuguese citizens towards the EU were still positive and instrumental. Nonetheless,

18 M. B. da Cruz, "National identity in transition", in R. Herr (ed.), *The new Portugal: democracy and Europe* (Berkeley, CA: Institute of International and Asia Studies, 1993), p. 157.

19 A. C. Pinto and M. C. Lobo, "Forging a positive but instrumental view: Portuguese attitudes towards the EU, 1986-2002", in A. Dulphy and C. Manigand (eds), *Public opinion and Europe: National identities and the European integration process* (Brussels: Peter Lang, 2004), pp. 165–81.

20 Pinto and Lobo (note 19), p. 181.

21 Magalhães, chapter 8.

increasing support for policy integration at the European level was grounded in the perception that the European political system was more efficient than Portuguese authorities when it came to enacting public policies.

Before moving to the section on national political elites' attitudes, we should remember the following lessons from the Portuguese experience. First, Portugal is a remarkable example of an elitist approach to European accession and integration. A key indicator is the absence of any referendum so far on European issues. Unlike the situation in most non-founding EU member-states, Portuguese citizens never had a direct say on the European polity, neither before accession in 1986 nor on the many treaties authorizing the delegation of more policy domains to the European level.

Curiously, since 1997 the Portuguese constitution has called for a mandatory referendum to decide upon the creation of autonomous sub-national authorities at the regional level, encompassing the transfer of a set of policy domains from the capital. In other words, a referendum has to be called if elites in Lisbon decide to delegate to a regional agent in Oporto, but such constraints are absent when the agent is outside Portugal, whether in Brussels or in Frankfurt.

Second, Portugal has been a remarkable case of executive elitism in EU matters, before, during and after accession. On the one hand, governments have dominated the European legislative process at the national level, on the other hand, the parliament has traditionally exerted weak control over governments and lacked the resources to deal with EU affairs.[22] This concentration of power in the executive seems to have been eased by electoral results and the distribution of parliamentary seats in

22 Resende and Paulo (note 7).

Portugal. From 1986 to 2009, governments were for 15 years backed by highly disciplined parliamentary majorities (including 12 years of single party majorities). At no time since accession have the mainstream PS and PSD shared less than two-thirds of the parliamentary seats, which has paved the way both for smooth constitutional reforms when needed to enact the European treaties and for a weaker parliamentary opposition to executive manoeuvres in those critical moments calling for "national unity"(e.g. the negotiation and approval of the Maastricht Treaty or the efforts to join the Economic and Monetary Union).

Portuguese governing elites seem to share the notion Portugal has to be fully pro-European, and that the government is a kind of guarantor of Portugal's pro-European stance. This may well be the reason the CDS had to abandon its anti-European position as a condition of entering into a coalition government with the PSD in 2002. This also might be the reason why the European manifestos issued by parties when in government never criticize any aspect of European integration.[23]

In such an executive-centred member state (within the framework of such an executive-centred EU), parliament has a limited decision-making role in respect of European affairs. Why, then, study the attitudes of parliamentary elites towards the EU?

There are at least four reasons not to disregard the stances of national legislators. First, the national parliament, even when imperfect, is the best national proxy for political diversity. Mapping the attitudes of representatives and comparing them with those of their constituents is quite an interesting challenge for those interested in the theory and practice of representation. The

23 E. R. Sanches and J. S. Pereira, "Which Europe do the Portuguese parties want? Identity, representation and scope of governance in the Portuguese Euromanifestos (1987–2004)", *Perspectives on European Politics and Society* 11, 2 (2010), pp. 183–200.

attitudes of the parliamentary elites may be approached through alternative means, for instance, through the analysis of party manifestos or of the legislative behaviour of deputies. Nonetheless, these methods do not fully grasp individual level attitudes, which we believe might differ from the viewpoints of the party central office expressed either through manifestos or through voting behaviour imposed on representatives through the mechanics of party discipline. Through interviewing deputies in a rather unconstrained context, we believe we can get closer to the way national representatives think (even if their opinions have no immediate political consequences).

Second, a national parliament is still an accurate barometer of political elite behaviour and of the extent of its internal grade of integration or consensus over important issues. It is the arena in which systematic and institutionalized political competition takes place between elections. Since the ideological scope of the Portuguese parliament is quite diverse, any significant underlying social or ideological tension will probably soon appear in the parliamentary arena as a form of political conflict.

Third, the national parliament is a crucial recruitment pool both for national government and for the European Parliament elite. Also many senior national representatives had previously held offices in national government or in European institutions. Monitoring the individual attitudes of national representatives might be a useful proxy of the political elite as a whole, and it may help trace the inter-institutional flows of ideas and of individual mental predispositions towards the EU. Furthermore, since mainstream parties have tended to be less rigid from a programmatic point of view, while often keeping silence on European issues that are currently not on the political agenda, the record of the attitudinal trends of the party members in parliament could be a helpful tool for predicting the possible stances taken by the party when those issues (re)emerge on the political agenda.

Fourth, while parliaments do not play a crucial role in the everyday business of European politics, in some critical circumstances—when a strong parliamentary majority is absent—they do emerge as central institutions, even when issues related to the EU are at stake. The resignations of José Sócrates in Portugal and of Italy's Silvio Berlusconi in 2011, both largely as a consequence of the European sovereign debt crisis, are recent and sound examples of such events.

Elite Attitudes towards the EU

Elite surveys are rare in Portugal, and to our knowledge the 2007 and 2009 IntUne surveys are the most comprehensive on European issues to date.[24] Within the framework of the IntUne project, 152 interviews were conducted with Portuguese deputies.[25]

The questionnaires were structured along the lines of the "compound" model of European citizenship, which refers to the idea that European citizenship is an amalgamation of two separate but intertwined dimensions: an indirect citizenship derived from the national citizenship of an EU member state; and a direct one that originates in and is established by the existence of a system of European institutions. According to this model, European citizenship is further characterized by a horizontal dimension that defines the membership linkage with the European polity (identity) and by two vertical dimensions that concern the relationship

24 This research was funded by a grant from the IntUne project (Integrated and United: A quest for Citizenship in an ever-closer Europe) financed by the Sixth Framework Programme of the European Union, Priority 7, "Citizens and governance in a knowledge-based society" (CIT3-CT-2005-513421).

25 Both samples were selected through a quota sampling procedure, the main criteria of which were party group and seniority.

between European citizens and EU authorities (representation and scope of governance).[26]

Here we will present and discuss descriptive data on these three major dimensions of European-ness. The topics covered range from the degree of attachment to different territorial communities and the basic elements considered as constituting European and national identities, the levels of trust in European and Portuguese institutions, the assessment of the future EU institutional design and attitudes towards EU common policy areas.[27] Where possible, our results will be compared with the findings from opinion polls and the analysis of European manifestos in Portugal, as well as with the results of the elite surveys of two

TABLE 2.1
General Support for European Integration
(mean, 0–10 scale)

	2007	2009
Mean	6.74	6.47
Standard deviation	2.42	2.30
N	77	70

SOURCE: *IntUne Elite Survey in Portugal* (2007; 2009).
NOTE: Respondents were asked to answer the following question: "Some say European unification should be strengthened, others say it already has gone too far. What is your opinion? Please indicate your views using a ten-point scale. On this scale zero means unification has already gone too far and ten means it should be strengthened. What number on this scale best describes your position?'

26 Cotta and Isernia (note 1).

27 Results of the 2007 survey have already been reported in Moreira et al., "Attitudes of the Portuguese elites towards the European Union", in N. Conti, M. Cotta and P. T. Almeida (eds), *Perspectives of national elites on European citizenship: A south European view* (New York, NY: Routledge, 2012), pp. 57–77. We expect the data to be quite consistent across waves, given the fact the composition of the Portuguese national parliament was basically the same in 2007 and in 2009.

groups of countries: southern European member-states and the IntUne group.[28]

We begin by mapping Portuguese deputies' attitudes according to a classic indicator of general support for European integration (Table 2.1). With a mean support for European integration of around 6.6, Portuguese deputies are in line with the average for legislators in all of the countries taking part in the IntUne survey (6.6), and below the 7.5 observed among deputies from southern European countries.

Identity

In order to explore identity—the horizontal dimension of European citizenship that comprises the links of citizens with their political communities—we analysed rates of elite attachment to different territorial levels and their understanding of what defines national and supra-national identity (Table 2.2).

Both in 2007 and in 2009 more than 90 per cent of Portuguese deputies considered themselves to be attached to the EU, their country and their region. Variation in territorial identities is therefore not a question of attachment or non-attachment, but of degree of attachment.

With respect to the degree of territorial attachment, we found Portuguese legislators consider themselves strongly attached to Portugal as a country, and more than half feel strongly attached to their town or village. A total of nine out of every ten deputies felt very attached to their country (as opposed to only four out of ten

---

28 The group of four southern European member states is composed by Greece, Italy, Portugal and Spain. The IntUne group, in which elite interviews took place, also includes six Western European member states (Austria, Belgium, Denmark, France, Germany and the United Kingdom), seven post-communist member states (Bulgaria, Czech Republic, Estonia, Hungary, Lithuania, Poland and Slovakia) and by Serbia, which applied to join the EU in December 2009.

Table 2.2
Attachment to Communities
(%)

	2007	2009
Attachment to the EU		
Very	45.0	43.7
Somewhat	51.3	53.5
N	80	71
Attachment to country		
Very	92.5	93.0
Somewhat	6.3	7.0
N	80	71
Attachment to region		
Very	61.3	81.7
Somewhat	32.5	14.1
N	80	71

Source: *IntUne Elite Survey in Portugal* (2007; 2009)

feeling a strong attachment to Europe). These results are consistent with another indicator of the 2009 survey. When asked if they regarded themselves (a) as European only, (b) as Portuguese only, (c) as European and Portuguese or (d) as Portuguese and European, four out of five Portuguese deputies regarded themselves as Portuguese (first) and European (then).

For most members of the elite European identity seems then to be "second order" compared to national identity.[29] This is also consistent with the weaker presence of references to European identity in European manifestos compared to references to national identity.[30]

29 G. Delanty, "Models of citizenship: Defining European identity and citizenship", *Citizenship Studies* 1, 3 (1997), pp. 285–303.

30 Sanches and Pereira (note 23).

The structure of territorial allegiances among Portuguese legislators follows the same pattern of the southern European member states and the IntUne countries, albeit with slightly—but consistently—higher numbers than the average of their (southern) European colleagues for all levels of identity.[31]

When compared to the public, elites report much stronger attachment to all of the polities considered, even if the order of allegiances (i.e. to country first, then to town/region and finally to the EU) remains unchanged. Indeed, the IntUne public opinion surveys show that no more than 70 per cent of Portuguese citizens feel very attached to their country, whereas only 25 per cent feel a strong attachment to the EU.

Deputies were also asked about the substantive elements deemed essential for being Portuguese or European (Table 2.3). Despite the small number of cases at the country level, results in Portugal were once again consistent between 2007 and 2009.

A first glance at the data gives rise to two related inferences. First, there seems to be a robust collinearity between elements of national and European identity that are equal or very similar in nature. Looking at the extremes of the scales, mastering a language of the polity and being Christian are the most and the least important elements of both Portuguese-ness and European-ness, respectively. Second, all elements—except for mastery of languages in 2007—are consistently more important in defining Portuguese-ness than they are for defining European-ness. Together, these findings seem to maintain the close connection between a national identity and a secondary and derivative European identity among Portuguese elites.

---

31 The results for (southern) Europe and for public opinion may be omitted for the reason of textual economy. Full access to these results is available by contacting ruivojp@fcsh.unl.pt.

TABLE 2.3
Elements of National/European Identity (%)

	2007	2009
To be a Christian		
Very important	5.0	2.8
	1.3	2.8
Somewhat important	21.3	15.5
	15.0	5.6
N	80	71
	80	71
To share national/European cultural traditions		
Very important	53.8	38.0
	41.8	18.3
Somewhat important	40.0	49.3
	45.6	56.3
N	80	71
	79	71
To be born in the country/in Europe		
Very important	33.8	31.0
	15.0	11.3
Somewhat important	32.5	33.8
	48.8	39.4
N	80	71
	80	71
To have national/European parents		
Very important	23.8	29.6
	17.5	8.5
Somewhat important	53.8	47.9
	36.3	43.7
N	80	71
	80	71
To respect the laws and institutions of the country/the EU		
Very important	63.8	64.3
	54.4	47.9

Somewhat important	33.8 31.6	31.4 36.6
N	80 79	70 71
To feel national/European		
Very important	75.9 73.4	81.7 73.2
Somewhat important	22.8 24.1	14.1 19.7
N	79 79	71 71
To master a national/European language		
Very important	71.3 75.0	67.6 62.0
Somewhat important	27.5 22.5	26.8 31.0
N	80 80	71 71
To be a national citizen		
Very important	52.5	
Somewhat important	41.3	
N	80	
To participate in national legislative elections/European Parliament elections		
Very important		56.3 40.8
Somewhat important		36.6 35.2
N		71 71

SOURCES: *IntUne Elite Survey in Portugal* (2007; 2009)
NOTE: Table shows results for both national identity (upper part) and European identity (lower part)

In order to make further sense of the data, we propose classifying the elements of identity as follows:

a) Strong majority elements: Those considered important by at least 75 per cent of respondents and very important by at least 50 per cent. In this segment we find respect for laws and institutions, being a member of the community and mastery of language, encompassing both Portuguese and European identities. Holding citizenship status and participating in national legislative elections also fall in this segment, but only for national identity.

b) Considerable majority elements: Those deemed important by at least 50 per cent of respondents and very important by 25-50 per cent. This group comprises the sharing of cultural traditions (for both identities), place of birth and having Portuguese parents (for national identity only) and participation in elections to the European Parliament (for European identity).

c) Weak majority elements: Those regarded important by at least 50 per cent of respondents and very important by less than 25 per cent. Here we find place of birth and family descent (for European identity only)

d) Minority elements: Those considered important by less than 50 per cent of respondents. Being a Christian is the only characteristic in this segment, for both national and European identities.

Conceptually, these elements of identity may also be placed in two categories: a) ascribed identity, i.e. inherited attributes that are not dependent upon the respondent's will, such as birthplace and family descent (and, to a certain extent, religion); and

b) achieved identity, i.e. attributes dependent on the respondent's actions, such as culture, respect for laws, sentiments and language.[32]

A closer look at our data suggest that, on the whole, for Portuguese deputies achieved components are more important than ascribed ones in respect of both Portuguese and European identities. Nonetheless, ascribed components (birthplace and family descent) are significantly more important for national identity than for European identity.

In order to assess the congruence of the ascribed and achieved components of identity at the individual level, Moreira et al. ran a factor analysis for the 2007 Portuguese elite sample.[33] The results confirmed an ascribed component to European identity, with birthplace and family descent being parts of the same factor. Likewise, there seemed to be an achieved dimension in which "respect for law and institutions" and "feeling European" were associated. A large and positive interaction with religious and cultural attributes was also found, suggesting that a significant proportion of deputies associated the cultural dimension of European identity with Christianity. It is interesting to note, however, that this was not the case with the cultural dimension of national identity.

With respect to the components of national identity, birthplace and family descent formed part of ascribed identity. Among the Portuguese elites, the feeling of being Portuguese, the mastery of the Portuguese language and the sharing of Portuguese cultural traditions—all elements that constituted achieved identity

---

32 The theoretical underpinnings of these concepts may be found in R. Linton, *Study of man* (New York, NY: D. Appleton-Century, 1936), and in T. Parsons, *The social system* (Glencoe, IL: Free Press, 1951).

33 Moreira et al. (note 27).

Table 2.4
Trust in EU Institutions
(%)

	2007	2009
Trust in the European Parliament		
Mean	5.93	6.31
Standard deviation	2.10	2.10
N	80	71
Trust in the European Commission		
Mean	5.90	5.65
Standard deviation	2.16	2.42
N	80	71
Trust in the European Council of Ministers		
Mean	6.24	5.73
Standard deviation	2.07	2.38
N	80	71

Source: *IntUne Elite Survey in Portugal* (2007; 2009).

on the European scale—were also positively contained into the same factor, which suggests there is also an achieved component to national identity.

Overall, and according to the findings of Jerez-Mir el al., which compares data from the 2007 IntUne elite and mass surveys, our results show that the attitude of Portuguese deputies is in line with the national representatives in a number of European countries.[34] Indeed, political elites across Europe seem to favour achieved components over ascribed ones, which means they have a concept of national and European identities that could extend

34 M. Jerez-Mir, J. Real Dato and R. Vázquez Garcia, "Identity and representation in the perceptions of political elites and public opinion: A comparison between southern and post-communist central-eastern Europe", *Europe-Asia Studies* 61 (2009), pp. 943–66.

citizenship beyond the closed boundaries of the *jus sanguinis* and of the *jus soli*.

The deputies' attitudes do not coincide completely with those of their constituents, however. In the 2009 citizens' survey, for instance, birthplace, family descent and Christianity were deemed very important factors of national identity by more than 50, 40 and 30 per cent of respondents, respectively. The higher scores these elements obtain have narrowed the gap between the achieved and the ascribed components of national identity among the population—a gap that gets narrower still in relation to European identity.

Representation

In this section, we analyse the second dimension of European citizenship, representation, is part of the vertical relationship between citizens and political institutions. On this topic, the IntUne survey includes two inter-related questions, the first designed to assess the degree of legislators' trust in the EU's three primary institutions—the European Parliament, European Commission and European Council of Ministers (Table 2.4), and a second to capture their prescriptive stances in respect of the EU's future institutional development (Table 2.5).

With respect to the first dimension, the aggregate level of trust does not vary greatly between institutions. Nevertheless, both in 2007 and in 2009 the European Commission scores lower than the European Parliament and the European Council. A wider standard deviation in the level of trust in the commission also indicates that support for this institution is more polarized. Indeed, the widest gap between parties in 2007 is found in the

Table 2.5
Future Institutional Setting of the EU
(%)

	2007	2009
The member states ought to remain the central actors of the EU		
Agree strongly	46.3	33.8
Agree somewhat	30.0	36.6
N	80	71
The European Commission ought to become the true government of the EU		
Agree strongly	8.8	11.3
Agree somewhat	33.8	35.2
N	80	71
The powers of the European Parliament ought to be strengthened		
Agree strongly	40.5	49.3
Agree somewhat	35.4	38.0
N	79	71
Majority voting should be extended in the European Council		
Agree strongly		28.6
Agree somewhat		45.7
N		70

Source: *IntUne Elite Survey in Portugal* (2007; 2009).

average trust in the commission, which was 7.31 among PSD deputies and 1.50 among PCP and Left Bloc deputies.[35]

These findings are in line with those found both in southern Europe and in Europe in general, where national representatives tend to trust the parliamentary institution more than they trust the executive institution. As for the population, the mean trust of Portuguese citizens in 2007 was also higher for the European

35 Moreira et al. (note 27).

Parliament than it was for the commission. On this particular point the Portuguese deputies and citizens agreed, unlike elsewhere in Europe.[36]

All in all mean trust levels both in Portugal and in (southern) Europe were never lower than 5.5 and never higher than 6.4 for all three institutions. This means that EU institutions received a mild degree of approval from Portuguese deputies. At the aggregate level, these results are consistent with another important indicator relating to the representation dimension of European citizenship: satisfaction with democracy in the EU. In 2009, almost five out of ten deputies were somewhat satisfied with the way democracy worked in the EU, while only one out of ten were highly satisfied.

When asked to prescribe future institutional developments in the EU political system, four out of ten deputies strongly agree that member states should retain a central role, while three out of ten would strongly support an extension of majority voting in the European Council. Both opinions gather more than 60 per cent of support (either strong or not), which may sound contradictory given that majority voting in the European Council plays against the centrality of member-states. What might explain this contradiction is the fact that the mode of decision-making in the EU, which can be simplified across lines of (a) national decision-making, (b) unanimity and (c) majority voting, has not been approached consistently by Portuguese parties in their manifestos. Lacking specific guidelines on this issue, deputies from the mainstream parties might feel free to express their diverse, and perhaps contradictory, personal preferences.

36 For a closer look at these cross-country comparisons, see Jerez-Mir, Real Dato and Vásquez García (note 34).

TABLE 2.6
EU Policies Over the Next 10 Years
(%)

	2007	2009
Unified tax system for Europe		
Strongly in favour	15.4	17.1
Somewhat in favour	56.4	45.7
N	78	70
Common system of social security		
Strongly in favour	22.8	19.7
Somewhat in favour	62.0	53.5
N	79	71
Single foreign policy		
Strongly in favour	43.8	47.9
Somewhat in favour	45.0	39.4
N	80	71
More help for regions in difficulties		
Strongly in favour	75.0	80.3
Somewhat in favour	25.0	18.3
N	80	71

SOURCE: *IntUne Elite Survey in Portugal* (2007; 2009).

As for the other two institutions, only one out of ten deputies strongly agrees that the commission should become the true government of the EU, while five out of ten advocate strengthening the powers of the European Parliament. At the aggregate level, then, the desire for a better future for the European Parliament, rather than for the commission, seems to correlate with the degree of trust in these institutions.

As Moreira et al. noted, these attitudes in respect of future institutional scenarios tend to follow the lines of mainstream/

radical party competition.[37] The closer one gets to the centre of the party system, the greater is the deputies' support for a strong European Commission and the lesser their enthusiasm for the idea that member states remain the central actors. However, in relation to the European Parliament, the divide extended along the left-right axis of the political spectrum, with the right less eager to strengthen the powers of the parliament.

Compared with their peers in (southern) Europe, Portuguese deputies show quite similar patterns of support for member states to retain a central role, for strengthening the European Parliament and for extending majority voting within the European Council. The most interesting differences are found between Portuguese deputies and their southern European counterparts, with the latter showing significantly less support for the role of member states and significantly more support for the role of the commission.

Scope of Governance

The third dimension of European citizenship—scope of governance—is also part of the vertical relationship between citizens and political institutions, but it is specifically concerned with the substantive content of that relationship, i.e. to the policies dealt with by political institutions. For the time being, there is a handful of very important policies still not delegated by the member-states to the EU institutions or that EU institutions have not fully developed. Asking whether these policies should be Europeanized over the next 10 years is a further way to approach attitudes towards the nature of the Europolity. The set of four policies under survey comprises two traditionally belonging to the realm of sovereign state functions (tax system and foreign policy) and another

37 Moreira et al. (note 27).

two related specifically to wealth redistribution functions among populations and regions (social security and regional policy).

The results on this topic (Table 2.6) show that further integration of each of the four policies into the European level enjoys the support of at least two-thirds of the national legislators. However, the degree of support varies significantly according to the policy in question. Roughly one-fifth of deputies were strongly in favour of both a unified tax system and a common system of social security, while four out of ten were sharply supportive of a common foreign policy and eight out of ten called strongly for more help for those regions experiencing difficulties.

Apart from the consensual and instrumental stance favouring more help for regions in difficulties—which is unsurprisingly more common among recipients of structural funds, such as Portugal and its southern and post-communist European peers— national deputies are still doubtful about whether more policies should be delegated to the EU.

The path towards a common foreign policy seems quite smoother. Support for this comes mainly from deputies in mainstream centre-left and centre-right parties,[38] which may be a consequence of the fact both PS and PSD regularly call for the EU to have a stronger role in the international arena.[39] Moreover, foreign policy is not such an important issue for Portuguese deputies: rather, it is an area in which the domestic parliament plays a more limited role than the executive and even than the president.

When it comes to the common tax and social security systems—policy areas in which member states remain central, and where, consequently, parliaments still have an important role—deputies are much less eager to give up their competences.

38 Moreira et al. (note 27)

39 Sanches and Pereira (note 23).

PORTUGUESE POLITICAL ELITES

No taxation without representation is a principle every deputy is aware of, and giving way the final say on key budgetary issues could result in a hollowed representation and the demise of the parliamentary institution as presently exists.

Conclusions

Parliamentary deputies in Portugal are supportive of European integration, but the degree of their support—which is close to the mean for the deputies of all EU member states—is not as high as the support found among deputies of other southern European member states. As in many other countries, the mainstream centre-left and centre-right parties in Portugal and their deputies have been solid reserves of political support for integration since the country's accession in 1986.

The underpinnings of the attitudinal relationship between national political elites and the EU may be analysed through the concept of citizenship, and in particular through three of its dimensions: identity, representation and scope of governance.

In respect of identity, deputies feel themselves to be Portuguese first, then members of their local/regional community and finally European. The sense of attachment to the EU is complementary and derived from the sense of attachment to the national community. The elements defining Portuguese-ness and European-ness converge among deputies, who tend to value achieved characteristics (language, respect for laws and institutions and sense of belonging) over ascribed components (birthplace and family descent). Political elites thus take citizenship beyond the narrow, traditional criteria of *jus sanguinis* and *jus soli*, and instead opt for an inclusive concept of both national and European identities. In doing so, they differ slightly from their fellow citizens, for whom the proportions of achieved and ascribed components are not so unbalanced.

In respect of *representation*, deputies tend only to be mildly satisfied with the way democracy works in the EU and tend not to display any deep trust for the European Council, the European Commission or the European Parliament. This suggests a weak link between national parliaments and parliamentary elites, on the one hand, and European political institutions (and European level elites), on the other. However, there is a distinction worth exploring: while the greatest amount of trust and support for strengthening institutional powers is placed in the European Parliament, the European Commission enjoys the least amount of trust and is the institution that deputies are most reluctant to give more power.

This seems to suggest there is an underlying critique of national legislators towards the executive elitism in Europe discussed at the beginning of this chapter. Indeed, deputies are aware of the role played by executive institutions in European politics: the government at the national level and the commission at the European level. When asked about the effective channels for influencing EU policy-making, national government and institutional lobbying within the EU (and the European Commission is the home of European lobbying *par excellence*) were deemed the most effective channels, while the national parliament was considered the least effective. Another indicator of the malaise of national deputies vis-à-vis current executive elitism is that while strongly supporting the existence of an EU president (a position equivalent to the current president of the European Council), they disagree with this position being in the gift of the European Council, as has been the case since the Lisbon Treaty came into effect. Indeed, 51 per cent of deputies call for the position to be directly elected by all EU citizens, while 33 per cent prefer the post to be filled by a vote of the European Parliament. In fact, only 16 per cent agree with the current process.

When asked about any future extension of the EU's *scope of governance*, Portuguese deputies show a considerable degree of interest-based pragmatism. They agree there should be more EU help for regions in difficulties (Portugal remains a net recipient state), but they are just as firm in their desire to close the door to the Europeanization of some national public policies, specifically those related to tax and welfare redistribution.

The 2007 and 2009 snapshot of Portuguese deputies' views have both uncovered a wide range of supportive attitudes towards the European Union. However, the surveys on which this chapter has been based were conducted prior to the banking collapse and European sovereign debt crisis.

Times have changed, and the challenge now is to understand how the European attitudes of national deputies will perform under the stress of political and economic crises. Will the deputies' weaker sense of European-ness and their critical acquiescence to European executive politics and the delegation of policy to Brussels survive in the current climate? Recent data from Eurobarometer seem to suggest that citizens might no longer believe the EU is a good thing from which Portugal has benefited? If that is the case, how will the elites react? Will they leap on the bandwagon with their fellow citizens, or will they act as the guardians of Portuguese European-ness? In Portugal, as across Europe, this has become a matter of crucial interest for political research, and for the very future of the European polity.

3 | Governing from Lisbon or Governing from Brussels? Models and Tendencies of Europeanization of the Portuguese Government

Carlos Jalali

The phenomenon of European integration is one of the clearest examples of transformation of political processes in post-war Europe. According to Nugent and Paterson, "the single most striking feature of government and politics in Western Europe in the modern era has been the creation of a European-level political system".[1] Moreover, this effect is also evident in terms of political discourse, as the perception of an impact of the European Union (EU) on governance processes permeates at the elite, media and mass levels.

National government is one of the areas in which adaptation at the European level has been most apparent. This is evident both in existing theoretical models and in empirical studies. In theoretical terms, the sharing of responsibilities and/or governmental authority with the supra-national level (amongst others) has led some authors to propose a model of national state hollowing out, as public policy processes involve a larger number of agents.[2] As

---

1   N. Nugent and W. Paterson, "The political system of the European Union", in J. E. S. Hayward and A. Menon (eds), *Governing Europe* (Oxford: Oxford University Press, 2003), p. 92.

2   R. Jessop, "The transition to post-Fordism and the Schumpeterian workfare state", in R. Burrows and B. Loader (eds), *Towards a post-Fordist welfare?* (London: Routledge, 1994), pp. 13–37.

Hall puts it, "sovereignty has little meaning in a context where the European Union has the authority to enforce regulations on its member states, without the agreement of their national governments".[3]

With regard to the loss of power of nation states, even the least pessimistic authors do not deny there has been a transformation. While emphasizing the central role of national governments in EU governance, Müller and Wright admit they are "more constrained", with "their actions [m]ore indirect, more discreet and more bartered".[4] Comparative studies at the European level tend to confirm this pattern. Müller confirms that national governments experienced significant transformations in their roles throughout the 1980s, although—as he also notes—these transformations involved a change in the role of nation-states rather than their demise.[5]

Research on governance processes in Portugal is relatively scarce. However, existing studies point to an impact of EU membership on domestic policy-making.[6] Equally, it is relatively easy to discern the apparent effects of European integration at the level of political discourse, with the European level being frequently used as a benchmark for economic development and national policy practices.

3   P. Hall, "Institutions and the evolution of European democracy", in Hayward and Menon (note 1), pp. 1–14.

4   W. C. Müller and V. Wright, "Reshaping the state in Western Europe: The limits to retreat", in W. C. Müller and V. Wright (eds), *The state in Western Europe: Retreat or redefinition?* (London: Frank Cass, 1994), pp. 1–11.

5   W. Müller, "The changing European state", in Hayward and Menon (note 1), pp. 369–79.

6   J. Magone, "Portugal", in H. Kassim, G. Peters and V. Wright (eds), *The national coordination of EU policy: The domestic level* (Oxford: Oxford University Press, 2000), pp. 141–60; J. Magone, *The developing place of Portugal in the European Union* (New Brunswick, NJ: Transaction, 2004); M. C. Lobo, *Governar em democracia* (Lisbon: Imprensa de Ciências Sociais, 2005).

This chapter aims to analyse both the extent and process of the Europeanization of executive power in Portugal, with particular emphasis on the post-accession period. Three main conclusions emerge: first, executive power in Portugal has not escaped the more general processes of transformation identified in comparative studies; second, the Portuguese experience tends to confirm the findings of Maurer, Mittag and Wessels, that European integration processes tend to generate an adaptation by national institutions to European demands rather than fundamental transformations;[7] and third, the Portuguese adaptation process paradoxically appears to contradict Schmidt's prediction that centralized and unitary states will experience a more difficult process of adaptation.[8]

As will be shown, this apparent paradox is accounted by the national executive's capacity to adapt to supra-national constraints. Specifically, the process of European integration has generated new opportunity structures at the domestic level, effectively increasing the room for manoeuvre of the national executive. In large measure, this derives from the executive's monopoly of representation at the European Union level, which effectively makes it the "official interpreter" of EU decisions. In this sense, the European level operates as an important additional "instrument" in the executive's armoury against domestic opposition.

7   A. Maurer, J. Mittag and V. Wessels, "National systems' adaptation to the EU system: Trends, offers and constraints", in B. Kohler-Koch (ed.), *Linking EU and national governance* (Oxford: Oxford University Press, 2003), pp. 53–82.

8   V. Schmidt, "Federalism and state governance in the European Union and the United States: An institutional perspective", in K. Nicolaidis and R. Howse (eds), *The federal vision: Legitimacy and levels of governance in the United States and the European Union* (Oxford: Oxford University Press, 2001), pp. 335–54.

What is Europeanization, and How can it be Measured?[9]

The concept of Europeanization is an increasing presence in the social sciences literature. According to Featherstone, between 1981 and 1995 the social sciences citation index contained 32 articles that had Europeanization as a subject term: from 1996 to 2001 this number more than doubled to 84.[10] This increased interest reflects a frequently ignored aspect of the European integration process, and consequently also of its effects—that it is a recent process, and one that is being constructed and reconstructed. As such, the EU is "fluid, ambiguous and hybrid", and research into its effects cannot escape the constraints of the "Neurath's boat" that is the EU, with inevitable impact on the Europeanization of domestic political institutions.[11]

In terms of definition, here we remain close to that initially used by Ladrech (1994). We are interested in analysing Europeanization as a process through which member-states are, due to the European level, obliged to alter their structures, policies, formal regulations and consolidated practices. Moreover, we seek to analyse the "adaptation of institutional settings in the broadest sense (of rules, procedures, norms, practices) at different political levels in response to the dynamics of integration".[12] Thus, the

9 This section is a revised version of a previously published analysis. C. Jalali, "A Europa como razão ou como desculpa? A europeização das instituições políticas nacionais", in P. Lains and M. C. Lobo (eds), *Em nome da Europa: Portugal em mudança, 1986–2006* (Lisbon: Principia, 2007), pp. 173–90.

10 K. Featherstone, "Introduction: In the name of 'Europe'", in K. Featherstone and C. M. Radaelli (eds), *The politics of Europeanization* (Oxford: Oxford University Press, 2003), p. 5.

11 J. P. Olsen, "European challenges to the nation state", in B. Steunenberg and F. van Vught (eds), *Political institutions and public policy: Perspectives on European decision-making* (Amsterdam: Kluwer, 1997), p. 165.

12 Featherstone and Radaelli (note 10), p. 19.

Europeanization of institutions becomes a matter of extent rather than of nature.[13] Giulani adopts a much wider definition of Europeanization, one that includes the "autonomization" of the European governmental arena from the preferences of member-states.[14] To the extent this avoids causal circularity, this dimension is legitimate for reaching an understanding of Europeanization as a phenomenon: national governments are, after all, an important part of European governance processes. Müller notes that national governments remain privileged actors in the European decision-making process while Heritier shows both the extent of choice national governments have within the EU and how they are able to adopt innovative methods in order to overcome decision deadlocks.[15]

However, this study departs from the assumption European level structures and regulations are effectively independent of national preferences, analysing Europeanization from a "top-down" perspective. This is a legitimate research strategy in the analysis of Europeanization processes.[16] In the Portuguese case, this assumption is all the more acceptable given the country's late accession to the European Union and its position on the EU's political and economic periphery.

The growing literature on the Europeanization of political institutions also integrates the much wider debate over neo-institutionalism (or neo-institutionalisms) as a methodology in political science. Börzel and Risse identify two competing methods of

13 M. Giulani, "Europeanization in comparative perspective: Institutional fit and national adaptation", in Featherstone and Radaelli (note 10), p. 135.

14 Guilani (note 13).

15 Müller (note 5); A. Héritier, *Policy-making and diversity in Europe: Escape from deadlock* (Cambridge: Cambridge University Press, 1999).

16 See, for example, T. Börzel and T. Risse, "Conceptualizing the domestic impact of Europe", in Featherstone and Radaelli (note 10), pp. 57–80.

conceptualizing Europeanization, in terms of rational choice and sociological neo-institutionalism.[17] With respect to the former, several authors have adopted Tsebelis' veto player model to explain domestic adaptation processes to the European level.[18] The model here is that the European level generates new opportunity structures within which agents can act, with the former in turn influenced by both the number of domestic veto players and by existing formal institutions. As such, the dispersal of power within the political system—both in terms of formal and informal veto players—limits the capacity for adaptation,[19] whereas the existence of institutions that can take advantage of the European level (for example, regions that are able to negotiate directly with Brussels without going through their national government) can accelerate adaptation. In terms of sociological neo-institutionalism, pressure for adaptation is a result of transformations at the political culture level. Thus, the rise of "European policies, norms and...collective understandings", combined with the presence of "change agents" and/or informal cooperative institutions, leads to the development of new identities, the adoption of new norms and, consequently, domestic adaptation and change.[20]

Here we adopt the former type of analysis, as it is easier to fit it into "consequentialist logic". In the meantime, it is worth noting the importance of the "goodness of fit", which is interpreted here as indicating the alignment between the European and national levels. As several authors have noted, the idea of Europeanization

17 Börzel and Risse (note 16), pp. 57–80.

18 G. Tsebelis, *Veto players: How political institutions work* (Princeton, NJ: Princeton University Press, 2002).

19 C. Radaelli, "The Europeanization of public policy", in Featherstone and Radaelli (note 10), pp. 27–56.

20 Börzel and Risse (note 16), pp. 57–9.

requires a de-alignment or "misfit" of these two levels: "there is no need for domestic changes" if pressures from the European level align perfectly with the domestic modus operandi.[21] Thus, "adaptational pressures are generated by the fact that the emerging European polity encompasses structures of authoritative decision making which might clash with national structures of policy making".[22] As Börzel and Risse note, this can result in two types of "misfit": in terms of public policies (when the member-states do not comply with European legislation); and that which interests us here—institutional de-alignment—to the extent the European level "challeng[es] domestic rules and procedures and the collective understandings attached to them".

In terms of research, the causal relationship between the pressure to change emanating from the European level and the domestic level's substantive adaptation is not easy to determine, thus becoming a sort of "missing link".[23] In the absence of formal institutional transformation—as in Portugal—this "missing link" becomes all the more difficult to find.

Thus, two related questions emerge. The first is regarding the literature's often vague definition of the concept of Europeanization. The fact that the concept can take on several meanings results in it being used to characterize a relatively large set of phenomena.[24] Because of this, Europeanization as a concept can lose discriminatory power and much of its analytical utility. The second question is concerned with the counter-factual to Europeanization. The existence of changes that are contemporary with

---

21 Börzel and Risse (note 16), p. 61.

22 Börzel and Risse (note 16).

23 K. Goetz, "European integration and national executives: A cause in search of an effect?", *West European Politics* 23, 4 (2000), pp. 211–31.

24 Radaelli (note 19).

European integration does not of itself imply a process of Europeanization. As such, the research strategy and the measurement of the effects of Europeanization must be capable of isolating the impact of European integration vis-à-vis a whole series of other factors that can also influence the patterns of institutional adaptation (such as internal pressures, social change, globalization processes, amongst others). The results are thus influenced not only by the degree of pressure emanating from the EU, but also by the extent of de-alignment between the European and domestic levels, and by extra-EU dimensions also.

The Europeanization of Executive Power: The Theoretical Context

One of the most important aspects of the analysis of the European integration process is its effect on national executive power. The debate about the existence of "new forms of governance" is a good example of this impact. The literature on "governance" re-conceptualizes government processes, outlining the need for a new "map" to help us understand its modern forms.[25] Stoker suggests this new map will involve an analysis of governance as a process involving a range of institutions and agents (that may or may not emerge from the state) and with ever less clear boundaries between the roles of different agents.[26] Within this new map, the European dimension is one of the more important new arenas for governance and decision-making.

25 R. Rhodes, "What is new about governance and why does it matter?", in Hayward and Menon (note 1), pp. 61–2.

26 G. Stoker, "Governance as a theory: Five propositions", *International Social Science Journal* 50, 155 (1998), pp. 17–28.

The impact of the EU also ties in with the popular concept of the "hollowed out state".[27] This concept suggests that functions that are traditionally performed by nation states are transferred to other institutions and levels, thereby creating a national state with an essentially unaltered "external façade", but within which there is ever less content. In this context, Europeanization is a good example of this transfer of responsibilities and of the hollowing out of nation states (and implicitly national executives). Stone, Fligstein and Sandholtz note European integration cannot be separated from more general interaction processes that weaken national government structures: "The move to European governance has been driven by firms trading more across national borders, by the economies of Europe becoming increasingly interdependent in other myriad ways, and by actors gradually finding that the forms and methods of supranational governance served their evolving conception of interests".[28] Yet, regardless of the origin of this phenomenon, the impact of Europeanization on national governments appears to be particularly strong.

The flow of responsibilities from the national to the supranational domain is not without its tensions and conflicts, however. As the study by Patrick Le Galès shows, the gradual resolution of conflicts between national governments and the EU tends to produce new equilibria (as well as potential tensions elsewhere), resulting in a "complex and deeply political" process of Europeanization that national governments—even ones historically as influential within the EU as France—cannot escape.[29] This process

---

27 Jessop (note 2); R. Rhodes, "The hollowing out of the state: The changing nature of the public service in Britain", *Political Quarterly* 65, 2 (1994), pp. 138–51.

28 S. A. Stone, N. Fligstein and W. Sandholtz, "The institutionalization of European space", in A. S. Sweet, W. Sandholtz and N. Fligstein (eds), *The institutionalization of Europe* (Oxford: Oxford University Press, 2001), p. 2.

29 P. le Galès, "Est maître des lieux celui qui les organise: How rules change when

may be slower and more difficult than some analysts or political actors might think or wish.[30] Nevertheless, there is a general sense that, over all, the swing of the pendulum is not unfavourable to the European level.

One model that captures well this gradual transformation of political processes in contemporary Europe is that of multi-level governance. Marks and Hooghe note that "formal authority has been dispersed from central states both up to supranational institutions and down to regional and local governments", and to this list we can also add the increasingly blurred boundary between the public and non-public sectors, which is noticeable in the role of the third sector in public policy processes.[31] Multi-level governance is defined as being characterized by "negotiated, non-hierarchical exchanges between institutions at the transnational, national, regional and local levels".[32] In this sense, the concept of multi-level governance allows us to overcome the separation in the study of international and national politics, a dichotomy that is increasingly inapplicable in the complex and changeable realities generated by the European integration process. As Scharpf posits, "the conceptual tools with which the political science sub-disciplines of international relations and comparative politics are

national and European policy domains collide", in Sweet, Sandholtz and Fligstein (note 28), p. 125.

30 See for example the comments of Romani Prodi and of Gerhard Schröder. For Prodi's perspective, see the October 1999 interview with the Spanish daily *El País*, which has been republished in *European Foundation Intelligence Digest* 8, 81 (22 October–4 November 1999). Available at www.europeanfoundation.org/docs/81id.htm. For Schröder's views, see the Schröder Plan of 2001.

31 G. Marks and L. Hooghe, "Contrasting visions of multi-level governance", in I. Bache and M. Flinders (eds), *Multi-level governance* (Oxford: Oxford University Press, 2004), p. 15.

32 B. G. Peters and J. Pierre, "Developments in intergovernmental relations: Towards multi-level governance", *Policy and Politics* 29, 2 (2001), p. 131.

approaching the study of European institutions are ill suited to deal with multi-level interactions".[33]

The use and development of the concept of multi-level governance by authors such as Marks and Hooghe also captures the notion that the relationship between different levels—and particularly of interest here, between the European and the national executives—is not defined by clear, hierarchical and formal jurisdictions.[34] Rather, these can vary across (formal and informal) public policy arenas and can also change over time. This distinction is captured in Marks and Hooghe's definition of type I and type II multi-level governance, each with a clear, and clearly distinct, implication for governance processes. Type I involves the existence of an explicit, hierarchical and largely stable jurisdictional structure between the different levels, and contrasts strongly with type II's complex and fluid structure, composed of numerous and overlapping jurisdictions. The impact of the European level is largely captured by this second type of multi-level governance, in which specific jurisdictions emerge in terms of functions, with intersecting and territorially overlapping jurisdictional levels, in a process captured by the concept of "fragmegration". This term, a contraction of fragmentation and integration, aptly illustrates the distinct and apparently contradictory impact when analysing multi-level governance in general, and the impact of Europeanization on national executives in particular.[35]

In this regard, it is worth noting Schmidt's prediction of the existence of a correlation between the impact of Europeanization

33 Cited in Bache and Flinders (note 31), p. 1.

34 Marks and Hooghe (note 31).

35 For more on this concept, see J. Rosenau, "Strong demand, huge supply: Governance in an emerging epoch", in Bache and Flinders (note 31).

and the pre-existing structure of the state.[36] Schmidt suggests that the impact of the EU's "quasi-federal" and "quasi-pluralist" policy formulation structures is more intense in unitary states than in either federal states or those in which there is a considerable degree of political decentralization, as in the former this involves a greater reduction in the executive power's autonomy and control.

The Europeanization of the Executive Power:
The Portuguese Case

Schmidt's hypothesis is particularly relevant with regard to the Portuguese case.[37] Le Galès shows Portugal as being one of the EU's most centralized states.[38] Yet Portugal represents a good example of how national institutions—and in this case, executive power—is able to adapt to supra-national pressures, confirming that:

> The requirement of adaptation has not led to dramatic modifications with regard to the overall systemic designs of the member states. Thus, comparing the changes at the European level to those in the 15 national systems, a clear asymmetry becomes obvious. The rate, frequency and cumulative effects of changes in the Brussels arena are larger and faster than those at the national level. Traditional national patterns are resistant and apparently flexible enough to be sufficiently capable of coping with the challenges from the European level. Thus, we note that the reactions to the EC/EU system on the national level have reached a certain prominence, but they do not constitute a dramatic turnaround from traditional patterns of policy-making.

36 Schmidt (note 8).

37 Schmidt (note 8).

38 P. le Galès, "The changing European state: Pressures from within", in Hayward and Menon (note 1).

Typically, we observe a mobilization of established actors within the existing constitutional and institutional framework.[39]

On the one hand, it is possible to see the impact of EU membership on the national administrative structure and culture, with Magone arguing Europeanization was an important factor in the democratization of Portugal's public administration.[40] At the same time, this impact of Europeanization is also reflected in transformations in government structures, with the creation of the office of Secretary of State for European Affairs (from 1985 on, with the tenth constitutional government that took office that year), which has support of the General-Directorate of Community Affairs (DGAC)/General-Directorate of European Affairs (DGAE).[41] Magone also notes the increasing share of DGAC resources, both in terms of personnel and of responsibilities at the level of European affairs, a reflection of the importance of the European level and of the need for support structures to deal with it within the executive.[42] The same conclusion can be taken from the creation of structures designed to interact with the EU level within several ministries, including the Ministry of Education's office for European Affairs and International Relations (GAERI) and the Ministry of Finance's General-Directorate of European Affairs and International Relations. In order to meet the need for governmental coordination, the Inter-ministerial Commission

39 Maurer, Mittag and Wessels (note 7), pp. 75–6.

40 Magone, 2001 (note 6).

41 The General-Directorate of Community Affairs (DGAC) became the General-Directorate of European Affairs (DGAE) in 2006 (see Decree-Law 204/2006 of 26 October, article 27/4).

42 Magone (note 6), p. 137.

for Community Affairs (CIAC) was also created.[43] As Magone notes,[44] this serves as the main structure for inter-ministerial and administrative coordination, even if its actual role does change over time, at times being superseded by more informal methods of coordination.

In practice, the impact of Europeanization on Portugal can be described as a mixture of transformation and inertia, to use the typology of Radaelli.[45] Radaelli outlines four distinct types of adaptation by national institutions to European pressures: inertia, absorption, transformation and retrenchment. This typology reflects the scale and direction of the Europeanization process which, in the case of retrenchment, can also be negative. In such a case, the reaction of domestic agents (for example, due to the existence of multiple points of veto against Brussels) may lead institutions to accentuate their de-alignment from Europe. Inertia can be seen as an absence of change, for instance through delays in the implementation of directives, or by resistance to changes introduced by the EU. Absorption indicates the adaptation—short of substantial transformations—of domestic structures in the European context. As Héritier notes, this implies an accommodation with European public policy requirements, without causing any real alteration in either the key structures or in the political system's behavioural logic.[46] Transformation, in turn, implies a change of paradigm, involving a fundamental modification of domestic political behaviour.

43   This is now the Inter-ministerial Commission for European Affairs (see note 41).

44   See note 41.

45   Radaelli (note 19).

46   Cited in Radaelli (note 19), p. 37.

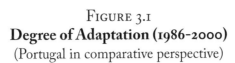

FIGURE 3.1
Degree of Adaptation (1986-2000)
(Portugal in comparative perspective)

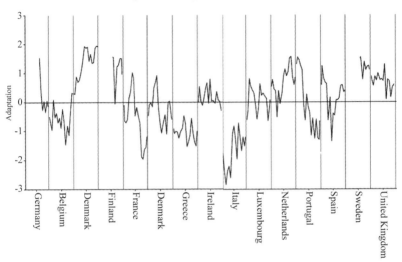

SOURCE: M. Giuliani, "Europeanization in comparative perspective: Institutional fit and national adaptation", in K. Featherstone and C. M. Radaelli (eds), *The politics of Europeanization* (Oxford: Oxford University Press, 2003), p. 138

This typology is useful to the extent it establishes analytical criteria. Naturally, results are influenced not only by the degree of EU pressure but also the extent of pre-existing de-alignment between the European and domestic levels. At the same time, it is worth noting this typology is incapable of fully dealing with the question of correlation versus causality in the analysis of the impact of Europeanization.

Figure 3.1 above shows the percentage of transpositions and the respective proportion of infractions in the various stages of the process. As can be seen, the adaptation in Portugal tends overall to be one of absorption, but one resulting from a mixture of transformation and inertia patterns.

This pattern suggests the inadequacy of the simplistic view of Portugal as a "good student" within the EU. It also highlights the degree of choice that domestic agents—and particularly here the executive—have vis-à-vis European pressures. Returning to the argument developed in Jalali,[47] the European level creates a new opportunity structure that domestic agents—again, especially the executive power—can exploit to their advantage, more specifically in creating support for their public policies.

The Executive Power's Room for Manoeuvre: External Ties in Theory

As Jessop notes, increasing "fragmegration" and transfer of responsibilities from national executives to other agents does not prevent the former from playing a crucial and central political role.[48] Equally, the analyses of Moravcsik and Dyson and Featherstone emphasise the room for manoeuvre of executives, and how their actions can alter their interaction with the context of "fragmegration".[49]

In particular, it is worth noting Dyson and Featherstone's concept of *vincolo esterno* (external tie or external binding).[50] In a

47 Jalali (note 9).

48 R. Jessop, "Multi-level governance and multi-level meta-governance: Changes in the European Union as integral moments in the transformation and reorientation of contemporary statehood", in Banche and Flinders (note 31) pp. 49–74.

49 A. Moravcsik, "Why the European Community strengthens the state: Domestic politics and international cooperation", *Center for European Studies Working Paper 52* (Cambridge, MA: Harvard University, 1994); K. Dyson and K. Featherstone, "Italy and the EMU as a 'vincolo esterno': empowering the technocrats, transforming the state", *South European Society and Politics*, 1, 2 (1996), pp. 272–99.

50 "External tie", see also K. Dyson and K. Featherstone, "Italian policy beliefs about EMU: External discipline versus internal protection", in Featherstone and Radaelli (note 10), p. 452. Radaelli and Franchino in turn translate it as "external lever", see C. Radaelli and F. Franchino, "Analysing political change in Italy", *Journal of European Public Policy*, 11, 6 (2004), p. 945. In either case, the sense of an external bind generating new opportunity structures is quite evident.

sense, this has as its point of departure Moravcsik's prediction that national executives may have strategic interests in agreeing to European commitments. [51] The European dimension thus serves as a form of binding the national political system to specific public policies. To use Tsebelis's model of veto players, this binding enables national executives to reduce the potential range of options that they present to subsequent veto agents, as well as altering their pay-offs, given the costs of non-compliance with European agreements.[52] At the same time, the European dimension also enables national executives to more easily adopt blame avoidance strategies with regard to the policies they adopt,[53] with these "external ties" acting as an important resource for national executives when taking potentially unpopular measures.

In contexts like that of Portugal, characterized by a weak direct articulation of civil society and interest groups with Brussels,[54] executives benefit even more disproportionately from this "European trump card". As Schendelen notes, Portuguese interest groups "play a marginal role on the input side of the EU machine".[55] This pattern implies that other agents, apart from the executive, have an extremely limited voice in European institutions and processes, and the resulting near-monopoly executives have in terms of the representation of national interests in the EU further facilitates this process of external binding. As Schendelen also highlights, "due to their lack of sufficient size and other resources, the private

51 Moravcsik (note 49).

52 Tsebelis (note 18).

53 R. K. Weaver, "The politics of blame avoidance", *Journal of Public Policy* 6, 4 (1986), pp. 371–98.

54 See Jalali (note 9) for more details.

55 R. van Schendelen, *Machiavelli in Brussels: The art of lobbying the EU* (Amsterdam: Amsterdam University Press, 2002), p. 126.

groups can hardly act self-reliantly. For the remote control of the EU, they remain dependent on their government and their national umbrellas, which are frequently linked to the government".[56]

This has two important implications. First, it means that decisions emanating from the European level have a negligible input from Portuguese interest groups, with the executive as the main representative of Portuguese interests. This implication is all the more relevant if we relax the assumption of a top-down only Europeanization process, and endogenize decisions taken at the European level to national preferences.

Second, the executive also sees its position reinforced in the top-down relationship, as its monopoly of representation within the EU also confers upon it a crucial role as the interpreter of European decisions at the national level and, consequently, room for manoeuvre.[57] In specific, this enables executives to emphasise or play down (as necessary) European pressures when drawing up public policies. This also allows for blame-avoidance, as executives can use the European dimension as a pretext for measures they consider desirable, but which they fear may be unpopular.[58] In this context, citizens' attitudes towards the EU are also important. Where citizens demonstrate more favourable attitudes towards the EU, and where trust in European institutions is higher, resorting to the European dimension by national executives may be more effective in attenuating and overcoming domestic opposition.

56 Schendelen (note 55), p. 127.

57 R. Roland, *Interpreters as diplomats: A diplomatic history of the role of interpreters in world politics* (Ottawa: University of Ottawa Press, 1999).

58 Jalali (note 9).

The Executive's Room for Manoeuvre:
The Portuguese Case[59]

This room for manoeuvre executives have obtained as a result of the Europeanization process is perceptible in the Portuguese case. First, the favourable attitudes of the Portuguese towards the EU facilitate the use of external binding. The Portuguese tend to have a more positive perception of the EU than the European average, and are characterized by higher levels of trust in European than in domestic institutions, as Figures 3.2 and 3.3 below indicate.

FIGURE 3.2
Evolution of Attitudes towards the EU (1989-2003, %)

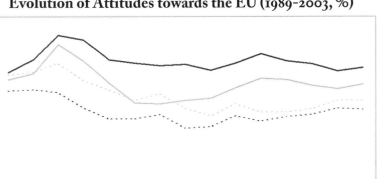

Source: M. V. Cabral, P. Magalhães, M. C. Lobo, F. Nunes and A. E. Santo, *Eurobarometer 59: Public opinion in the European Union, national report Portugal* (European Opinion Research Group, 2003), p. 7.

An example of the national executive's recourse to external binding may be perceived in the policies of the 15th constitutional government, headed by José Manuel Durão Barroso, and which

59 This is a revised version of the analysis published in Jalali (note 9).

FIGURE 3.3
Trust of the Portuguese in National and European Institutions, Annual Average
(1999–2003)

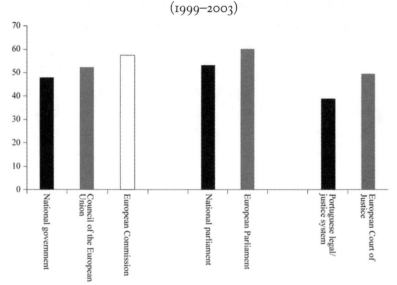

SOURCE: M. V. Cabral, P. Magalhães, M. C. Lobo, F. Nunes and A. E. Santo, *Eurobarometer 59: Public opinion in the European Union, national report Portugal* (European Opinion Research Group, 2003), p. 34.

was in office in the period 2002-05. This government very rapidly adopted as its main goal the reduction of Portugal's budget deficit to within the three per cent of GDP criterion of the Euro zone's growth and stability pact, even if the election manifesto of the main coalition partner—the centre-right Social Democrats (PSD—Partido Social Democrata)—gave few indications of a public expenditure containment programme. Figure 3.4 shows the results of a content analysis of the PSD's election manifesto, resulting from the Euromanifestos project.

This external tie emerged very early on in this government's life. The government took office on Saturday, 6 April 2002. Less

FIGURE 3.4
2002 PSD Election Manifesto Policy Positions
(number of quasi-sentences indicating specific
positions and preferences)

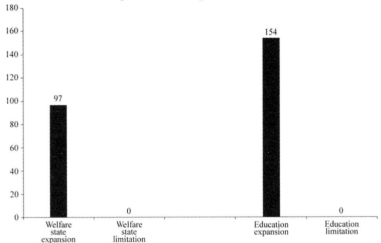

SOURCE: *Euromanifesto* project dataset.

than two days later the new finance and state minister, Manuela
Ferreira Leite, declared the 2001 budget deficit situation as being
"extremely serious". Four days later—on the eve of the government completing its first week in office—the prime minister emphasized the budget deficit question in a speech to the congress of
the National Association of Portuguese Municipalities. Speaking
to an important audience in terms of domestic politics, Barroso
explained the need to contain the budget based on the European dimension. Balancing the public accounts was described as a
"patriotic duty given the serious situation in which we find our-
selves", with the prime minister asking those in power at the local level to make "an effort to avoid Portugal being outside the
stability pact".[60] The escalating dramatization of the budget deficit

60 *Portugal Diário*, "Durão dramático" (12 April 2002), www.portugaldiario.iol.pt/
noticia.php?id=35152&div_id=291.

and of the existence of entirely exogenous penalties should the stability pact criteria not be met was to continue later in the same month: alluding to the penalties Portugal could face, Barroso said he "pray[ed] that the 2001 deficit remain below three per cent".[61]

In July 2002, having already implemented a series of austerity measures, Barroso revealed that the 2001 deficit was 4.1 per cent of GDP. At the same time, Europe was used as a justification for the continued implementation of budgetary control policies. While the prime minister indicated he did not believe Brussels would impose sanctions, he also indicated the need to carry on with budgetary restraint: "It would be absurd if, at a time when Portugal is making an effort to adjust, they fine us and make this adjustment more difficult".[62] Once again, the association between internal austerity policies (for example, through a public sector wage freeze) and European pressure was stressed.

However, if the political message stressed that the executive's main concern was meeting the stability pact criterion regarding the budget deficit, the government's actual programme—as submitted to parliament—enunciated a related, although not necessarily identical, objective. Thus, Barroso's government's programme defined its economic policy objectives to be the enlargement of the role of the market in the Portuguese economy, and defined the state's weight in the economy as excessive. Many of the Barroso government's policies could only be indirectly related to its apparent goal of controlling the budget deficit in order to avoid sanctions under the terms of the stability pact, being rather more clearly directed at eliminating constraints on market

61 *Portugal Diário*, "Orçamento rectificativo de rigor e austeridade" (24 April 2002), www.portugaldiario.iol.pt/noticia.php?id=37447&div_id=291.

62 *Portugal Diário*, "Durão Barroso não acredita em sanções de Bruxelas" (26 July 2002), www.portugaldiario.iol.pt/noticia.php?id=55129&div_id=291.

forces. A good example of this is the labour legislation reform of 2003–04, which introduced greater labour market flexibility. The stress Barroso's government laid on the budget deficit exemplifies the notion of binding externally to bind internally. Its recourse to Europe gave it an additional weapon in the formation and implementation of potentially unpopular public policies.

Final Notes

The change in the standards and processes of government that is captured by concepts such as governance, multi-level government and "fragmegration" are inevitably reflected in the operation and role of executive power. One of the important driving-forces behind such changes is the European integration process, with the resulting transfer of responsibilities to the supra-national level. This effect of Europeanization is particularly significant in cases such as Portugal, given its politically and economically peripheral position within the EU.

At the same time, echoing Maurer, Mittag and Wessels, the European integration processes do not necessarily generate fundamental transformations, and the Portuguese executive also demonstrates autonomy of action that enables it to adapt to European demands. In particular, European integration creates new domestic opportunity structures, which executives have used to increase their room for manoeuvre.[63] The European level thus emerges as not only a constraint on national executive power, but also as an instrument enabling it to overcome domestic opposition and veto players who resist its public policies.

It is also worth highlighting aspects that merit examination in future research. In particular, the rapid growth of regulatory bod-

63 Maurer, Mittag and Wessels (note 7).

ies in Portugal since the beginning of the present century must be noted, confirming the assertion regulation is the (only) component of modern government that continues to expand.[64] In part, this is a consequence of the process of Europeanization, to the extent European integration is a creator of regulatory policies. At the same time, this emerging regulatory web may come to represent a constraint on executive autonomy, to the extent it overlaps with and constrains executives' prerogatives.

---

64 C. Hood, O. James, G. Jones, C. Scott and T. Travers, *Regulation inside government: Waste-watchers, quality police and sleaze-busters* (Oxford: Oxford University Press, 1999).

4 | Implementing the Treaty of Lisbon: The Portuguese Parliament as an Actor in the European Legislative Arena

Madalena Meyer Resende and Maria Teresa Paulo

Introduction

This chapter analyses the institutional and political factors shaping the Portuguese parliament's response to the pressures for the adaptation to the Treaty of Lisbon's provisions on the involvement of national parliaments as scrutinizers of European legislation. In its inquiry into the factors shaping the response to pressures the chapter follows a conception of Europeanization as adaptation to the conditions imposed by the European institutions.[1] Until 2006 the parliament had no involvement in the European legislative cycle, mainly because it had no access to the legislative initiatives of the European Commission (EC), even those within its exclusive legislative competence.

The peculiarity of the Portuguese case in its response to the European Union's (EU) pressure for adaptation derives both from its participation in the political dialogue with the EC since 2006,[2]

---

1 T. A. Borzel and T. Risse, "Conceptualizing the domestic impact of Europe", and C. M. Radaelli, "The Europeanization of public policy", in K. Featherstone and C. M. Radaelli (eds), *The politics of Europeanization* (Oxford: Oxford University Press, 2003), pp. 57–82, 27–56; K. H. Goetz and K. H. F. Dyson, "Europeanization compared: The shrinking core and the decline of state power", in K. H. Goetz and K. H. F. Dyson (eds), *Germany, Europe, and the politics of constraint* (Oxford: New York: Oxford University Press, 2003), pp. 349–76.

2 European Commission, Communication from the Commission to the Euro-

and following that the way it implemented the Treaty of Lisbon's provisions—namely the subsidiarity control of EU pieces of legislation. Parliaments that developed a systematic scrutiny system of European legislation are usually those with a strong tradition of control over the government in the national sphere or the presence of Eurosceptic parties.[3] In Portugal both these conditions are absent: the parliament has some constitutional powers for controlling the government but no tradition of using them and political parties have a positive consensus on integration.[4] Moreover, parliament dedicates relatively scarce resources to the management of European affairs.

Consensus among parliamentary parties—rather than the usual factors contributing to the implementation of strong control powers over the government in the scrutiny of EU affairs, such as the allocation of resources or an institutionalized conflict over integration—was key to the parliament's success in shedding its legacy and in instituting an ex-ante scrutiny of European legislation. The Portuguese parliament thus earned a place among the eight most active national parliaments as EU legislation scrutinizers. In this it was helped by the direct transmission of information by the EC to national parliaments.

pean Council: A citizens' agenda—delivering results for Europe, COM 211 (10 May 2006).

3   A. Maurer, "National parliaments in the European architecture: From latecomers' adaptation towards permanent institutional change?", in A. Maurer and W. Wessels (eds), *National parliaments on their ways to Europe: Losers or latecomers?* (Baden-Baden: Nomos Verlagsgesellschaft, 2001), pp. 27–76; R. Pahre, "Endogenous domestic institutions in two-level games and parliamentary oversight of the European Union", *Journal of Conflict Resolution* 41, 1 (1997), pp. 147–74.

4   C. Leston-Bandeira, "The Portuguese parliament during the first two decades of democracy", *West European Politics* 24, 1 (2001), pp. 137–56; M. C. Lobo and P. Magalhães, "Room for manoeuvre: Euroscepticism in the Portuguese parties and electorate 1976–2005", *South European Society and Politics* 16, 1 (2011), pp. 81–104.

The analysis of the parliament's assertion of its position as a monitoring body at the national and European levels carried out in this chapter takes into account the statutory and informal arrangements of the parliament's scrutiny process, in particular the 2006 European Scrutiny Law (ESL) and the initiatives at European level—the Barroso initiative to share directly information on European legislation with the national parliament—and the early warning mechanism's eight-week deadline for the national parliament's pronouncement on the legislative initiatives imposed by the Treaty of Lisbon (protocol number two).[5] These two initiatives reinforced and complemented the ESL by providing direct and timely access to draft legislation and by imposing deadlines for the parliament to pronounce its opinion of the draft legislation.

Following studies on the Europeanization of national parliaments in the EU this chapter describes the adoption and implementation of the ESL and assesses the first year of the implementation of the provisions of the Treaty of Lisbon.[6] The parliament's implementation of ESL resulted in an impressive number of laws being scrutinized. From 2006 the parliament became one of the most effective scrutinizers of European legislation in the EU, forwarding 162 parliamentary opinions on EU institutions

5   Law 43/2006, *Diário da República*, 1 Série—No 164, 25 August 2006, pp. 6201–3.

6   K. Auel, "Adapting to Europe: Strategic Europeanization of national parliaments", in R. Holzhacker and E. A. Cheltenham (eds), *Democratic governance and European integration: Linking societal and state processes of democracy* (Northampton: Edward Elgar, 2007), pp. 157–79; L. Besselink, "National parliaments in the EU's composite constitution: A plea for a shift in paradigm", in P. Kiiver (ed.), *National and regional parliaments in the European constitutional order* (Groonigen: Europa Law Publishing, 2006), pp. 117–31; A. Fraga, *Os parlamentos nacionais e a legitimidade da construção europeia*, (Lisbon: Cosmos, 2001); E. Miklin, "Visibility of choices and better scrutiny? The effects of politicization and EU decision-making", paper prepared for the 5th ECPR Conference (Potsdam, 10–12 September 2009); A. Pliakos, "National parliaments and the European Union: Necessity of assigning a supranational role", *Revue Européenne de Droit Public* 19, 3 (2007), pp. 757–88.

and coming on top of the EC's rankings. The implementation of the Treaty of Lisbon provided a further boost to the working of the system: within one year of the treaty being implemented, parliament had forwarded more than 100 parliamentary opinions to EU institutions. However, in addition to the number of EU legislative proposals scrutinized, there is a qualitative impact of the legislative scrutiny onto the parliament's participation in the European multi-level governance that is still understudied. Based on a preliminary assessment of several cases of legislative scrutiny undertaken by parliament, this chapter proposes that the implementation of ESL had an effect on parliament's relations with the government, with the EU institutions (EC, European parliament and the European Council), other national parliaments in the EU, as well as on the establishment of parliament's role as a link between Portuguese civil society and European institutions.

Internal factors of Europeanization: The 2006 ESL and the 2007 and 2010 Internal Scrutiny Procedures

The adoption of the ESL, which foreshadowed the institutionalization of a systematic scrutiny system in the summer of 2006, was a key factor for the success of parliament's record of scrutinization of European legislation, which resulted in the strengthening of the oversight of parliament over government on European affairs and the establishment of a direct dialogue between parliament and European institutions in the EU legislative process. By establishing an obligation on government to consult with parliament in areas of its exclusive or partially-exclusive competence (although with non-binding effects) it opened the way for parliament to assume a role in European affairs. The ESL established the European Affairs Committee (EAC) as the coordinating body for scrutiny, while also involving sectoral committees in the scrutiny process. ESL also anticipates an increase in plenary and EAC discussions on European issues.

Since the 1992 Maastricht Treaty, national parliaments have been called to take a more active part in the European legislative process, in particular by establishing systems for scrutinizing their governments' stances on European legislation in the Council of Ministers. Parliamentary scrutiny systems vary considerably, and they have been classified in three types: informal information; authorized parliamentary consultation; and the mandate system.[7] Until 2006 the Portuguese parliament ran a scrutiny system of informal information, and had no commitment to take a stance on European affairs (Spanish, Greek and Portuguese—before Law 43/2006). In 2006, parliament adopted a system of authorized parliamentary consultation, which meant there had to be a formal exchange of information with the government, and which included regular meetings between members of parliament and ministers as well as the systematic scrutiny by parliament of matters that fall within its legislative remit (e.g. Germany, Cyprus, France, Ireland, Malta). This system falls short of the powers granted parliament within the mandate system, where government actions are bound by parliament's position (e.g. Austria, Denmark, Finland, Latvia, Poland, Slovakia, Sweden and the United Kingdom).[8]

7   Fraga (note 6).

8   COSAC, "Eighth bi-annual report: Developments in European Union procedures and practices relevant to parliamentary scrutiny. Prepared by the COSAC Secretariat for the XXXVIII Conference of Community and European Affairs Committees of Parliaments of the European Union" (2007); COSAC, "Thirteenth bi-annual report: Developments in European Union procedures and practices relevant to parliamentary scrutiny. Prepared by the COSAC Secretariat for the XLIII Conference of Community and European Affairs Committees of Parliaments of the European Union" (2010), available at www.cosac.eu/en/documents/biannual.

The literature points to two factors triggering the creation of strong systems of parliamentary scrutiny: a tradition of parliamentary control over the government and the contestation of European integration by Eurosceptic parties.[9] The two conditions do not apply in the Portuguese case: all Portuguese parliamentary parties support the EU and parliament has limited control over the government. The analysis of the discussion of Law 43/2006 by the EAC's working group points to a broad consensus on European integration among parliamentary parties and how it facilitated the adoption of the law by the plenary. All parliamentary parties presented bills along the lines of a systematic scrutiny system. The Socialist Party (PS—Partido Socialista) recommended "the strengthening of the power and ability of parliament",[10] the PSD called for a strengthening of "the role of the EAC, by granting it a coordinating role", in "closing the gap between citizens and the European decision-making process" and "assuring democratic control over the government and its ability to influence its positions.[11] The Popular Party (CDS—Centro Democrático Social) called for the fulfilment of constitutional provisions, whereas the Communist Party (PCP—Partido Comunista Português) called for the "adoption of a legal mechanism obliging the government to take into account the opinions of parliament" and the Left Block (BE) sought "a more active and decisive role on European affairs" for parliament.[12]

The authors of the law were operating in the wake of the debates on the involvement of national parliaments in the European

9   Maurer; Pahre (note 3).

10 PS, Draft Law 266/X, 24 May 2006.

11 PSD, Draft law 250/X, 11 April 2006.

12 PC, Draft law 245/X, 7 April 2006; CDS-PP, Draft law 249/X, 11 April 2006; BE, Draft law 270/X, 31 May 2006.

decision-making process during the EU convention on the European constitution, and were thus aware of the growing importance of national parliament participation in EU affairs. During the plenary debate preceding the vote on the EAC's report on 2 June 2006, the "urgency in overcoming the limitations of the national debate on European integration" and "preventing the distancing of parliament from the full exercise of its competences on European affairs" were stressed.[13] That the formulation of national positions should be the result of a process of co-decision between the government and the parliament in order to "fight the distancing of parliamentarians from European affairs" was defended.[14]

The ESL anticipated the Treaty of Lisbon's views on national parliaments' scrutiny of European legislation by three years. Article 3 of the scrutiny law referred to the possibility of issuing a "duly substantiated formal written opinion" on the compliance of an EU initiative with the principle of subsidiarity. The law established a compulsory pronouncement by parliament on matters reserved to it either exclusively or partially, although its character was non-binding. It also obliges government to inform parliament of its position on particular legislation, but does not impose any deadlines, instead using the general formula that the government should inform the parliament "in good time". Thus, in the absence of systematic governmental information to parliament on the ongoing European legislative process, the Barroso initiative's direct linking of draft European legislation from the EC to national parliaments prevented the ESL from being a dead letter prior the implementation of the Treaty of Lisbon in December 2009.[15]

---

13 Respectively, Armando França (PS) and Honório Novo (PCP), in *Diário da Assembleia da República* (DAR), I Série, 131, 3 June 2006, p. 6027.

14 Almeida Henriques (PSD), DAR I Série, 131, 3 June 2006, p. 6031–3.

15 AR, Law 43/2006, article 2.2.

The law strengthens parliament's oversight of government, rather than establishing it as a (co-)legislator. Other instruments typical of parliamentary control over the executive were also established: three annual plenary debates with the government, two meetings with the Secretary of State for European Affairs in the EAC before and after the European Councils, and the possibility of meetings between the EAC/sectoral committees and the ministers involved in European Council meetings.

The EAC's role in the scrutiny process is central and, one can argue, it is the main motor of parliament's scrutiny system. Indeed, since the introduction of the ESL, the EAC has played a key role in the articulation of the scrutiny process within parliament. Responsibility for initiating and concluding the scrutiny procedure is given to the EAC (article three of the ESL): the EAC "shall draw up the formal written opinion in consultation with the sectoral parliamentary committees with responsibility for the matter in question…the formal written opinion shall be submitted in form of a draft resolution to the plenary for debate and voting by simple majority, except in cases in which there are grounds for urgency, when the committee's decision shall suffice". The EAC, upon receiving draft EU laws (usually from EC) forwards it to the relevant sectoral committee(s), which decide whether to nominate a *rapporteur* to draft a report.[16] Unless the EAC specifically requests their opinion, specialist committees freely decide whether to draft a report, draw up concrete proposals, prepare the documents for the EAC's consideration or remain silent on the matter. When a scrutiny document arrives the EAC decides on the effect it is given. The committee may designate one or more rapporteurs (*deputado relator*) for the purpose of drafting a written opinion (or reasoned opinion, if a breach of

---

16   Article four of the second protocol in the appendix to the Lisbon Treaty.

subsidiarity is identified), which—if adopted—is sent to the president of the parliament, who sends it to the EU institutions and the government. In the case of non-approval, as in the case of the refusal of the opinion on one of the initiatives of the EC's package for economic governance at the beginning of 2011, the EAC may decide to forward the existing specialized committee report. The committee may also decide to adopt a motion for a parliamentary resolution and send it to the plenary for debate and vote (being the only committee with this power). As a rule, the EAC finalises the scrutiny process by approving a final opinion and either submitting a resolution to the plenary for discussion and approval or sending it directly to parliament's speaker for forwarding to the government and EU institutions. Although the ESL refers to the approval of the plenary as the rule, in fact the EAC vote has been the consensual practice for concluding the scrutiny process. The Portuguese parliament follows the trend among national parliaments, where the EAC is, as a rule, the arena for the adoption of scrutiny opinions.[17]

The role of the specialist committees has been developed by regularly providing specialized inputs to the scrutiny process on the substance of the proposals falling under their scope. This is why the EAC only plays a substantive role if the committee with responsibility for the matter in question decides not to take action or when a parliamentary group considers a proposal politically relevant. Otherwise, the EAC forwards the substantial remarks of the sectoral committee and analyses the legal basis of the EU proposal, as well as it compliance with the subsidiarity principle. Often the opinion sent to the government and EU institutions

---

17 T. Raunio, "National parliaments and European integration: What we know and what we should know", *Arena Working Paper* 2/2009.

includes a report by the specialist committee. Nevertheless, ultimately the EAC's opinion prevails.

In order to implement the provisions stated in law 43/2006 the EAC developed and approved some procedural rules in 2007 for managing the legislative and non-legislative initiatives submitted by the EC. Considering these procedures each week the EAC distributes legislative initiatives to the relevant sectoral committees. These procedures also provide the EAC with the task of prioritizing areas of parliamentary EU scrutiny, both in the short- and in the long-term (on an annual basis). According to the 2007 rules the EAC's chairman could have the initiatives monitored according to the political relevance of the European initiative for Portugal. This list of priorities for political assessment was discussed at an EAC meeting according to three fundamental criteria: reserved parliamentary responsibility, the principle of subsidiary and the strategic interest for Portugal. Since the Treaty of Lisbon, this distribution is made every eight weeks, which means all initiatives sent by EU Institutions under the treaty's second protocol are subject to prioritization and included on the agenda of the committees' weekly meetings.

As a result of the January 2010 revision of the internal scrutiny procedure following the September 2009 general elections in Portugal and the implementation of the Lisbon Treaty in December 2009, the EAC began distributing EU initiatives on a daily basis—from all EU institutions—to the competent committees. For those initiatives falling under the Lisbon Treaty's "early warning mechanism", parliament has eight weeks to take a position. When no report is presented by a sectoral committee within the first six weeks, the EAC decides whether to present an opinion. Nonetheless, when a sectoral committee provides the EAC with a report, the committee analyses and debates it and, usually, produces a "rubberstamp" final opinion. The EAC often adds some additional notes, reflecting the additional information it collected through its informal channels of information with the government, the permanent representative (PERMREP) in Brussels and within the network of national parliaments, through the Portuguese parliament's permanent representative in Brussels.

The EAC may propose formal mechanisms to implement an effective monitoring and assessment of and pronouncement by parliament on EU matters within its reserved legislative competence. For that purpose the EAC is entitled to ask for a sectoral view from permanent committees in order to ascertain parliamentary opinion on EU initiatives—on the substance (sectoral committees), on the legal basis and the observance of the subsidiarity principle. The ESL invites the EAC to "act with the sectoral parliamentary committees with responsibility for the matter in question to ensure the exchange of information and appropriate ways of working".[18]

The amendments to the internal scrutiny procedure in 2010 also instituted the system of enhanced scrutiny, in which parliament defines six annual priorities for scrutiny, with a specific road map and monitoring methodology. Enhanced scrutiny begins with a pre-selection process using the criterion of the political relevance of an EU initiative for Portugal. Each parliamentary committee prepares its annual opinion on the EC's legislative and work programme and notifies the EAC whether it intends to submit any EC initiative—legislative or otherwise—to the enhanced scrutiny procedure. Upon the receipt of these notices, the EAC organizes a meeting with the Secretary of State of European Affairs, Members of the European Parliament (MEPs) and members of the two regional parliamentary assemblies in order to

18 Article 6d.

debate the EC working programme and the priorities for scrutiny. The EAC may, after this comprehensive consultation process, choose six initiatives every year for enhanced scrutiny. The EAC will, in cooperation with the relevant parliamentary committee, draft a broader work programme for each of the selected initiatives. Enhanced scrutiny proceeds on the basis of these individual tailor-made scrutiny roadmaps.

The legislative and non-legislative priorities for enhanced scrutiny include joint meetings with the responsible sectoral committees, an exchange of information with the government, the PERMREP and inter-parliamentary exchange of information among the 40 EU parliamentary chambers.

The External Factors of Europeanization: The Barroso Initiative and the Treaty of Lisbon

Although the adoption of this law implies the convergence of the Portuguese parliament's scrutiny system to the model of systematic consultation practiced by Germany, France, Sweden and the Czech Republic,[19] its omission of parliamentary specific scrutiny procedures, the difficulty of connecting with the daily political work of deputies, the lack of human resources and the deadlines for government passing information European initiatives to parliament has been a crucial weakness in the implementation process. During 2006 and 2007 the government seldom notified parliament on new European legislation related to matters of the former pillars II (common foreign and security policy [CFSP]) and III (freedom, security and justice [AFSJ]). The timely reception of the government's position by parliament is a crucial condition for the success of the scrutiny procedure.

19 COSAC 2007 (note 9).

Therefore in such legislative areas as AFSJ and CFSP, which are the main matters reserved exclusively to parliament, the legislature was prevented from performing its duty to scrutinize for lack of access to legislative initiatives.

The ESL's modesty in establishing an obligation on the government to inform parliament timeously of EU legislative initiatives predictably results in parliament being impeded in its duty caused by a lack of information. However, almost simultaneously with the approval of the law in September 2006, as a result of the Barroso initiative, parliament began receiving draft EU proposals and consultation documents directly from the EC. As a consequence the EC initiated a political dialogue with national parliaments on all aspects of its plans, asking parliaments to pronounce on issues of subsidiarity, on proportionality, the legal basis, and the substance of draft proposals or political considerations.[20] The direct dispatch of information to parliaments gave the Portuguese parliament well-timed access to the text of legislative proposals issued by the EC prior to the onset of the EU legislative decision-making process. This effectively reduced parliament's dependence on government for access to this information. This measure improved parliament's ability to fulfil its scrutiny obligations in the ESL.

The coincidence between the adoption of the ESL and the promotion of the Barroso initiative in the summer of 2006 led the EAC to tailor its scrutiny procedures specifically to the newly-established political dialogue with the EC. This allowed parliament to pronounce on all sorts of issues and influence both the government's position and the European institutions directly. The success of this new approach to EU affairs is highlighted in EC

20 European Commission, *Annual report 2009 on relations between the European Commission and national parliaments of 2 June 2010*, COM (2010), 2009.

reports, which recognise Portugal's parliament as a "particularly active chamber", which has so far sent most reasoned opinions. From 2006 to 2008 the Portuguese parliament sent 84 opinions to the EC, the French senate sent 53, the German Bundesrat 39; the Swedish parliament 33; the British House of Lords 30; the Danish Folketing 23 and the Czech senate 22,[21] in 2009 the Portuguese parliament sent 47 opinions, leaving the Czech senate behind with 27 and the Dutch houses of parliament with 18,[22] while in 2010 it sent 106 opinions, followed by two upper chambers—the Italian senate with 71 and the Czech senate with 29.[23]

In addition to the Barroso initiative, the European Parliament sends parliament those of its resolutions relevant to national parliaments and gives notice of the European parliament committee to which Portuguese parliamentary opinion on EU legislation was forwarded for consideration. From September 2008, the permanent representative of the parliament to the EU,[24] with a seat in Brussels, regularly forwards reports on European parliament debates on matters of interest to parliament and, moreover, enables the connection between the Portuguese PERMREP approach in the Coreper (Committee of Permanent Representatives) and the parliamentary work of the EAC's *rapporteur* on the same EU draft.

21 European Commission 2009 (note 20).

22 European Commission 2009 (note 20).

23 European Commission 2009 (note 20); European Commission, *Annual report 2008 on relations between the European Commission and National Parliaments*, CO (2009) p. 343, 7 July 2009 and European Commission, *Annual report 2010 on relations between the European Commission and National Parliaments*, COM (2011) p. 345, 10 June 2011.

24 The Portuguese parliament has had permanent representation in Brussels since 1 January 2007, first in the form of a representative of the parliament to the COSAC secretariat, then since 24 June 2008 in the form of a permanent representative to the EU. The main task of parliament's representative in Brussels is to relay information about the EU decision-making process as a "qualitative support" for parliament's scrutiny of the EU.

The Treaty of Lisbon enhances the potential for the involvement of national parliaments in the European decision-making processes, by recognizing national legislatures actively contribute to the good functioning of the EU and that governments are democratically accountable to them. More concretely, the treaty describes the parliaments' involvement by guaranteeing the subsidiarity principle is respected, by taking part, within the framework of the area of freedom, security and justice, in the evaluation mechanisms for the implementation of EU policies in those areas and through being involved in the political monitoring of Europol and in the evaluation of Eurojust's activities.

In order to guarantee the greater involvement of national parliaments in the EU, the treaty enabled all parliaments to receive all consultation and planning documents from the EC, as well as draft legislation issued by any institution or group of member states. Consequently, national parliaments may, within eight weeks, submit to the presidents of the European Parliament, the European Council and EC a reasoned opinion on the observance of the subsidiarity principle. Through the early warning mechanism, if one-third of national parliaments (or one-quarter on matters relating to the AFSJ) oppose any measure, the EC is required to reconsider.[25] After analysing the draft, the EC may maintain, withdraw or amend the draft.

The implementation of the treaty introduced an added argument and stimulus for the Portuguese parliament to actively scrutinize the EU's performance, enriching its practice and promoting its development through the involvement of the main parliamentary bodies. The treaty introduced two of the key scrutiny factors:

---

25 Each national parliament has two votes out of a total of 54, with 18 representing one-third (nine parliaments or 18 chambers) and one-quarter representing 14 (seven parliaments or 14 chambers).

the possibility for national parliaments to speak out on EU bills; and a timeframe for this pronouncement. These factors contributed to strengthening parliamentary scrutiny, mostly by providing a legal basis and an additional political reason for the exercise of scrutiny. It has also had a remarkable spill-over effect, both on the closer relationship between parliament and government and on the dynamics of the relationship between the 40 parliamentary chambers in the 27 member states, with reflects the Portuguese parliament's way of working in this field. The real need to issue an opinion within an eight-week time frame made national parliaments more aware of the importance of exchanging information between themselves.

Assessment of the Impact of the Treaty of Lisbon on Parliament

The ESL's provision and the Barroso initiative were key factors in the systematic parliamentary scrutiny of European legislation. The Lisbon Treaty provided a further dynamic to parliament's activities by inaugurating the early warning mechanism's eight-week deadline for compliance with the subsidiarity principle. An analysis of the early years of its operation shows the initiation and conclusion of an impressive number of scrutiny processes, with the Portuguese parliament among the eight most active parliaments in the EU.

This section contains a qualitative evaluation of the content and effects of the scrutiny process. While most opinions consist of a synthesis of EU initiatives and approval of the proposals, some processes went beyond formal approval of European legislation and consisted of a debate on the initiative's substance and its effects on the national economy and society. The higher profile of the scrutiny procedures also demonstrated the implications of parliament's more substantive debates and opinions. In the following section we outline landmark cases and the main changes to parliament's relations with the government, other parliaments and civil and economic society in respect of the European legislative process.

The Impact on the Relationship between Government and Parliament

As Maurer asserts, the system of scrutinizing European law adopted by parliaments is closely related to their relationship with their executives.[26] The systematic scrutiny initiated in 2006 strengthened parliament's oversight of government through the development of accountability mechanisms vis-à-vis the executive. Instead of merely rubber-stamping treaties by ratifying them, ESL provides parliaments with instruments for the *ex ante* examination of government positions regarding EU matters, which provides parliament greater control mechanisms.

The main goal of the scrutiny process is to hold the Portuguese government accountable for its positions in the council of ministers, and for that the ESL gives governments a duty to provide information to and to consult with parliament. This focus on government as an object stems from the constitutional link between parliament and government at the national level. The Portuguese constitution grants parliament substantial powers of control over the government: the government is politically responsible only to parliament. Members of parliament have an effective means of controlling the executive. Prime ministers and ministers are regularly called to account by parliament, with greater use of the

26 Maurer (note 3).

mechanisms for ensuring accountability being clearly observable, particularly following the reform of parliamentary procedures in 2007 that strengthened the control mechanisms it had over government activity.[27] There is, however, no procedure for mandating ministers.

The emerging relationship between government and parliament in relation to the European legislative processes is an aspect of parliament's reassertion of its powers in after decades of decline. While before 2006 parliament's views on EU matters were of little interest to the government, since the adoption of ESL, and in particular following the implementation of the Lisbon Treaty, there has been an increase in the extent of consultation between parliament and government in relation to on-going European legislative projects. This is because of parliamentary activism and the adoption of opinions that do not follow those of the government. It is already true that government provides information on its positions before parliament issues its opinions and asks for the positions of different parliamentary groups on particular draft European projects. The parliamentary groups have also become more pro-active in taking stances on draft European legislative projects.

The following cases illustrate the changing relationship between government and parliament in this respect. The first case is parliament's adoption of a position contrary to the government's regarding the EC framework decision on the use of the Passenger Name Record (PNR) for law enforcement purposes. This decision was taken in the wake of the attack on the twin towers in New York on 11 September 2001, and meant European countries would provide the United States with information about air pas-

27 AR, Standing Orders of the Assembleia da República 1/2007, 20 August 2007, *Diário da República* 159, 20 August 2007, Serie I.

sengers. The initiative was examined by three special committees: on constitutional affairs, on rights, freedoms and guarantees, and on foreign affairs and the Portuguese communities and European affairs. Once the committee reports had been received, in accordance with the rules ensuring the proportional representation of all parliamentary parties, the EAC nominated a *rapporteur* from the Left Bloc (BE—Bloco de Esquerda). The opinion of the specialist committees notwithstanding, the BE *rapporteur* believed the EC's decision violated the subsidiarity principle.[28] Because of the controversial nature of this dossier the speaker of parliament decided to present it to a plenary session for decision. The EAC drafted a motion withdrawing the charge that the proposal violated the principle of subsidiarity, following which the resolution was approved by parliament.[29]

The PNR case was a landmark. From then on the centre parties became alert to the sensitivity of possible conflictual stances as a consequence of parliament's scrutiny of EU legislation. The fact the scrutiny process takes place within specialist committees and the EAC, where all parliamentary political parties are represented, resulted in an increase of pluralism and in an increasingly ideological debate along left-right lines.

The possibility that parliament's opinion could contradict those of the Portuguese government in the council of ministers triggered a change of heart by the parliamentary parties in respect of the importance of parliament's examination: government institutions became more aware of its disruptive potential. Now, whenever a sensitive initiative is on the table, the EAC and the

28 Available at www.ipex.eu/ipex/cms/home/Documents/dossier_CNS20070237/pid/47348.

29 AR, *Resolution of the Assembleia da República* 71/2009; Proposal for a framework decision, COM (2007) p. 654; Final SEC (2007) 1422 and 1453, on the use of passenger name record data for law enforcement purposes approved on 23 July 2009.

government attempt to coordinate positions, which has led to an increase in the information exchanged between the executive and the legislature in respect of their positions towards European legislative projects.

One other case in which parliament's position contradicted that of government occurred with the vote on a proposal limiting the number of legislative initiatives to be scrutinized by national parliaments. Immediately after the Lisbon Treaty took effect, a proposal from the United Kingdom called for a restricted definition of "draft legal act", which would result in the exclusion of a number of directives and regulations from scrutiny by national parliaments with regards their compliance with the subsidiarity clause. The interpretation of the UK government was adopted by the council on 22 March 2010. Following this, both the European Commission (27 April 2010) and the European Parliament (May 2010) expressed agreement with the council's position.[30] Consequently, national parliaments will be prevented from examining regulations and directives put forward under by Article 103 European Union treaty, which includes competition policy.

Reacting to this attempt by its government to reassert its exclusive competence, the UK House of Commons asked for the matter to be discussed within the Conference of Community and European Affairs Committees of Parliaments of the European Union (COSAC) framework by all NP. COSAC considered this limited interpretation would take some acts that are legislative in substance out of parliamentary scrutiny and called on the EC and the European Council to review their position. The Portuguese parliament went against the restrictive approach approved

---

30 See letters from these institutions at www.cosac.eu/en/meetings/Madrid2010/ordinary.doc.

by council,[31] arguing the decision would lead to parliament's reception of fewer initiatives for parliamentary scrutiny.

These cases show how the application of the Lisbon Treaty has contributed to the growing importance of the Portuguese parliament's opinions to ministers and the PERMREP in Brussels. As a result both the government and the PERMREP began providing information to parliament about governmental views during the scrutiny procedure, and after parliament's opinion is adopted, obtained detailed information about the positions of parliamentary groups. The relationship between parliament and government on EU legislation has thus been built up, with parliament establishing informal information channels with government—particularly with the secretary of state for European affairs and the PERMREP. This has been one of the major positive side effects of the Lisbon Treaty, making both parliament and government aware of each another's position and, whenever possible, allowing the establishment of a common position that strengthens the Portuguese views at the EU level.

The Strengthening of Relations between EU National Parliaments

The Lisbon Treaty's early warning mechanism raised the need for an intense and timely exchange of information among national parliaments. Going beyond the institutionalized participation in inter-parliamentary meetings such as COSAC, Conference of Speakers from EU Parliaments, European Parliament meetings and the use of the inter-parliamentary information system (IPEX), the Portuguese parliament increased it direct contacts

31 AR, *Written opinion of the Assembleia da República on the definition of "legislative act" in the Treaty of Lisbon*, 13th bianuual COSAC report, available at www.cosac.eu/en/meetings/Madrid2010/ordinary.doc.

with other national parliaments concerning the on-going scrutiny process. The exchange of information helps parliaments influence each other's positions on matters of interests to Portuguese deputies.

One example of this was on the proposal for a directive on the liberalization of the right of entry for seasonal workers, which gained the highest number of reasoned opinions in 2010 (nine out of 23 of the chambers that examined this proposal).[32] The sensitive nature of the proposal ensured a great deal of attention would be paid to it by national parliaments. Nine chambers said the proposal violated the subsidiarity principle and expressed reservations on the social rights provided for in the proposal. Although the one-third threshold was not reached, the pronouncement of 23 parliamentary chambers provided the EU institutions with a strong political signal and represented a warning for similar future initiatives.

Parliament as a Link between Portuguese Civil Society and European institutions

In addition to its increased importance in the scrutiny process as the main institutional counterpart to government, parliament has become link between civil and economic societies and EU institutions. As the main interlocutor with the European institutions in the Lisbon Treaty's early warning mechanism, in political dialogue with the EC and in the inter-parliamentary cooperation with the European Parliament and the institutional relationship

---

32 The Portuguese parliament's opinion raised several questions on the substance of the proposal, which were also quoted by the government while negotiating at the Coreper level. Parliament's opinion is available at www.ipex.eu/ipex/cms/home/Documents/dossier_COD20100210/pid/55295.

with the European Council, parliament has assumed an increasingly important role as a multi-level player.

The action of the Portuguese parliament on the 2007 initiative on a sustainable European wine sector illustrates this new role as a mediator between the national and the European levels.[33] In its usual process of scrutiny, the EAC nominated a *rapporteur* from the committee of economic affairs, innovation and regional development's sub-committee for agriculture. It also called a public hearing with wine producers, the government, Portuguese MEPs and the responsible European commissioner. The debate was preceded by a public consultation and resulted in a lively discussion on the contents and possible consequences of the proposal for the Portuguese agriculture and wine sector. The public exchange on the proposal's contents resulted in the concerns expressed by the Portuguese wine sector to be taken into account in the final version of the directive. Finally, it allowed the wine sector to prepare early for the changes resulting from the directive.

Conclusion

The chapter outlines the institutional shape of scrutiny procedures and the importance of the transmission of EC legislative initiatives to national parliaments. Parliament's adaptation to the emerging conditions illustrates the impact of timely interaction between the pressure for change (the Treaty of Lisbon provisions for national parliaments) with reform of internal procedures of parliamentary scrutiny (ESL) and the availability of new informational resources provided by the EC (Barroso initiative). Rather than a result of the politicization of European questions at the national level, the adoption of a systematic scrutiny system by

33 AR, COM 319 (2007), available at www.ipex.eu/ipex/cms/home/Documents/dossier_COM20060319.

parliament was the result of the deliberate coalition of cross-party political actors, along with the presence of several high-ranking EAC chairmen and motivated speakers responding to EU pressures to ensure the involvement of national parliaments in the European legislative arena. The preparatory work by parliament in establishing its EU scrutiny system through the formulation and implementation of the ESL was key to the full participation of national parliaments in exercising the powers, possibilities and mechanisms that the Lisbon Treaty contained three years later.

Parliament adapted to the opportunities by accommodating its internal procedures to the new realities—in particular by strengthening the competences and the resources of the EAC and calling on specialist committees to undertake the task of scrutinizing EU legislation. This new routine took root during the years before the treaty and was already common practice when it entered into force. Trying to go beyond the rubberstamp approach of the ratification process, *ex post*, the instruments of *ex ante* and on-going scrutiny of government positions foreseen in the ESL provide parliament with an increase in its control mechanisms. This is key to understanding the extent to which the Lisbon Treaty's early-warning mechanisms have been implemented.

The analysis of some landmark cases shows the qualitative change in parliament's role in the European legislative arena following the implementation of the Lisbon Treaty. In particular, relations between parliament and government on the European legislative processes have now been routinized and parliament is on a path that will lead it to develop its role as a counterpart to government in the EU legislative process. In addition parliament now has a well-established procedure for daily contact with other national parliaments, and has taken steps to establish itself as a multi-level actor and as a bridge between national stakeholders and European institutions.

5 | The Europeanization of the Portuguese Courts

Nuno Piçarra and Francisco Pereira Coutinho

Introduction

The treaties, which during the 1950s created the foundations of what is today the European Union (EU),[1] granted—albeit discretely—an important role to the courts of the member states: that of applying EU law as common courts.

EU law is directed towards individuals and not only towards member states and has a binding force superior to that of international law. The Europeanization of national courts has thus been essentially a consequence of their duty to apply a common European law, primarily of an economic nature, to private parties.[2] Each

---

1 The European Coal and Steel Treaty (ECS), which was signed in Paris on 18 April 1951, entered into force on 24 July 1952 and was abolished on 23 July 2002. The European Economic Community and the European Atomic Energy (EAE) treaties were signed in Rome on 25 March 1957 and came into force on 1 January 1958. In contrast to the ECS, they contain a clause that expressly states their permanent application. In 1992, with the entry into force of the Treaty on the European Union (TUE), the European Economic Community Treaty became the European Community Treaty. The Lisbon Treaty, which has been in force since 1 December 2009, states in article 1(3) in fine that the "Union shall replace and succeed the European Community". From that date, the Treaty of Rome became the Treaty on the Functioning of the European Union (TFEU). This text will refer only to the Union. All the articles from the TEU and the TFEU will be quoted with their new numeration.

2 The EU treaties also attribute to the member states' public administrations the role of "common enforcers" of EU law. Litigation between member states and individuals concerning the interpretation and the enforcement of EU law must be settled by the national courts.

of the three treaties originally created a single central court—the European Court of Justice (ECJ)—conceived as a special court endowed with the competences national courts could not exercise properly. Amongst those competences is the guarantee of the uniform interpretation and application of EU law across all member states. The relationship the EU treaties originally established between the ECJ and national courts was not hierarchical but cooperative.[3] This feature of the EU jurisdictional system remains unchanged.[4]

Within the scope of that "cooperation between courts", an important set of European duties has been assigned to national courts. Such duties have been creatively extracted mainly from the most important of the founding treaties—the Treaty of Rome. These Europeanizing impulses, largely jurisdictional in origin—and of which national courts are also co-authors—will be briefly identified before determining the extent to which the Portuguese courts have adapted to them since Portugal's accession to the EU.

The Essential Features of the EU Jurisdictional System

The European duties conferred upon member states' courts can be explained with reference to the nature of the EU jurisdictional system. Therefore, it is first worth recalling the essential features

---

3   P. Magnette, *Au nom des peoples: Le malentendu constitutionnel européen* (Paris: Cerf, 2006), pp. II, 31. According to the author, the original European Communities sought "an improved means of inter-state diplomacy". Therefore the treaties were a continuation of the European diplomatic tradition, without prejudice that they constitute "a greater rupture with the European Machtpolitik tradition".

4   The establishment of the Court of First Instance in 1988 (now the General Court) and the European Civil Service Tribunal in 2004, both of which were granted specific competences that cannot be properly exercized by national courts, in no way changes the deeper logic of the EU jurisdictional system.

of this system, within the parameters of which these obligations have been delineated.[5]

National Courts as EU Common Courts

Since its foundation, the EU has organized itself according to the principle of subsidiarity. This meant rejecting the creation of its own system of courts to apply EU law. The Treaty of Rome gave that responsibility to national courts, which thereby became EU common courts. In other words, the member states' courts took on the obligation to apply EU law in addition to their duty of applying national law. The powers at their disposal as national courts do not necessarily coincide with their powers as EU courts. In the latter capacity, the ECJ has vested them with the power to either set aside national norms conflicting with EU law or to suspend their application.[6]

In this regard, it must be emphasized that the legal orders of several member states, including the Netherlands and Sweden, deny such powers to their courts, which are thus compelled to apply national legislation even when they consider it to be unconstitutional.

---

5   The fundamental legal basis of these obligations is now in article 4 (3) of the TEU. It is worth remembering its wording: "Pursuant to the principle of sincere cooperation, the Union and the member states shall, in full mutual respect, assist each other in carrying out tasks which flow from the treaties. The member states shall take any appropriate measure, general or particular, to ensure fulfilment of the obligations arising out of the treaties or resulting from the acts of the institutions of the Union. The member states shall facilitate the achievement of the Union's tasks and refrain from any measure which could jeopardize the attainment of the Union's objectives".

6   These "Europeanizing impulses" for the national courts were made explicit by the ECJ in two well-known decisions: the Simmenthal case, 106/77 (9 March 1978) and the Factortame case, 213/89 (19 May 1990).

*The European Court of Justice as Guarantor of the Uniform
Interpretation and Application of EU Law by National Courts*

One power that obviously had to be reserved to the ECJ is that
of guaranteeing the uniform interpretation of EU law. However, a
federalist solution was rejected in the process of achieving this objective. This would grant the ECJ the final power to set aside national judicial decisions inconsistent with EU law and would thus
entail the establishment of a hierarchical relationship between
national courts and the ECJ. One of the most original aspects of
the EU jurisdictional system is the result of the approach adopted
by the Treaty of Rome, aimed at preventing the establishment of
divergences on questions of EU law. It is thereafter outlined in article 267 of the Treaty on the Functioning of the European Union
(TFEU) that if a national court has doubts on the interpretation
of EU law it may refer the question directly to the ECJ.[7] However,
if the court which has doubts is the court of last resort, this faculty
becomes an obligation.

This is the so-called preliminary ruling procedure; the framework within which the relationship between the ECJ and the national courts operates.

*Relations between the European Court of Justice and the
National Courts in the Preliminary Ruling Procedure*

The Nature of the Preliminary Ruling Procedure

References to preliminary rulings are an instrument for national courts but not for parties. Such procedure consists of three
phases: (1) the national judge refers the question to the ECJ, (2)
the ECJ answers through a preliminary ruling and (3) the national

---

7   The national judge's doubts may also concern the validity of a EU act vis-à-vis
the treaties and the principles contained therein.

judge applies the ECJ's preliminary ruling to the pending case. This has important consequences for individuals: they have neither the right to refer a question to the ECJ nor can they prevent the national court from referring questions. The decision to do so rests exclusively with the national courts, which choose whether or not to request a preliminary ruling, regardless of the preference of the parties in the case.[8]

Nevertheless, once the national court has decided to make a reference to the ECJ, all parties in the national case may take part in the correspondent proceedings opened before the ECJ.[9] In such proceedings there are no cross-examinations and replies are restricted to the oral phase of the process. In order to ensure continued cooperation with national courts, the ECJ established a presumption that questions referred are pertinent. Such presumption can only be rebutted in exceptional circumstances, such as (1) when it is manifest that the interpretation of EU law has no relation to reality or with the object of the litigation in the national court, (2) when the problem is of an hypothetical nature and (3), when the ECJ does not have the factual and legal elements necessary to present a useful response to the questions referred. In these

---

8   The decision to refer can be subject to an internal appeal, but this appeal cannot restrict the power of the lower court to refer a question to the ECJ. As the ECJ stated in Cartesio, C-210/06, paragraph 53, a lower court remains "subject to the remedies normally available under national law. Nevertheless, the outcome of such an appeal cannot limit the jurisdiction conferred by article 234 EC (now article 267 of the TFEU) on that court to make a reference to the court if it considers that a case pending before it raises questions on the interpretation of provisions of community law necessitating a ruling by the court".

9   In addition to the parties in the main process, EU institutions and member states may also present their observations to the ECJ in the framework of a preliminary procedure. For more information on the observations presented by the Portuguese state, see F. P. Coutinho, "Os estados-membros e os processos prejudiciais: Um balanço da participação portuguesa nos 20 anos da adesão à União Europeia", *Negócios Estrangeiros* 9, 1 (2006), pp. 231ff.

exceptional circumstances, the ECJ can declare the reference inadmissible.[10]

Cases of Mandatory Reference for a Preliminary Ruling

The aim of article 267 (3) of the TFEU—ensuring the uniform interpretation and application of EU law—is to determine those cases in which a reference to the ECJ should not be considered an option for the national court, but rather as an obligation.[11] The most obvious example occurs when the reference for interpretation or validity of EU law is, to quote article 267 (3) of the TFEU, "raised in a case pending before a court or tribunal of a member state, against whose decision there is no judicial remedy under national law". If the court was not obliged to refer the matter to the ECJ, and was able to reach a decision alone, the objective of ensuring the uniform interpretation and application of EU law would be frustrated. This solitary interpretation or appreciation of the validity of an EU provision could result in a solution contrary to that of any other national court of last instance.

It follows from article 19(1) *in fine* of the Maastricht Treaty (TEU—Treaty of the European Union) that the ECJ has the final word in cases involving the interpretation and validity of EU law.[12] This explains why the ECJ has interpreted article 267 (3) of the TFEU in order to provide a very strict delimitation of cases in which an exception to the obligation to refer can be accepted.

10 See, among others, the ECJ decision in Beck and Bergdorf, C-355/97 (7 September 1999), paragraph 2.

11 In the ECJ's own words, the "obligation to refer is...particularly designed to prevent a body of national case law that is not in accordance with the rules of community law from being established in any member state". See the Gomes Valente case, C-393/98 (22 February 2001), paragraph 17.

12 See J. H. H. Weiler, "The transformation of Europe", *Yale Law Journal* 100 (1991), p. 2414.

According to consistent case law, such an exception is only acceptable if the national court of last instance can invoke the following: (1) that the EU law question is not pertinent for the resolution of the national judicial case, (2) that the question raised is materially identical to a previous ECJ decision or (3), that the correct application of EU may be so obvious as to leave no scope for any reasonable doubt. The latter possibility must be assessed on the basis of the characteristic features of EU law and the particular difficulties to which its interpretation gives rise, as well as the risk of divergences in judicial decisions within the EU.[13]

The other less obvious case the ECJ has identified as being subject to a mandatory reference for a preliminary ruling occurs when the national court does not decide in the last instance and has doubts about the validity of EU law vis-à-vis the treaties. In this case, and contrary to the text of article 267(2) of the TFEU, the ECJ transformed this court into one "against whose decisions there is no judicial remedy under national law". Therefore, this court is obliged to refer a question whenever it considers EU law to be invalid.[14]

---

13 According to the ECJ, it must be borne in mind EU legislation is drafted in several languages and that the different versions are all equally authentic. An interpretation of a provision of EU law thus involves a comparison of the different language versions. Even where the different language versions are entirely in accord with one another, EU law uses terminology which is peculiar to it. Furthermore, legal concepts do not necessarily have the same meaning in EU law and in the law of the various member states. In addition, "every provision of community law must be placed in its context and interpreted in the light of the provisions of community law as a whole, regard being had to the objectives thereof and to its state of evolution at the date on which the provision in question is to be applied". In order to limit as far as possible the exceptions to the duty to refer, the ECJ further emphasizes that in any case the national judge must be convinced the matter is equally obvious to the courts of the other member states and to the ECJ. This somewhat rigid and dated case law, which might have become to some extent impractical in an enlarged EU, was expounded in CLIFIT, 283/81 (6 October 1982), paragraphs 16–21 and was reiterated in Intermodal, C-495/03 (15 September 2005), paragraph 45.

14 See Foto-Frost, 314/85 (22 October 1987).

National Courts' Duties as EU Courts

The Duty to Enforce EU Law

As stated above, the keystone of the EU jurisdictional system is the preliminary rulings procedure, which has potential consequences that were unforeseen by the authors of the treaties. In fact, within the framework of such procedure it has been possible to confer upon EU law a binding force similar to that of national law. This became clear when, in a decision of 5 February 1963, the ECJ responded in the affirmative to the question of whether article 12 of the Treaty of Rome (now article 30 of the TFEU)—which was directed to member states—produced an "internal effect".[15] In other words, a Dutch court asked if parties could "lay claim to individual rights which the national courts must protect".

The question concerned the company Van Gend & Loos, which imported urea formaldehyde from Germany. The company invoked article 12 to contest the decision of the Dutch administrative authorities obliging it to pay more customs duties. The principle of the direct effect implies that the Treaty of Rome "is more than an agreement which merely creates mutual obligations between the contracting states". According to the ECJ, the task assigned to it under article 267 of the TFEU confirms that the member states have acknowledged EU law has an authority which can be invoked by their nationals before the national courts and tribunals. Moreover, "the vigilance of individuals concerned to protect their rights amounts to an effective supervision in addition to the supervision entrusted by articles 169 and 170 (now

15 In its original version this article said "member states shall refrain from introducing, as between themselves, any new customs duties on importation or exportation or charges with equivalent effect and from increasing such duties or charges as they apply in their commercial relations with each other".

articles 258 and 259 of the TFEU) to the diligence of the Commission and of the member states".

In the case Van Gend & Loos, the ECJ also established the supremacy of EU law over conflicting national law—albeit implicitly. In effect, EU law is able to produce immediate internal effects and to confer individual rights the national courts must protect, only if conflicting national law—whether prior or posterior to EU law, constitutional or infra-constitutional—is not applied by those courts.[16] National courts thus began to increase the frequency of preliminary references to the ECJ in order to obtain decisions on the compatibility of national law with EU law, understood as a higher law.[17] Indeed, this soon came to represent the largest proportion of cases referred to the ECJ. However, the ECJ never considered itself competent to answer such questions directly in the framework of article 267 of the TFEU[18].

Notwithstanding, instead of declaring them inadmissible, the ECJ reformulates these questions when necessary, seeking always to give the national court all the elements necessary to enable it to decide by itself on the compatibility of national law with EU law.[19] To that effect, the ECJ demands from national courts the

16 See Costa-ENEL, 6/64 (15 July 1964).

17 Among the cases referred by Portuguese judges see, for example, the case referred by the Tribunal da Relação de Lisboa, 1140/90 (10 December 1990), Colectânea de Jurisprudência V (1990), pp. 160–1. In this case the Portuguese court expressly asked the ECJ to rule on the compatibility of a decree-law provision with the Treaty of Rome's provisions on the free movement of people and services.

18 See Pretore di Salò, 14/86 (11 June 1987), paragraph 15.

19 According to a former ECJ judge, "having paid lip service to the language of the treaty and having clarified the meaning of the relevant community measure, the court usually went on to indicate to what extent a certain type of national legislation can be regarded as compatible with that measure. The national judge is thus led hand-in-hand as far as the door: crossing the threshold is his job, but now a job no harder than child's play". See Federico G. Mancini, "The making of a constitution for Europe", *Common Market Law Review* 26 (1989), p. 606.

factual and legal framework of the national case in which the reference is made. Failure to do so may result in the reference being declared inadmissible.[20] Once the ECJ enacts such a ruling, the referring court is obliged to set aside any national law incompatible with EU law and must decide the pending case based on this decision.[21] In this sense, a reference to the ECJ has an outcome that is comparable to that which occurs in federal systems when state law conflicts with federal law.[22]

Corollaries of the Duty to Enforce EU Law

The principles of direct effect and supremacy contributed decisively to the autonomization of EU law as a new type of law,[23] more compelling than international law and almost as compelling as national law.[24] The ECJ, always in cooperation with the national courts, proceeded to develop a collection of supplementary means to guarantee the effectiveness of EU law. Amongst the most relevant are the principle of consistent interpretation and the principle of member states' responsibility for the violation of EU law.

20 See Telemarsicabruzzo, C-320/90, C-321/90 and C-322/90 (26 January 1993).

21 "The national courts are presented, in the legal order of the respective member states, as the final recourse against the national norms conflicting with Community law". See O. Dubos, *Les juridictions nationales: Juge communautaire* (Paris: Dalloz, 2001), p. 56.

22 This confirms the single nature of the European integration project, which has proved itself capable of achieving a level of legal integration similar to far more advanced federations, while retaining strong member states. See P. Magnette (note 3), p. 142. The author notes that if the EU member states submit themselves to a constitutional discipline, it is by the force of their own will and not because they are subordinated to the sovereignty and the state authority of a European people—which obviously does not exist (p. 152).

23 Among the reasons for the absence of direct effect of an EU law provision is the possibility its content is not unconditional and sufficiently precise.

24 See P. Magnette (note 3), p. 152.

The Principle of Consistent Interpretation

According to this principle, member state courts must interpret national norms in conformity with EU law. This results from article 4(3) of the TEU, which imposes on all national authorities—including (within the ambit of their responsibilities) courts and tribunals—the obligation to adopt any appropriate measure, general or particular, to ensure fulfilment of obligations arising out of EU treaties or resulting from the acts of the EU institutions. This principle assumes special importance in relation to directives. The direct effect of these acts can only be invoked in proceedings between individuals and public authorities (direct vertical effect),[25] and not between individuals (direct horizontal effect). Moreover, the direct effect of a directive can only be invoked in cases in which there has been no transposition into national law within the established deadline, or where the transposition was concluded in an incorrect manner.[26]

It follows from the principle of consistent interpretation that "national courts are required to interpret their national law in the light of the wording and the purpose of the directive in order to achieve the result referred to in the third paragraph of article 189 [now article 288 of the TFEU]".[27] This "indirect direct" effect to

25 In this context, the ECJ interprets the concept of public authority in very wide-ranging terms. See Foster, C-188/89 (12 July 1990), paragraph 20.

26 See Ratti, 148/78 (5 April 1979), paragraphs 23 and 24.

27 See Von Colson and Kamann, 14/83 (10 April 1984), paragraph 26. According to the Arcaro ruling (C-168/95 [26 September 1996]), the obligation of the national court to refer to the content of the directive when interpreting the relevant rules of its own national law reaches a limit "where such an interpretation leads to the imposition on an individual of an obligation laid down by a directive that has not been transposed or, more especially, where it has the effect of determining or aggravating, on the basis of the directive and in the absence of a law enacted for its implementation, the liability in criminal law of persons who act in contravention of that directive's provisions" (paragraph 42).

a large extent mitigates the absence of the directive's direct horizontal effect.[28]

The Principle of Member States' Responsibility for the Violation of EU Law

This principle, the most recent of the corollaries to the principle of the effectiveness of EU law, was initially invoked by the ECJ against the Italian state for not transposing within the established deadlines a directive the provisions of which were not unconditional and sufficiently precise. That meant such provisions could not be invoked before a national court. According to the ECJ, in such cases "the full effectiveness of community rules would be impaired and the protection of the rights which they grant would be weakened if individuals were unable to obtain redress when their rights are infringed by a breach of community law for which a member state can be held responsible".

The ECJ has held this right to reparation depends on the fulfilment of three conditions: (1) the EU provision infringed must be intended to confer rights on individuals, (2) the breach must be sufficiently grievous and (3), there must be a direct causal link between the breach of the obligation resting on the member state and the loss or damage sustained by the injured parties.[29]

More recently, the ECJ—always within the preliminary rulings framework—extended the principle of responsibility for the infringement of EU law to the decisions of the national courts

28 The principle of conforming interpretation was even extended to the framework decisions of the former EU's third pillar through the ECJ's ruling on the Pupino case, C-105/03 (16 June 2005). This has contributed towards a considerable strengthening of the efficacy of these legal acts, which were closer to international law, and particularly attenuated the reach of the former article 34 (2) (b) of the TUE, which stated "framework decisions do not produce a direct effect".

29 See Francovich et al., C-6/90 and C-9/90 (19 November 1991), paragraph 33, and Brasserie du Pêcheur et al., C-46/93 and 48/93 (5 March 1996), paragraphs 51–2.

adjudicating at last instance. Nevertheless, state liability for such an infringement "can be incurred only in the exceptional case where the court has manifestly infringed the applicable law".

Among the factors the competent national court hearing a claim for reparation due to a judicial decision of that nature must take account are "in particular, the degree of clarity and precision of the rule infringed, whether the infringement was intentional, whether the error of law was excusable or inexcusable, the position taken, where applicable, by a Community institution and the non-compliance by the court [adjudicating at last instance] in question with its obligation to make a reference for a preliminary ruling under the third paragraph of article 234" (now article 267 TFEU).[30]

Developing this case law, the ECJ, prompted by an Italian court that had referred a question for preliminary ruling concerning the state's responsibility for an infringement of EU law allegedly committed by one of the country's supreme courts, ruled EU law precludes national legislation which (1) excluded state liability, in a general manner, for damage caused to individuals by an infringement of EU law attributable to a court adjudicating at last instance by reason of the fact that the infringement in question "results from an interpretation of provisions of law or an assessment of facts or evidence carried out by that court", and (2) limited such liability solely to cases of intentional fault and serious misconduct on the part of the court, if "such a limitation were to lead to exclusion of the liability of the member state concerned in other cases where a manifest infringement of the applicable law was committed, as set out in paragraphs 53 to 56 of the Köbler judgment". Since the interpretation of legal norms and the assessment of facts and evidence are the true essence of the

30 See Köbler, C-224/01 (30 September 2003), paragraphs 53–6.

jurisdictional function, such law would be tantamount to rendering meaningless the principle of state responsibility for the violation of EU law by a national court adjudicating at last instance.[31]

With this decision, the "Europeanizing impulses" emitted to national courts by the ECJ case law reached a new peak. It becomes possible for a lower court competent to hear claims for reparation to judge and eventually sanction the actions of a higher court for infringements of EU law and particularly for infringing the duty to refer imposed by paragraph three of article 267 of the TFEU. This has been seen as a curious inversion of roles in the national legal hierarchy.[32]

The Principle of Procedural Autonomy and its Limits

In the absence of provisions adopted by the EU, the national courts competent to apply EU law are in principle bound by their procedural judicial organization laws. It is therefore within this framework that individuals must seek to protect their rights granted by EU law. The principle, according to which national courts must comply with national procedural law when applying EU law is called the principle of procedural autonomy of member states.[33]

Since differences in procedural law can have serious repercussions on substantive law, the principle of the effectiveness of EU law had to impose limits on the principle of procedural autonomy of member states. These limitations are two-fold: (1) national procedural law cannot make a distinction between the demands of individuals based on EU law and their demands based on national

---

31   See Traghetti del Mediterraneo, C-173/03 (13 June 2006), paragraphs 36, 40.

32   See A.-S. Botella, "La responsabilité du juge national", *Revue Trimestrielle de Droit Européen* 2 (2004), pp. 283–315.

33   See Rewe, 33/76 (16 December 1976).

law (the principle of equivalence) and (2) even if such distinction is not made, national procedural law cannot render virtually impossible or excessively difficult the exercise of rights conferred by EU law (the principle of effectiveness).[34]

EU law proscribes, as a breach of the principle of equivalence, that in order to exercise rights conferred by EU law—such as the right of reparation for damages caused by the member state for the non-transposition of a directive—the individual must pay legal expenses and meet deadlines more onerous than those that would result from the exercise of a similar right based on the national law. The injured party can invoke such principle before the national court in order to eliminate the discrimination.

Similarly, EU law proscribes, in the name of the principle of effectiveness, that national procedural law, despite being applied indiscriminately, establishes rules of proof that create a practical impossibility for an injured party to exercise the right of refund for any undue payments. In such a case, the injured party can invoke the principle of effectiveness in order to prevent the application of national norms demanding such a proof.

These principles represent strong "Europeanizing impulses" for the national courts, leading them to set aside when necessary any conflicting national provisions. These "impulses" also extend to the national legislator and lead it to establish procedural rules compatible with EU law.

It remains to be seen to what extent the principle of state responsibility for the infringement of EU law by a national supreme court will imply the adaptation of the judicial organization of the member states in order to prevent or limit the effects of the "hierarchical inversion" mentioned above. In any case, it is essential to avoid an eventual scenario whereby a supreme court could review,

34 See Aprile, C-228/96 (17 November 1998), paragraph 18.

on appeal, a decision of a lower court that imputes on the same supreme court an infringement of EU law. Otherwise, the principle of impartiality would be impaired.[35]

A Weak Point of the EU Jurisdictional System: The Precarious Nature of the Guarantees for Compliance with Article 267 (3) of the TFEU

The preliminary ruling procedure has succeeded to such an extent that the ECJ has become a so-called "victim of its own success".[36] This disguised the main weaknesses of this procedure: the precarious nature of the guarantees provided by the EU legal order itself for compliance with the duty to refer set out in article 267 (3) of the TFEU.[37]

It has been claimed a member state can, under article 258 of the TFEU, be called before the ECJ for infringements of EU

35 See, however, the judgement of the Supremo Tribunal de Justiça of 3 December 2009, P. 9180/07.3TBBRG.G1.S.1, Cadernos de Justiça Administrativa, 79 (2010), pp. 29–37, with a critical annotation of Maria José Rangel de Mesquita, "Irresponsabilidade do Estado-juiz por incumprimento do direito da União Europeia: Um acórdão sem futuro", pp. 37–45. See also Alessandra Silveira, "Da (ir)responsabilidade do estado-juiz por violação do direito da União Europeia—Anotação ao acórdão do Supremo Tribunal de Justiça de 3 de Dezembro de 2009", *Scientia Iuridica*, vol. LVIII, 320 (2009), pp 773–804 and N. Piçarra, "As incidências do direito da União Europeia sobre a organização e o exercício da função jurisdicional nos Estados-Membros", encontrosdireitopublico. blogspot.com, pp. 12–16.

36 See T. Koopmans, "La procédure préjudicielle—victime de son succès?", in F. Caportorti, C.-D. Ehlermann, J. Frowein, F. Jacobs, R. Joliet, T. Koopmans and R. Kovar (eds), *Liber Amicorum Pescatore* (Baden-Baden: Nomos Verlagsgesellschaft, 1987), pp. 347–57.

37 At the national level, some member states have developed internal mechanisms to guarantee compliance with the duty to refer questions to the ECJ. For example, the German Federal Constitutional Court, the Austrian Constitutional Court and the Spanish Constitutional Court have all declared themselves competent to control failures to refer by courts or tribunals against whose decisions there is no judicial remedy under national law. For a discussion of the Portuguese case, see N. Piçarra, *O Tribunal de Justiça das Comunidades Europeias como juiz legal e o processo do artigo 177 do tratado CEE: As relações entre a ordem jurídica comunitária e as ordens jurídicas dos estados-membros na perspectiva dos tribunais constitucionais*, (Lisbon: AAFDL, 1991).

law by its courts. Nevertheless, the European Commission (EC) only recently initiated infringement proceedings in cases related to failures to refer in breach of article 267 (3) of the TFEU.[38] It could also be argued that as a result of the Köbler case law, state responsibility emerges if the duty to refer is breached. Nonetheless, article 267 (3) of the TFEU was never intended to confer rights upon individuals, and particularly the right to a preliminary reference. This has always been rejected in the name of the "inter-court" procedural nature of such mechanism. Nevertheless, as a result of the Köbler and CILFIT decisions, a supreme court that wishes to avoid the serious risk of giving rise to member state responsibility must carefully assess the necessity to make a preliminary reference and cannot—except when a case is materially identical to one on which the ECJ has already made a ruling—simply resolve the question ex officio, through the simple invocation of the clarity of the EU provisions in question.[39] This is the most recent "European duty" national courts are pledged to fulfil in this context.

Portuguese Courts' Reactions to the "Europeanizing Impulses"

The evolution of EU law has been the result of some proactivity on the part of the ECJ; however, it has never ceased to be supported through a real legal dialogue with the national courts

---

38 In a case concerning the Swedish supreme court's failure to refer cases to the ECJ, see Schmauch, "Lack of preliminary rulings as an infringement of article 234: European Commission case COM 2003/2161, procedure against the Kingdom of Sweden", *European Law Reporter* (2005) pp. 445ff, and U. Bernitz, "The duty of supreme courts to refer cases to the ECJ: The commission's action against Sweden", *Swedish Studies in European Law* 1 (2006) pp. 37ff.

39 See P. J. Wattel, "Köbler, CILFIT and Welthgrove: We can't go on meeting like this", *Common Market Law Review* 41 (2004), p. 178.

TABLE 5.1
Preliminary References by Member State
(1986–2005)

Year	Austria	Belgium	Denmark	Finland	France	Germany	Greece	Ireland	Italy	Luxembourg	Netherlands	Portugal	Spain	Sweden	UK	Total
1986		13	4		19	18	2	4	5	1	16	0	1		8	91
1987		15	5		36	32	17	2	5	3	19	0	1		9	144
1988		30	4		38	34	0	0	28	2	26	0	1		16	179
1989		13	2		28	47	2	1	10	1	18	1	2		14	139
1990		17	5		21	34	2	4	25	4	9	2	6		12	141
1991		19	2		29	54	3	2	36	2	17	3	5		14	186
1992		16	3		15	62	1	0	22	1	18	1	5		18	162
1993		22	7		22	57	5	1	24	1	43	13	7		12	204
1994		19	4		36	44	0	2	46	1	13	1	13		24	203
1995	2	14	8	0	43	51	10	3	58	2	19	5	10	6	20	251

	Austria	Belgium	Denmark	Finland	France	Germany	Greece	Ireland	Italy	Luxembourg	Netherlands	Portugal	Spain	Sweden	UK	Total
1996	6	30	4	3	24	66	4	0	70	2	10	6	6	4	21	256
1997	35	19	7	6	10	46	2	1	50	3	24	2	9	7	18	239
1998	16	12	7	2	16	49	5	3	39	2	21	7	55	6	24	264
1999	53	13	3	4	17	49	3	2	43	4	23	7	4	5	22	255
2000	31	15	3	5	12	47	3	2	50	0	12	8	5	4	26	223
2001	57	10	5	3	15	53	4	1	40	2	14	4	4	4	21	237
2002	31	18	8	7	8	59	7	0	37	4	12	3	3	5	14	216
2003	15	18	3	4	9	43	4	2	45	4	28	1	8	4	22	210
2004	12	24	4	4	21	50	18	1	48	1	28	1	8	5	22	247
2005	15	21	4	4	17	51	11	2	18	2	36	2	10	11	12	216
Total	276	358	92	42	436	946	103	33	699	42	406	57	163	61	349	4063

through the preliminary reference mechanism. By making references to the ECJ, the national courts have allowed EU law both to expand its ambit and ensure its progressive and systematic internal consolidation. The almost complete acceptance of the ECJ's preliminary rulings gave EU law practically the same binding force attributed to domestic law.

The second part of this chapter provides a brief outline on how Portuguese courts have reacted to the "Europeanizing impulses" cited above during the first two decades of Portugal's membership of the EU. This will also enable an assessment of the dialogue established between Portuguese courts and the ECJ, as well as their contribution towards the development of EU law.

It is important first to analyse the way in which Portuguese courts have used the preliminary rulings procedure, which is the main framework for the establishment of such a dialogue.

Portuguese Courts and Article 267 of the TFEU

What the Figures Reveal

Table 5.1 shows the number of references made by member states' courts between 1986 and 2005.[40] Taking the absolute figures as a starting point, it should be noted that, compared to Portuguese courts, only the Irish, Luxembourgeois and Finnish courts have demonstrated less interest in making references to the ECJ. Portuguese preliminary references represent only 1.4 per cent of the total sent to the ECJ during the period in question.

The rate of references from Portuguese courts has also been erratic. Following a slow start up in the 1980s there was a gradual increase that reached its peak in 2000. In recent years there has

---

40 The 12 most recent member states have not been included since there is no data available to enable a useful comparison.

TABLE 5.2
Preliminary References and Population of Member States
(1986–2005)

	Number of references	Population (in millions)	Ratio references/ population
Austria	276	8.20	33.65
Belgium	357	10.40	34.32
Denmark	92	5.40	17.03
Finland	42	5.20	8.07
France	436	60.50	7.20
Germany	946	82.50	11.46
Greece	103	11.10	9.27
Ireland	42	4.10	10.24
Italy	699	58.50	11.94
Luxembourg	33	0.46	71.73
Netherlands	406	16.30	24.90
Portugal	57	10.50	5.42
Spain	163	43.00	3.79
Sweden	61	9.00	6.77
UK	349	60.00	5.81

SOURCE: Author's own figures

been a sharp fall in the number of referrals, which contrasts with the general trend across member states. Since 2001, Portuguese courts have referred an average of just more than one case per year. To some extent, this undermines the thesis proposed by Sweet and Brunnel, who claim there is a direct link between the evolution of a country's gross domestic product (GDP) and the level of trade with other member states on the one hand, and the number of cases referred to the ECJ by the national courts on the other.[41]

41 See A. C. Sweet and T. L. Brunell, "Constructing a supranational constitution: Dispute resolution and governance in the European Community", *American Political Science Review* 91, 1 (1998), p. 73.

One of the possible explanations for these figures is Portugal's small population in comparison with other member states. The population variable—which must not be considered decisive—allows for the calculation of the relative value of the total number of cases referred (see Table 5.2).

The introduction of this scale element worsens Portugal's relative position, since its courts are the penultimate in terms of the ratio of population to number of references (5.42), exceeding Spain (3.79) and coming in some distance behind courts of member states with similar populations, such as the Netherlands (24.90), Austria (33.65) and Belgium (34.32).

The Authors of the Portuguese Preliminary References

Analysing Portugal's references from the perspective of their authors—that is to say, the courts that made the reference to the ECJ (see Table 5.3)—produces a conclusive set of data.[42]

The first fact to note is the disproportionate number of cases referred by the administrative courts (80 per cent) and those referred by the civil courts (20 per cent). Nevertheless, this may be partially justified by the fact EU law continues to be essentially of an economic and administrative nature.

The second fact worth noting is that only approximately one-third of the cases referred originated in lower courts, which are by far the most numerous courts in the Portuguese jurisdictional system—as indeed they are in every jurisdictional system.

This figure clearly contrasts with the situation in the majority of member states and, therefore, casts some doubts on Weiler's judicial empowerment thesis, which states it is essentially the

---

42 For more on Portugal's preliminary references, see R. Chambel Margarido, "O pedido de decisão prejudicial e o princípio da cooperação jurisdicional", *Working Papers da Faculdade de Direito da Universidade Nova de Lisboa* 8/99 (1999).

TABLE 5.3
Origin of the Preliminary References in Portugal
(1986–2005)

	Number of references	%
Constitutional Court	0	0.0
Supreme Court of Justice (STJ)	1	2.0
Supreme Administrative and Tax Court	32	56.0
Second Instance Administrative and Tax Court	3	5.0
Court of Appeal (Civil)	2	4.0
First Instance Administrative and Tax Court	11	19.0
First Instance Civil Court	8	14.0
Total	57	100.0

SOURCE: Author's own figures.

lower courts that feel a greater need to refer cases to the ECJ for a preliminary ruling. Weiler argues that through this mechanism lower courts obtain "powers reserved to the supreme courts".[43]

In the case of Portugal, the Supreme Administrative Court (STA) made more references (32) than all the lower administrative and tax courts combined (14). The same cannot be said of the civil courts. The statistics reveal it took the Supreme Court of Justice (STJ)—which for the purposes of article 267 (3) of the TFEU is one of the highest courts in the land—20 years to make its first reference to the ECJ.[44] All the country's lower civil courts have, together, referred fewer than ten cases to the ECJ.

43 See J. H. H. Weiler, "The transformation of Europe", *Yale Law Journal* 100 (1991), p. 2426.

44 This occurred on 3 November 2005, in Process 05B1640, which was heard by a former Portuguese judge in the ECJ, José Carlos Moitinho de Almeida.

It should also be noted in this context that the Portuguese Constitutional Court has never made a reference to the ECJ within the framework of article 267 of the TFEU, a fact consistent with the general trend in other member states. However, the Portuguese constitutional court has recognized its duty to refer in a manner that is uncommon amongst its peers.[45]

Portuguese Preliminary Reference Subject

Figure 5.1 shows the existence of a scale of priorities concerning matters referred to the ECJ: a scale that reflects the fact the administrative and tax courts make the greatest number of references.

As the graph clearly shows, tax questions and those relating to customs duties accounted for 18 and 14 respectively, representing 56 per cent of the total. Following far behind are questions relating to the approximation of laws (4), social policy (4), competition (3) and the free movement of goods (3).

Close analysis of the preliminary references also allows the collection of other conclusive data. The first is connected to the fact that such cases generally pertain to the interpretation of highly specific and technical norms of EU law. Perhaps it is for this reason that ECJ preliminary rulings have only very rarely had a significant impact on the Portuguese legal order. The main exceptions, however, have been some cases regarding notary and registry emoluments and cases concerning the maximum cost of car insurance. Both resulted in legislative changes.

45 See ruling 163/90 (23 May 1990), in *Acórdãos do Tribunal Constitucional* 16 (1990), p. 301, and ruling 606/94 (22 November 1994), in *Acórdãos do Tribunal Constitucional* 29 (1994), p. 161. See also J. L. Cruz Vilaça, L. M. Pais Antunes and N. Piçarra, "Droit constitutionnel et droit communautaire: Le cas portugais", *Rivista di Diritto Europeo* 2 (1991), p. 301.

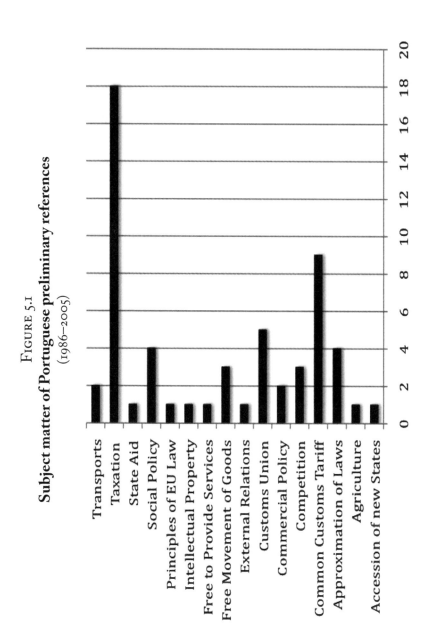

Figure 5.1
Subject matter of Portuguese preliminary references (1986–2005)

The ECJ's Reaction to Portuguese Preliminary References

The picture outlined would be incomplete without a generic comment on the responses the ECJ has given to Portuguese preliminary references.

In this respect, there have been several cases in which the ECJ has refused to provide an answer, since it considered the reference to be either inadmissible or poorly based, or because it had to be reformulated before it was able to decide. This seems to reveal a certain lack of understanding on the part of some Portuguese courts as to how the preliminary rulings procedure works.

Portuguese Courts and the Duty to Refer

A closer examination of the judicial cases involving the application of EU law but did not result in references for preliminary rulings reveals some infringements of article 267 (3) of the TFEU—including frequent examples of clear misunderstandings of the fundamental duty to refer. It is worth mentioning those cases in which the national court recognized the existence of doubts in the interpretation of EU law, but decided to resolve such doubts without the ECJ's support. In other cases, the same court has concluded a reference is only necessary when confronted with unavoidable interpretative doubts. On the other hand, numerous rulings that refused parties' requests for referrals invoked—either explicitly or implicitly—the so-called theory of *acte clair*, without taking into account the criteria established by the ECJ in the CILFIT case.

Moreover, there have been several cases in which the courts refused an *ex officio* power to refer, or where they excluded a reference concerning certain EU acts, such as recommendations. Finally, it should be noted that, paradoxically, all the cases mentioned were heard in the STA, which is the Portuguese court responsible for most of the country's preliminary references.

Portuguese Courts and the Duty to Enforce EU Law: The Portuguese Peculiarity

Contrary to what may be observed in other member states, the assimilation of European obligations has occurred rather uneventfully in Portugal.

The principles of supremacy and the direct effect of EU norms were quickly accepted by Portuguese courts, although in many cases article eight of the constitution provided the basis for rather than recognition of the autonomy of EU law. In contrast to certain French and German courts, Portuguese courts had no difficulty accepting their duty to directly enforce European directives. The same is true with respect to the principles of consistent interpretation and the state's responsibility for infringements of EU law.

During the first 20 years of EU membership there have been few examples of rebellious attitudes by Portuguese courts vis-à-vis their European obligations. How, then, can we explain this apparent peculiarity: the small number of cases referred to the ECJ given the acceptance by the Portuguese courts of their "European obligations" related to the application of EU law? There are a number of possible factors that should be considered in providing an answer to this question.

First, when Portugal joined the EU, the member states' courts had to a significant extent overcome the resistance originally surrounding some of the more "revolutionary" principles of EU law, such as those of supremacy and the direct effect. Second, the revisions of the Portuguese constitution have in some ways incorporated these principles and facilitated the acceptance of newly created ones. Third, the Portuguese constitution explicitly entitles each court to set aside provisions considered unconstitutional—a competence that gives all courts equal status. With this embedded autonomy, the Portuguese courts may have felt less need than their European counterparts to seek support from the ECJ on the interpretation and application of EU law.

Conclusions

More than 20 years after Portugal's accession, EU law still does not have an impact on the Portuguese legal order comparable to the impact experienced in other member states.

Without prejudice to the fact some Portuguese courts are still not completely familiar with the preliminary reference procedure, the limited use of this mechanism by lower courts is largely rooted in the particular status they have been vested with by the 1976 constitution. This status allows them to decide upon the most important questions of law without the need to seek advice or rulings from superior courts. Concerning the highest courts, while the absence of references for preliminary rulings by the STJ may be perplexing, the STA's successive violations of the duty to refer might also have something to do with the rigidity of the criteria set out in CILFIT.

6 | The Europeanization of Portuguese Interest Groups? Trade Unions and Employers' Organizations

Sebastián Royo

Introduction

The process of European integration has exerted significant influence in the industrial relations realm, not only through the implementation of the *acquis communautaire* and European regulation on social affairs, but more importantly by fostering the opening of the Portuguese economy to increasing competition, which has led to privatizations, downsizing and internal restructuring of economic sectors, and the liberalization of the economy.

These developments have generated pressures and have had an enormous influence on the social actors contributing to the emergence of a new pattern of industrial relations. Yet the legacies of authoritarianism and the experience of the revolutionary period have hindered efforts to institutionalize a modern and stable industrial relations setting that is based on trust and cooperation. This chapter will look at the transformation of the Portuguese trade unions and employers' associations, and outline the main features of the Portuguese industrial relations framework.[1]

---

1   This chapter borrows from S. Royo, *A new century of corporatism? Spain and Portugal in comparative perspective* (Westport, CT: Praeger, 2002).

Historical Background

In Portugal, a military coup installed a new authoritarian regime in 1926. During the 1930s the establishment of the authoritarian corporatist New State by the new dictator, António Salazar (1932–68) and the approval of a new constitution in 1933 led to the replacement of all independent political parties by the National Union (UN—União Nacional) and the banning of all independent unions in favour of new corporatist bodies. This regime lasted for more than 40 years.

The legacy of intervention by an authoritarian corporatist regime has left a strong imprint on the configuration of the Portuguese labour market and its trade union structure. The regime was also characterized by direct state intervention in the economy and authoritarian regulation of labour relations through corporatist institutions. The state was in charge of licensing new firms, setting external tariffs, foreign investment, finance, planning and control over prices, wages and rents.[2] A modified version of the Italian National Labour Statute (Estatuto de Trabalho Nacional) was introduced. It would regulate labour relations and interest group representation for the next 40 years. The authoritarian government sought to overcome the class struggle. In the realm of industrial relations, the regime created a corporatist system of industrial relations based on *sindicatos nacionais* (national trade unions) and *grémios* (employers' guilds), which had a legal monopoly of representation and were directly controlled by the government. While union membership was voluntary, non-members were forced to pay dues, and the government promoted collective bargaining very early, although it was a state-directed process, and

2   J. Barreto, "Portugal: Industrial relations under democracy", in A. Ferner and R. Hyman (eds), *Industrial relations in the new Europe* (Cambridge: Blackwell, 1992), pp. 445–81.

since it was voluntary it happened very rarely at company level. Until the 1960s, wages and most labour regulations were directly established by the government. The law admitted only individual grievances: strikes were illegal and repressed.

The heritage of authoritarian corporatism led to a state-dominated industrial relations setting. During the last period of the regime, the new leader—Marcelo Caetano—tried to foster more union autonomy and strengthen collective bargaining—which became legally compulsory—in order to improve productivity, management and to increase wages. These reforms introduced limited autonomy and fostered collective bargaining. Strikes remained illegal, but the government developed state-sponsored conciliation and arbitration procedures to address industrial disputes. The organization of free elections within unions resulted in the penetration of these organizations by people opposed to the regime, particularly by the communists. They mobilized workers against the regime, which led to repression during the regime's final years and a dramatic radicalization of class relations in the transition period. These activities resulted in a renewed membership drive, fostered by the new status and respectability of these organizations.

The fall of the regime in 1974 resulted in the dismantling of the corporatist system. In 1974, military officers, concerned about the future of the country and disaffected by the colonial wars, staged a coup that ended the authoritarian regime. This triggered a democratic transition process that had enormous consequences for Portugal's labour market and economic institutions. However, the transition to democracy was not smooth: democratization was threatened in 1974–75 by a revolutionary communist movement that sought to construct a socialist society, and which took the country to the brink of civil war. The social and political climate during the revolution was radically anti-capitalist, and the Communist Party (PCP—Partido Comunista Português) gained control of the ministry of labour and another government post. This resulted in a shift in the balance of power in favour of the workers, who exerted pressure—including intimidation and violence—and led to a spectacular increase in pay and social security benefits.

This revolutionary period, although short, left an enduring legacy in the country. In contrast to Spain, where the unions largely submerged their ambitions within the overall project of gradual reform, in Portugal the revolutionary nature of the transition process fostered workers' radicalization, deepened resentment between workers and employers and hindered the development of a new bargaining culture based on compromise. This legacy is still felt in the country, and has hindered the modernization of the Portuguese industrial relations system. In addition, state intervention increased during the revolution and the constitution enshrined a new system of industrial relations that was very favourable towards workers. All national banks and insurance companies, as well as many manufacturing firms, were nationalized. At the same time, the revolutionary government approved new and inflexible labour laws. For instance, norms regulating redundancies, dismissals and the rules on severance pay were very restrictive.[3]

Moreover, the 1976 constitution enshrined the right to job security, and this prevented successive governments from reforming the labour laws. Social security was extended to the whole population in 1974, but benefits remained low by European standards. Furthermore, most workers were covered by statutory regulations:

3   One paradox, however, is that legal rules covering temporary hiring were permissive allowing Portuguese employers to hire workers on a temporary basis, thus bypassing restrictions covering dismissals and the high severance pay costs. The result of this development has been—as in Spain during the second half of the 1980s—the increasing segmentation of the labour market and a sharp increase in temporary employment.

the government introduced a minimum wage in 1974 that is revised every year, and it approved a new law in 1975 that made collective dismissals difficult. These measured were slowly reversed during the 1980s when successive governments led by the liberal-conservative Social Democratic Party (PSD—Partido Social Democrata) reformed the constitution and approved labour laws introducing a more flexible legislation facilitating collective dismissals and reducing the costs associated with severance of employment.[4] These developments resulted in a dramatic deterioration of economic conditions, with mass unemployment, high inflation, huge budget deficits and recession that exerted heavy pressures on the labour market and companies, and led to deflationary policies by subsequent governments. Failed coup attempts in 1974 and 1975 gave way to a new phase in the transition process that culminated in free elections based on universal suffrage in 1975 and 1976. After the elections, the Socialist Party (PS—Partido Socialista) led by Mário Soares became the largest party, and the PCP was excluded from power. A new constitution was approved in 1976 that paved the way for the establishment of a new industrial relations framework. The following sections will outline this development.

The Main Actors

Trade Unions

The communist-led union coalition Intersindical emerged from the illegal and clandestine union opposition movement during the authoritarian regime. This union formed the basis of a national labour confederation after the revolution,

4   Barreto (note 2), pp. 454–5; J. Barreto and R. Naumann, "Portugal: Industrial relations under democracy", in A. Ferrer and R. Hyman (eds), *Changing industrial relations in Europe: Portugal* (Cambridge: Blackwell, 1998), p. 402.

Intersindical Nacional, which emerged in 1974 when it gained control over most national unions. Two-thirds of existing unions joined Intersindical in 1974–75. Intersindical sought to monopolize the labour movement and advocated a unitary labour organization.[5] The communists' influence during the revolutionary period facilitated this objective, and Intersindical achieved legal monopoly of representation under the 1975 union law; however, it failed to control the rank and file. New representative bodies, such as the workers' commissions, emerged spontaneously in workplaces outside of union control. The leaders of these commissions got involved in negotiations with employers, organized strikes and, in some cases, even managed small companies. Yet the leaders of these commissions opposed the PCP and challenged the dominant position of the Intersindical. They received support from organizations and individuals opposed to the PCP, which viewed them as an alternative to Intersindical.[6] In 1976 these commissions were recognized by the constitution. Subsequently, they were regulated by a 1979 law restricting their role, attributing them the duty of supervising management and participating in the administration of welfare issues within the company.

The end of the revolutionary period resulted in the approval of the 1976 constitution that abolished Intersindical's legal

5 United union activism during the dictatorship had been facilitated by the common struggle for democracy; however, the unions pursued different strategies. The radical left, the communists and the Catholic labour movement sought to overthrow the existing capitalist system, while the social democrats supported a more reformist strategy. These contrasting political strategies became critical during the transition and hindered efforts at unification. The struggles between labour activists were mirrored by partisan conflicts that split the union movement into two groups. See R. Naumann and A. Stoleroff, "Portugal", in B. Ebbinghaus and J. Visser (eds), *The societies of Europe: Trade unions in Western Europe since 1945* (New York, NY: Grove's Dictionaries), pp. 552–3.

6 Barreto and Naumann (note 4), p. 409.

monopoly.[7] The new constitution adopted a model of pluralist representation that allowed for the establishment of trade unions at any level. Pluralism reflected the divisions of the revolutionary period. Disputes within the left between the communists and the socialists and social democrats, who resented the PCP's control of the labour movement, resulted in the organization of new unions in all sectors. After the collapse of the authoritarian regime, all parties sought roots in the working class, and party activists played an important role in the emergence of new unions. At its 1977 Congress, Intersindical changed its name to the General Confederation of Portuguese Labour (CGTP—Confederação Geral dos Trabalhadores Portugueses).

Immediately after the formal abolition of the unity clause, 30 unions, led by those representing banking, insurance and office employees, came together and with the support of the PS and the liberal-conservative Popular Democratic Party (PPD—Partido Popular Democrático),[8] founded the General Workers' Union (UGT—União Geral de Trabalhadores).[9] The major aim of the new organization was to challenge Intersindical's monopoly of the labour movement. This development led to union pluralism and inter-union competition in the workplace. As a matter of fact, the UGT was able to achieve a near monopoly in certain sectors—such as the financial sector—and expanded rapidly in the

7   Barreto and Naumann (note 4), p. 410; D. Nataf, *Democratization and social settlements: The politics of change in contemporary Portugal* (Albany, NY: State University of New York Press), p. 131.

8   The PPD later changed its name to the Social Democratic Party (PSD).

9   At that time, the PS and PPD had very limited influence with the unions. The PS was founded in 1875, but had virtually disappeared by the 1930s. The PPD was founded shortly after the fall of the authoritarian regime. In contrast, the PCP survived the dictatorship and infiltrated its corporatist unions, which, because the unions were at the forefront of the transition, gave it leverage. See Barreto and Naumann (note 4), p. 409.

manufacturing sector by signing collective agreements the CGTP had rejected. However, Intersindical has been able to maintain its position of dominance within the labour movement, with 150 affiliated unions against the 63 affiliated to the UGT. The CGTP is dominant in manufacturing, construction, electricity, road and urban transport, post and telecommunications and large sections of the civil service, while the UGT is dominant in banking, insurance, several industries and services and education, as well as in white-collar occupations.

During the 1980s, the number of unions increased dramatically as new groups sought to represent particular groups of workers. These new groups, however, do not consider themselves part of the union movement. This development has resulted in the fragmentation of the labour movement. The CGTP represents 60 per cent of unionized workers, the UGT 30–35 per cent and independent unions less than ten per cent.[10] As we will see below, despite repeated attempts by the UGT to consolidate and concentrate the union movement, fragmentation and divisions have remained: it was not until 1988 that the CGTP and the UGT established formal relations with one another. During the 1990s there was a process of rapprochement between both unions, and some initiatives for both organizations to merge. Nevertheless the relationship between the two confederations remains strained.

At this point it is important to stress the Portuguese legislature has not given preferential treatment to either union confederation: all unions are the same and have equal rights. Despite being highly interventionist (for example, in the procedures covering collective bargaining), Portuguese law does not include any criteria for representatives or recognition procedures.

---

10 Barreto (note 2), pp. 464–6; Barreto and Naumann (note 4), p. 412.

An important feature of Portuguese unions is their relative weakness and their lack of financial resources.[11] As we will see below, union membership declined dramatically during the 1980s following the conclusion of the democratic transition. As a result, the organizations lack adequate financial resources, and often depend on external help for their survival. They also have few employees. A major feature has been the support given to unions by political parties. Up until the late 1980s, Portuguese communist and socialist trade unions have maintained historically interlocking directorates between the parties and the union organizations. Their different ideological orientations were mirrored in their statutes and programmes. Up until the late-1980s, union leaders had party responsibilities and, in many cases, political jobs: they have also been elected to parliament. In Portugal, the PS and the PSD have been dominant within the UGT, and the PCP within the CGTP. These institutional links between unions and parties still prevail, although partisan control of unions is waning.[12]

Finally, Portugal experienced high levels of labour conflict during the 1970s, most of which was politically motivated and concerned with the transition to democracy. Industrial conflict declined sharply during the second half of the 1980s, despite the

11 Barreto and Naumman (note 4), pp. 412–15.

12 Ibid, p. 414. Although formally only personal ties exist between the unions and political parties, in reality union leaders and activists share political jobs and party responsibilities, with union officials frequently being appointed to executive positions within the parties (although union rules prohibit this). During the 1980s, between five and nine per cent of parliamentary deputies were also officers within unions affiliated to the UGT or Intersindical, or occupied leadership positions within the confederations: consequently, unions are vehicles of political influence. Some of the factors explaining the predominance of political activity within Portuguese trade unionism include the historic role of societal self-regulation compared to statutory regulation, partisan control of the unions, the endemic weakness of the unions and the tendency of employers to rely on the government to achieve their goals for them: these tendencies were reinforced during the economic crisis of the 1980s. Unions have used political action—including calling a general strike in 1988—to defend the employment legislation inherited from the revolution.

success of the general strike organized separately by all major unions in 1988 to oppose the government's plan to liberalize the labour market and facilitate collective dismissals.

The Union Structure

Union fragmentation has had deleterious consequences for collective bargaining in Portugal, because it has hindered efforts to centralize and rationalize the outdated structure of collective bargaining. The combination of political cleavages between the major unions, and the craft and territorial divisions imposed in the "vertical unions" during the authoritarian regime have hampered the development of strong and articulated union structures. This problem is particularly acute in Portugal, where centrifugal pressures caused by regional, political and occupational rivalries have generally impeded the development of concerted and unitary strategies by unions.

Dispersion and fragmentation are the predominant features of the Portuguese union structure.[13] Political schisms within Intersindical, coupled with the emergence of the UGT and resistance from certain occupational groups (particularly office workers and professions with special functions) to integrate into centralized organizations, hindered efforts to centralize and rationalize the outdated union structure.

While the number of individual unions increased from 307 in 1974 to 383 in 1996, this was the result of two main processes: new unions were created in sectors in which union activity was banned during the dictatorship (that is, the public sector in central and local administration, education, health services and public

---

13 Naumann and Stoleroff (note 5), p. 557.

enterprises),[14] while political competition and class consciousness intensified centrifugal pressures hindering rationalization efforts.

The CGTP and UGT remain confederations of vertical units in which the degree of organizational consolidation varies. CGTP is a confederation of about 12 vertical units complemented by unions at the local level that are organized within 20 autonomous district unions within the confederation. To further complicate matters, many of the CGTP's small union affiliates—and even some federations (for example, the teachers' union)—are not officially affiliated with the CGTP, but are associated and integrated into its structure. For its part, the UGT has a dual regional and functional organization. Its structure is unbalanced: it has 63 affiliated organizations led by the three regional unions of bank employees, by the office workers' unions with an average of about 15,000 members and by a large group of smaller organizations.[15] In addition, federations are less important within UGT, and they focus mostly on the coordination of collective bargaining. Furthermore, nearly 100 independent unions, mostly concentrated in the public service sector, are not affiliated with either of the two main confederations.[16]

14 Barreto and Naumann (note 4), p. 410. There are now more than 150 independent unions, most small and occupational based (for example, airline pilots, train drivers, civil servants and dock-workers), many of which function as little more than as employment market cartels and lobbying groups, although they tend also to be highly cohesive and effective. These unions seek to defend the particular interests of their members and to preserve their autonomy while opposing policies of solidarity with other organized workers. They are deeply resented by both the UGT and CGTP, which view them as egocentric organizations defending the privileges of certain groups.

15 Barreto and Naumann (note 4), p. 410. With close links to both Scandinavian and central European unions, the UGT wanted to follow the example of Germany and Austria, with their limited number of national industrial unions. The opposition from existing unions (particularly the more powerful banking, insurance, services and education unions) has hindered plans to achieve vertical integration. National industry-based UGT unions in sectors such as clothing, chemicals, textiles, metal, construction etc. are weaker than their Intersindical peers.

16 A group of independent unions was formed by the PSD's labour wing; however, they have been unable to challenge the dominant position of the major confederations.

Union fragmentation intensified further with the foundation of public sector unions after the revolution and the emergence of new associations to cater for the specific interests of certain groups of workers and professionals during the latter-half of the 1980s. Political competition and status consciousness have intensified these processes. The consequence of these developments has been that, since the revolution, the number of service sector unions has increased considerably.[17] Finally, at the end of the 1980s, the PSD's labour organization, the Social Democrat Workers (TSD – Trabalhadores Social Democratas), decided to create a third confederation of its own, and terminate the alliance with the PS. This attempt failed when the majority of PSD activists within the UGT rejected this proposal and remained within the UGT. Consequently the Convention of Independent Unions (CSI—Convenção dos Sindicatos Independentes) has a limited social base and low representation, with only seven occupational unions and five sector unions. In total, during the 1980s and 1990s there was a contradictory evolution within the trade union structures. On the one hand, both the CGTP and UGT attempted (with limited success in the case of UGT) to reorganize their structures and deepen their vertical integration, on the other, the emergence of new independent occupational unions intensified the fragmentation of Portuguese unionism. There are now 370 unions compared to the 328 that existed in 1974.[18]

At the beginning of the new century, the basic institutions of Portuguese industrial relations were clear. Union members at the enterprise level elect union delegates who become the main interlocutors with management. When there are several unions present, the delegates establish an enterprise-based inter-union

17 Naumann and Stoleroff (note 5), pp. 554–7.

18 Barreto and Naumann (note 4), pp. 410–11.

committee.[19] Based on a 1979 law, in a limited number of firms the workers elect worker commissions, which in most cases were run by the dominant union representatives.[20] Hence, in some medium-sized firms, and in the majority of large companies, there is a dual model of workers' representation with trade union representation (in the form of shop stewards, joint shop-steward committees, or union commissions [*comissões sindicais*]) and the workers' commission. In practice, though, this dual system of workers' representation stipulated by law is the exception. The existence of these representative bodies depends largely upon company size, and to a lesser extent upon union membership density within the company.[21] Moreover, as we will see below, these workers' commissions exist in a considerably smaller proportion of companies than do the trade union organizations and have limited statutory rights to be kept informed and to be consulted.[22] Additionally, the right to call strikes, to negotiate and to sign collective agreements is reserved for union representatives. This institutional setting is closed at the macro-level, with the tripartite Standing Social Concertation Committee (CPCS—Conselho Permanente de Concertação Social) being in charge of social bargaining.

Union Membership

During the dictatorship membership of the "vertical" unions was compulsory except in sectors such as the civil service—where unions were illegal; hence, the collapse of authoritarian regimes

19 Naumann and Stoleroff (note 5), p. 550.

20 A. Stoleroff, "Elementos do padrão emergente de relações industriais em Portugal", *Organizações e Trabalho* 13 (1995), pp.11–42.

21 Stoleroff (note 20).

22 Barreto and Naumann (note 4), p. 415. An Intersindical survey in 1993 revealed that about 60 per cent of 1076 registered commissions were inactive.

allowed unions to inherit a large number of members. In addition, the disappearance of official unions, which motivated workers to join new unions that could articulate their demands, coupled with the euphoria associated with the transition to democracy and the wish of Portuguese workers to participate in public life and contribute to the democratization processes, fostered high levels of union affiliation.[23] Consequently, during the first years of the transition process, union membership was high: between 1979 and 1984 membership (as a percentage of wage and salary earners) reached 58.8 per cent.[24]

This development proved short-lived. The political and economic conditions for union participation deteriorated sharply during the second half of the 1970s. After the highs of the transition period, unions failed to live up to expectations and were unable to achieve outcomes favourable to their members. They also failed to develop services to their affiliates that would have made membership more attractive. Once the euphoria of regime transition dissipated, workers decided to cancel their memberships. In Portugal, this process was hastened by the PS government's decision in 1977 to repeal the automatic deduction of union dues from wages: a move aimed at weakening the CGTP.[25] The economic crisis that resulted in rising unemployment, the significant rise in temporary work and informal employment in the black

23 Naumann and Stoleroff (note 5).

24 M. da C. Cerdeira, *A evolução da sindicalização portuguesa de 1974 a 1995* (Lisbon: Ministério para a Qualificação e o Emprego), p. 46; A. Stoleroff and R. Naumann, "A sindicalização em Portugal: A sua medida e a sua distribuição", *Sociologia: Problemas e Práticas* 14 (1993); Naumman and Stoleroff (note 5), p. 557.

25 Barreto and Naumann (note 4), p. 412. Since 1977, public enterprises have deducted union fees from their members' wage packets; however, private companies and employers' associations have refused to follow suit, with the result unions have to make arrangements to collect the membership dues themselves.

economy,[26] coupled with the growth of the service sector and the underground economy, as well as the emergence of new forms of business organizations in which traditional blue-collar unskilled workers were no longer dominant, have also been mentioned as some of the reasons for the sharp decline in union membership. Other explanations for falling membership include poor member services, inter-union rivalry, union politicization and employers' pressure.[27] Finally, other authors have stressed the impact of the statutory extension of collective agreements to non-members: since all workers benefit from the agreements, there is little incentive for anyone to join trade unions and pay their dues.[28]

As a result of these developments, the proportion of union members in the labour force has declined sharply over the past two decades, with the number of members reaching its lowest point during the mid-1980s.[29] Between 1988 and 1990, there were approximately one million union members—representing 30 per cent of the employed workforce.[30] Since then, union membership (as a percentage of all wage and salary earners) declined by 44.2 per cent between 1985 and 1995, and by 2000 stood at 25.6 per cent. This places Portugal in the group of Western European countries

26 Barreto and Naumann (note 4). This problem is particularly acute in economic sectors such as construction (where the estimated proportion of informal employment is as high as 50 per cent, and union membership is barely ten per cent), the clothing and footwear industry and certain service sectors.

27 J. Ribeiro, P. Granjo, N. Leitão and A. Harouna, *Posições face à sindicalização: Desafios de mudança* (Lisbon: Cosmos, 1993).

28 M. A. Malo, "Elecciones sindicales y comportamiento de los sindicatos españoles: Una propuesta", *Estudios sobre la Economía Española*, 93 (2001); O. Bover, P. García Perea and P. Portugal, "A comparative study of the Portuguese and Spanish labour markets", *Servício de Estudios, Documento de Trabajo* 9807 (Madrid: Banco de España, 1997).

29 Cerdeira (note 24); Stoleroff and Naumann (note 24); Naumann and Stoleroff (note 5).

30 Naumman and Stoleroff (note 5), p. 557.

with low- to medium-union density, although it is significantly ahead of both France and Spain. Union density is also unequally distributed: it is higher in the primary sector and the public services and is slightly below the general level in private industries and services. It is important to be aware that in Portugal, union membership is close to 100 per cent in sectors where unions have a monopoly of health care provision (for example, in banking, insurance and telecommunications).[31] For instance, in contrast with the general trend, banking unionism in Portugal approaches 90 per cent and membership has doubled since the revolution.[32] Levels of unionization are particularly strong in the railways, banking, insurance, transport and public companies, and rather weak in construction, commerce, textiles, food industries and ceramics. In Portugal, the combination of increasing union fragmentation and an overall decline in union density, has resulted in a decline in the total number of unionized workers per union (from 2600 members per union in the late 1980s to 2000 in the late 1990s) (see Table 6.1). At the end of the 1990s the CGTP and its associated unions represented more than 71 per cent of all union members, and UGT less than 23 per cent.[33]

Business Organizations

The authoritarian corporatist legacy also left an important imprint in the configuration of employers' associations; however, in Portugal the business associations were not integrated into the

31 Bover, García Perea and Portugal (note 28), p. 14.

32 Barreto and Naumann (note 4), p. 413. In the banking sector the services provided to union members are well developed, collective bargaining and industrial disputes procedures work very effectively, strikes are subject to ballots and the internal elections to the governing bodies are well contested with high participation rates.

33 Naumann and Stoleroff (note 5), pp. 557–8.

Table 6.1
Reported Membership by Selected Unions in Portugal
(1995–2008)

	Sindicato dos Trabalhadores da Função Pública do Sul e Açores (STFSA)	35.7
CGTP	Sindicato dos Trabalhadores das Indústrias Metalúrgicas e Metalomecânica de Portugal (STIMMDP)	19.8
	Sindicato dos Trabalhadores do Comércio, Escritórios e Serviços de Portugal (CESP)	26.8
	Sindicato de Enfermeiros Portugueses (SEP)	17.4
CGTP*	Sindicato Nacional dos Trabalhadores da Administração Local (STAL)	44.6
	Sindicato dos Professores da Grande Lisboa (SPGL)	19.9
UGT	Sindicato dos Bancário do Sul e Ilhas (SBSI)	49.7
	Sindicato dos Bancários do Norte (SBN)	18.9

* CGTP associated (cooperating) union.
Sources: R. Naumann and A. Stoleroff, "Portugal", in B. Ebbinghaus and J. Visser (eds), *The societies of Europe: Trade unions in Western Europe since 1945* (New York, NY: Grove's Dictionaries, 2000), Table PO19, p. 572.

corporatist "national vertical unions". Businesses in Portugal created their own organizations, the national guilds, although they remained reluctant to participate in them. As long as they were not organized, companies did not have to bargain with labour, and this offered them a powerful incentive to remain outside guilds that lacked power and autonomy. The inefficiency of the system led to a profound transformation in the late 1950s. Unions and guilds up until that time were increasingly perceived to be classic organizations preventing the overthrow of the class struggle. The government introduced a new system based on corporations, which excluded single-peak associations.[34]

34 Barreto (note 2), p. 453.

Before the revolution, seven corporate groups that had grown under the New State's protection dominated the Portuguese economy. This situation changed dramatically during the democratic transition: indeed, one of the main consequences of the revolution was the expropriation of the entire domestic financial sector and important industrial and service companies (including oil, breweries, steel, transportation and telecommunications). This development proved short lived, however, as Cavaco Silva's governments privatized practically all of them by 1995.

After the collapse of the authoritarian regime, the Portuguese business guilds were disbanded. While during the democratic transition employers lagged behind in establishing their association, now businesses are organized into two separate structures: the employers' associations and the regional associations. In 1974, the employers created the Confederation of Portuguese Industry (CIP—Confederação da Industria Portuguesa), which—with the support of influential members of the Lisbon and Oporto Portuguese Industrial Associations (AIP—Associação Industrial Portuguesa) that had functioned throughout the dictatorship—claimed to represent all sectors. Its main organizational foundations lay in regional associations in textiles, metallurgy and construction. CIP is the main employers' body, and was created to protect their interests at a time they were threatened by the impetus of the revolutionary movement. At that time, it waged campaigns against state intervention, restrictive labour regulation, "Marxist" economic strategies and nationalizations, while leading the employers' struggle for survival. In more recent years its priorities have been to reduce the role of the state in the economy and improving the competitiveness of Portuguese firms.[35]

---

35 Barreto and Naumann (note 4), pp. 406–8.

The Portuguese Confederation of Commerce and Services (CCP—Confederação do Comércio e Serviços de Portugal) was established in 1974. Largely as a result of conflicts of interest between it affiliates (for example, the wholesale versus retail sectors), and the fact some important service sectors (such as, transport, banking and insurance) are not included, it is not as powerful as CIP. The third employers' confederation, the Confederation of Portuguese Farmers (CAP—Confederaçao dos Agricultores de Portugal), represents the interests of industrial-scale farmers.[36] These organizations have sought to defend business interests and act as channels of communication with the government. Their major objective during the 1980s was reform of the pro-labour legislation that had been approved during the revolutionary period. CIP rejected any bilateral negotiations with the union confederation until 1990, but were active participants in the CPCS.

While these organizations provide a wide range of services to member firms, membership data is not reliable. The CPI is the most powerful of them, claiming to represent 35,000 private companies—75 per cent of all Portuguese companies.[37] Internal differences over strategies (for example, on state intervention, economic policy, European integration and competitiveness), and regional rivalries have hampered their ability to function effectively. CIP gained further legitimacy and strength with the affiliation of AIP-Porto and AIP-Lisboa in the late-1980s and early-1990s. Internal challenges are more deeply rooted in the other two organizations: the CCP remains split between its wholesale and retail

36 Naumann and Stoleroff (note 5), pp. 549–50. Small- and medium-sized farmers are mainly represented by CAN.

37 Barreto (note 2), p. 461; Barreto and Naumann (note 4), p. 407. This claim is disputed. Other scholars argue new empirical evidence indicates a 60 per cent affiliation rate. However, unions argue membership of the employers' organizations is lower than that of the unions. See J. L. Cardoso, J. Brito and F. Mendes, *Empresarios e gestores da indústria em Portugal* (Lisbon: Dom Quixote, 1990).

members, while the major supermarkets have established their own association, the Portuguese Association of Distribution Companies (APED—Associação Portuguesa de Empresas de Distribuição) outside the confederation, which has resulted in a series of disputes between supermarkets and other retailers. In addition, employers' associations in banking, insurance and transportation continue to remain outside the confederate structures. Finally, CAP's social base is being challenged by a new organization, the National Agricultural Confederation (CAN—Confederação Nacional da Agricultura), which organises small- and medium-sized farmers, which constitutes the majority of agricultural employers.[38]

The business sector is also represented by regional associations providing services such as sales promotion, fairs, training and technological advice to their members. These organizations are smaller, but they are better organized at the local level. The largest is the Lisbon-based AIP. These associations differ over critical issues such as the role of the public sector and the state, economic policies, the EU, trade barriers and competition policies, differences that have prevented their integration as successive attempts to set up unitary organizations have failed. Only the CIP, the CCP and CAP are officially recognized by the state as employers' representatives at top-level bodies such as the CPCS.[39]

Industrial Relations under Democracy

Collective Bargaining and Wage Setting

A legal minimum wage is set each year and collective bargaining agreements establish a starting wage for each of the

38 Barreto and Naumann (note 4), p. 408.

39 Barreto and Naumann (note 4), p. 408; Barreto (note 2), p. 461.

occupational categories in the agreement. Wage flexibility in Portugal is high, with the base wage in each categories being established through collective bargaining agreements at a much lower relative level, giving employers greater flexibility in determining wage levels.[40]

Portuguese legislation does not define any criteria for representation with respect to collective bargaining rights. Representation criteria and the rules governing the authority to negotiate agreements are key factors in limiting union bargaining power. Trade union representation and the ability of unions to negotiate and sign collective agreements largely depends on the level of trade union membership.[41] The absence of a representation criteria means all unions are considered representative, with all having equal rights.[42] Since 1976 the right to negotiate and sign collective agreements has been reserved by law to union representatives. Workers' commissions only have statutory rights of consultation and information. Furthermore, collective bargaining is voluntary, since few sanctions can be imposed and any union—including minority unions—are able to negotiate with management. Collective bargaining therefore depends largely on the employers' willingness to negotiate with a particular union. Both sides must comply with all legal requirements only after they have formally

40 Bover, García Perea and Portugal (note 28), p. 11. A consequence of this development has been that actual wages in Portugal generally exceed industry wage agreements. By contrast, in Spain any nationally agreed wage-rates are legally binding for all unskilled and semi-skilled workers.

41 One of the key outcomes of the 2001 agreement on working conditions, hygiene and safety, and reduction of workplace accidents is that it helps clarify the actual representation role of the unions. This agreement renews the commitment, initially established in 1991, to create workplace health and safety committees and establishes a six-month deadline for the development of legally-regulated procedures for the election of employee representatives to these committees.

42 Barreto and Naumann (note 4), p. 411. Although there are some legal requirements, they are not enforced on the grounds they may be unconstitutional.

agreed to negotiate. These provisions have contributed towards weakening Portuguese unions by allowing employers to ignore the strongest workplace unions and instead reach agreement with the more accommodating.[43]

Since the Portuguese trade union structure is characterized by several unions acting in an uncoordinated fashion, the consequence of these developments has been that unions do not have as much leverage vis-à-vis employers. Other factors have also contributed to limiting union power: they are financially dependent on the contributions they receive from their relatively small memberships and inter-union coordination remains limited.[44]

Collective agreements only apply to workers who are represented by signatory unions; however, since the law does not permit differentiated workplace conditions based on union membership, these agreements in practice extended to all workers.[45] As previously stated, this helps explain the low levels of trade union membership in Portugal: since all workers will benefit from the agreements, there is little incentive for people to join the union and pay its membership fees.[46]

Given there is no requirement for an absolute majority of union representatives to reach an agreement, and there are no recognition procedures or representation criteria, Portuguese

---

43 Barreto and Naumann (note 4), p. 411.

44 Bover, García Perea and Portugal (note 28), p. 115. The government grants unions a small "allowance" for their participation within the CPCS (generally no more than ten per cent of their total annual income). Declining membership numbers has resulted in unions facing increasing financial difficulty, particularly now that aid from foreign union movements has largely dried up. Increasingly, the confederations rely on contributions from a small number of unions and European state agencies. In 1990, more than 50 per cent of the UGT's income came from just one of its (then) 61 affiliates: the Southern Portugal Union of Banking Employees. See Barreto and Naumann (note 4), pp. 412–15.

45 Barreto (note 2), p. 470; Barreto and Naumann (note 4), p. 417.

46 Malo (note 28).

employers have been able to open negotiations with moderate unions (mainly independent unions, although in some cases with the UGT) with which they expect to reach more favourable agreements. This has enabled employers to break the almost complete "bargaining monopoly" enjoyed by the CGTP in such sectors as manufacturing, construction, electricity, urban transport, post and telecommunications, as well as in large sectors of the civil service. A union that is in a minority position within the sector is able to reach an agreement with management that covers workers who are not members of that union for the simple reason that only one agreement is enforceable for the same group of workers within any company. This has limited union bargaining power in Portugal, and hindered the establishment of uniform conditions at the national level and has resulted in widely varying wage levels across sectors.[47] The consequences of an over-regulated and legalistic framework, coupled with voluntary collective bargaining, helps explain the near absence of company-level bargaining in the private sector and the minimal impact it has on working conditions.[48]

Once an agreement is obtained and it is registered and published by the Ministry of Employment, it remains in force until superseded by a subsequent agreement, which overall, and by law, must not be less favourable to the workers than the one it replaces. A consequence of this is that employers view agreements as potential milestones that once concluded will form the basis of further union demands.

Local unions and federations negotiate with the employers' associations, groups of companies and—in some cases—large individual firms, on both wage and non-wage issues. Traditionally, the

47 Bover, García Perea, and Portugal (note 28), p. 13.

48 Barreto and Naumann (note 4), p. 418.

major objective of bargaining has been the settlement of wages; however, with the annual revision of the minimum wage this is now largely done by the government—employers are only able to negotiate variations between the national and industry minimum rates,[49] although in practice deviations from sector-level bargaining are common.[50] The highly regulated collective bargaining framework has resulted in limited collective bargaining within the private sector. Managers are reluctant to negotiate at the company-level out of fear of encouraging union activity; unions, which are weak at the company-level, also prefer industry-level bargaining. Consequently, collective bargaining mainly takes place at the industry-level, and government regulations still play an important role. Company-level collective agreements are possible only by establishing more favourable conditions than the corresponding industry-level agreement, which helps explain the lack of company-level agreements.[51] As we have seen, since the 1990s there has been a tendency to move from regional to national industry agreements.

Differences in the union structure have also had a significant impact on wage bargaining. The weakness of unions has hindered their attempts to set wages above the national minimum—particularly for the lower and middle occupational categories. It is not uncommon for employers to seek to negotiate conditions that will be less favourable to their employees than those they presently enjoy through established industry-level agreements: a process that requires intermediation from the Ministry of Employment.[52]

49 Barreto (note 2), p. 472.

50 Stoleroff (note 20).

51 Bover, García Perea and Portugal (note 28), p. 14.

52 Bover, García Perea and Portugal (note 28), pp. 13–14.

Social Concertation

Following the revolutionary upheavals, intense efforts by governments and social actors to normalize industrial relations in Portugal led to the development of social bargaining. Despite the antagonistic relationship between union and employers and the ideological divisions within the labour movement that had their roots in the revolution, the social actors have moved towards a less polarized industrial relations model. Indeed, globalization and European integration have encouraged—rather than undermined—social bargaining. Unable to escape from economic interdependence, Portugal has experimented with the social concertation model in which centralized agreements between employers' and labour organizations seek to resolve tensions between economic interdependence and political sovereignty and between monetary and exchange rate policies.[53]

53 As I have argued elsewhere (S. Royo [note 1], pp. 245–6), social concertation describes those centralized agreements reached between union and business leaders in the pursuit of shared macro-economic objectives. Although this term is less common in the United States, it is used in neocorporatist literature throughout Western Europe and Latin America. Through these agreements, unions are willing to moderate and limit wage growth. The participation of governments is not mandatory, since the agreements are usually negotiated and signed by trade unions and business organizations with centralized structures and hierarchical powers and then followed (and implemented) by the majority of businesses and workers. Amongst other things, concertation agreements cover incomes policies, industrial relations, productivity, absenteeism, working hours, training etc. They also include provisions dealing with macro-economic issues such as redistribution, inflation targets, competitiveness etc., as well as institutional issues, including the participation of social actors in economic policy-making and participation in state institutions etc. Social democratic governments have often participated in these agreements in an attempt to achieve their economic objectives, and have offered compensation, such as subsidies, increases in public expenditures, public jobs, fiscal benefits etc. to the social actors for their cooperation. See P. C. Schmitter, *Corporatism and public policy in authoritarian Portugal* (Beverly Hills, CA: Sage, 1974). Some Spanish authors may use the term corporativismo to refer to "old" corporatism, and the neologism, corporatismo to mean "new" corporatism. In Portugal this system of interest representation is known as corporativismo. J. Martínez-Alier and J. Roca, "Spain after Franco: From corporatist ideology to corporatist reality", *CES working paper series* 15 (Cambridge, MA: CES-Harvard University, 1986), pp. 23–6.

TABLE 6.2
Social Concertation in Portugal
(1986–2001)

Agreement	Year	Signatories
Prices and incomes policy	1986–7	CIP, CAP, CCP, UGT, government
Prices and incomes policy	1988	CAP, CCP, UGT, government
Economic and social	1991	CIP, CCP, UGT, government
Incomes policy	1992	CIP, CAP, CCP, UGT, government
Short-term social dialogue	1996	CIP, CAP, CCP, UGT, government
Strategic social pact	1996–9	CIP, CAP, CCP, UGT, government
Employment policies and vocational training	2001	CIP, CAP, CCP, UGT, CGTP-IN, government
Workplace working conditions, hygiene and safety and to reduce workplace accidents	2001	CIP, CAP, CCP, UGT, CGTP-IN, government

SOURCE: Author's own data

In Portugal, social concertation began in 1987 and was consolidated during the 1990s. Social concertation agreements were established in 1987, 1988, 1990, 1992 and 1996, there was an agreement of strategic concertation covering the 1997–99 period, and a further two concertation agreements were reached in 2001.[54]

The emergence of national social bargaining in Portugal took place at the outset of a dramatic economic crisis of 1983–85. To give an idea of the magnitude of the crisis, in 1984 alone the country's GDP declined by 1.6 per cent, investment fell by 18 per

54 In 1991 the social actors signed two complementary agreements regulating professional training, hygiene and security in the workplace.

cent, unemployment rose to 8.3 per cent, inflation reached 29.3 per cent, disposable family income decreased by 3.7 per cent and private consumption declined by three per cent. The 1983 legislative elections resulted in the formation of the Centre Bloc coalition consisting of the conservative PSD and the PS, with the PS's leader, Mário Soares, becoming prime minister. This government implemented an International Monetary Fund (IMF) stabilization plan and in 1984 created the CPCS. The positive outcome of these polices became evident in 1985 when the economy emerged from recession. The rewards were reaped by the PSD, which won the 1985 legislative election under the leadership of Aníbal Cavaco Silva.

Helped by the country's accession to the European Community and a generally improving international situation, the Portuguese economy continued to improve during 1986. In order to reduce inflation, the government pursued incomes policy agreements with the social actors. Under the guise of "recommendations on incomes policy", in 1986 the CPCS (which included the UGT, the government, and the three employers' associations: CIP, CCP and CAP) reached an agreement on incomes policy that fixed wage increases at seven per cent, subject to actual inflation.[55] This agreement dealt almost exclusively with the rate of growth of nominal wages for 1987, and was based on inflation forecasts that proved accurate, thus contributing to the curbing of inflation.

The process of social concertation continued after the 1987 legislative elections at which the PSD won a parliamentary majority. In October of that year, the CGTP—with the support of the PCP—decided to participate in CPCS. The unions' linked the government's programme of structural reform (aimed at revising labour legislation, introducing privatization, constitutional

55 The CGTP refused to participate.

revision and agrarian reform) to the incomes policy. On 18 January 1988, the social actors represented in the CPCS—with the exception of the CGTP and the CIP, which both refused to sign—reached a new incomes policy agreement.

Contrary to expectations, the process of deinflation halted in 1988 and UGT withdrew its support for the agreement following the government's refusal to adjust wage increases to recognize rising inflation. The consequence of this was that no agreements were reached during 1989 and 1990, although moderation continued to prevail in collective bargaining. Rising inflation, fuelled by huge budget deficits, forced the social actors to return to the bargaining table. In 1990, the government proposed a social pact: the Programme of Economic and Social Progress for the 1990s (Programa de progresso económico e social para os anos noventa). This initiative resulted in intense negotiations that led to the Economic and Social Agreement (AES—Acordo Económico e Social), which was signed by all members of the CPCS except the CGTP.

This pact included a reduction in the working week from 48 to 44 hours, and included a commitment for a further gradual reduction to 40 hours by 1995. It also addressed a wide range of other issues that were to be resolved by legislation, including: dismissals, health, safety and hygiene at work, unemployment benefits, vocational training, working-time flexibility, supplementary social security in cases of industrial restructuring and the employment of minors. The AES also covered collective bargaining and included a recommendation on wage policy that capped wage increases to 13.5 per cent. Furthermore, for the first time in the course of tripartite negotiations, the AES also included the annual revision of the national monthly minimum wage, which was set at

40,000 escudos (approximately $254).[56] The AES also led to a new labour package (*pacote laboral*) in 1991, which revised legislation on dismissal for non-adaptation, employment of minors, working hours, holidays, collective bargaining rules and the arbitration of industrial disputes. In July 1991 all CPCS members—including the CGTP—signed two subsidiary agreements governing work safety and hygiene, and professional training.

Following the PSD's victory at the 1991 legislative elections, the social partners re-opened CPCS negotiations in order to reach agreement on a new economic and social agreement. After some difficult and protracted negotiations over wage increases (owing to the government's insistence on containing wage costs), the three employers' confederations, the UGT and the government signed the new agreement on 15 February 1992. This agreement limited wage increases to 9.75 per cent, while increasing the minimum wage by 11 per cent.

The PS's victory in the 1995 legislative election led to a resurgence of social bargaining through the 1996 short-term social dialogue agreement. This pact was followed by the 1996 strategic concertation agreement, which covered the years 1997–99. The strategic concertation agreement consisted of a catalogue of macro-economic aims as well as a programme for employment and competitiveness. Among the issues included were: the contractual distribution of productivity gains, the promotion of competitiveness amongst Portuguese companies and a policy of overall wage growth consistent with the goal of achieving international competitiveness and Portugal's integration into European Monetary

56 The CGTP, demanding a 15 per cent wage increase and a minimum wage of 41,500 escudos, refused to sign the agreement, although its secretary general, Carvalho da Silva, insisted "positive things have been negotiated" and agreed to take the agreement to the CGTP plenary for debate. The CAP also refused to sign this agreement. A. Stoleroff, "Between corporatism and class struggle: The Portuguese labour movement and the Cavaco Silva governments", *West European Politics* 15, 4 (1992), pp. 118–50.

Union. This agreement covered most areas of macro-economic and social policy, including the direction of economic policy, incomes policy (the agreement capped average wages and pensions), employment policy, professional training, labour legislation, collective bargaining, social security and the contribution to the competitiveness of Portuguese companies. The agreement also established a commission to supervise and guarantee its signatories complied with its provisions.[57] In 2001, the social partners reached two more social agreements: the employment policies and vocational training agreement and the working conditions, hygiene and safety and reduction of workplace accidents agreement.

The overwhelming belief in Portugal is that the process of concertation was very positive.[58] By allowing for the reduction in unit labour costs, the agreements improved the country's international competitiveness, contributed to the reduction in inflation from 13.4 per cent in 1990 to less than three per cent in 1999, and kept unemployment at levels below those in other European countries (around six per cent). The agreements also contributed to the maintenance of an extended period of good industrial relations and social peace. Portugal, which as late as 1997 was considered to be an unlikely candidate for membership of the European single-currency zone, was able to comply comfortably with the Maastricht criteria, and—partly as a result of the concertation process—it was able to do so relatively painlessly: it was the only country able to reduce its budget deficit to below the three per cent of GDP set out in the Maastricht criteria while simultaneously increasing government spending. This stands in stark contrast to

---

57 J. da S. Lopes, "El consejo económico y social de Portugal", in F. Durán López (ed.), *El dialogo social y su institucionalización en España y Iberoamérica* (Madrid: CES, 1999), pp. 95–6.

58 Lopes (note 57), p. 95; Stoleroff (note 56).

TABLE 6.3
Consumer Price Index (CPI), Contractual Wages, Productivity and Unemployment in Portugal
(1987–2000, % change over previous year)

Year	1987	1988	1989	1990	1991	1992	1993	1994	1995	1996	1997	1998	1999	2000
CPI	9.4	9.6	12.6	13.4	11.4	8.9	6.5	5.2	4.1	3.1	2.3	2.8	2.3	2.9
Contractual wages	14.4	9.9	10.6	14.1	14.2	10.9	7.9	5.1	5.0	4.7	3.6	3.3	3.6	3.4
Real wages	5.0	0.3	-0.2	7.0	2.8	2.0	1.4	-0.1	0.9	1.6	1.3	0.4	1.3	0.5
Average earnings	–	–	–	–	–	–	6.4	5.9	6.1	6.2	5.1	5.0	5.1	–
Real average earnings	–	–	–	–	–	–	-0.4	0.5	1.9	3.1	2.7	1.9	2.3	2.9
Unemployment	7.0	5.7	5.0	4.5	4.3	4.1	5.5	6.9	7.2	73	6.8	5.0	4.4	4.0
Productivity	3.7	2.3	2.6	2.3	-0.7	8.8	2.4	3.4	3.1	3.0	1.7	1.3	1.1	1.5
Unitary labour costs	–	–	–	–	–	–	7.9	2.4	3.7	3.2	3.5	4.1	3.9	3.4

SOURCES: ILO, Yearbook of labour statistics (various years) and OECD, Economic surveys: Portugal (various years). The average productivity increase 1987–96 was 2.7 per cent.

the Spanish economy's disappointing performance following the failure of concertation there in 1986.

The process of social concertation in Portugal has also been credited for its contribution to social bargaining, solidarity and social cohesion. It helped develop institutional mechanisms that have allowed social partners to participate in the decision-making process, thus deepening democracy and fostering social peace.

The resurgence of social concertation in Portugal was the result of the re-orientation of the social partners' strategies: a new set of constraints and opportunities facilitated the emergence of new strategies. First, in the context of the 1980s and 1990s, trade union organizations supported tripartite bargaining as a defensive strategy enabling them to retake the initiative and influence policy outcomes. The decision by the unions to return to the bargaining table was motivated to a degree by their weakness at the company-level (as is evident with the relative decline in union membership) and their inability to mobilize workers effectively in response to employment policies designed to liberalize the labour market. In other words, with their support for these macro-economic agreements, organized labour sought both to mitigate the decline of its bargaining power at the workplace level and to participate in the policy-making process.[59]

Additionally, the resurgence of social bargaining has been fostered by a process of institutional learning, which has led the social partners to conclude previous confrontational strategies were detrimental to the interest of their constituencies and threatened their own survival. This development also reflects an attempt by the social partners to reconcile the need to control costs through greater flexibility in hiring practices and the need for cooperative relations at the company-level in order to remain competitive. In

59 Royo (note 1).

other words, these agreements have constituted an institutional mechanism supporting business competitiveness through consultative practices.[60]

The emergence of new institutions to promote tripartite social bargaining (for example, the CPCS) has resulted in the institutionalization of the political struggle between the government, the employers and the trade unions, and has contributed to a transformation in patterns of industrial relations. In other words, the choices the social partners made were less conditioned by the pre-existing institutions: the changing balance of power made the partners more predisposed to pursue their goals within the new institutions. Simultaneously, newly emerging constraints and incentives to change largely determined their interaction and strategies.[61]

The Portuguese Social Bargaining Model

Institutional and structural conditions in Portugal provide fruitful ground for analysing the arguments developed in the neo-corporatist literature. Portugal lacks some of the conditions specified as characterizing neo-corporatist settlements: its trade unions do not organize a high proportion of the working population and neither do they have a monopoly of representation. Indeed, Portugal has divided and weak trade unions with relatively small memberships. Fragmentation is particularly acute, although two major confederations, the UGT and CGTP, dominate the movement. These two organizations have a tradition of ideological confrontation, with the pro-communist confederation having been dominant for a long time. While the CGTP has taken steps to break

---

60 M. Regini, "Still engaging in corporatism? Recent Italian experience in comparative perspective", *European Journal of Industrial Relations* 3, 3 (1997), pp. 259–78.

61 Royo (note 1).

some of its links with the PCP, the party remains influential and plays an important strategic role within it—effectively preventing the establishment of cordial relations with the social-democratic UGT. The union confederations are also understaffed and lack the organizational and financial clout of their European peers. The employers' organizations are also fragmented, with three separate confederations vying for the support of Portuguese business. Finally, Portugal's collective bargaining system is relatively decentralized, which according to the literature on neo-corporatist is not conducive to wage moderation.

However, other factors have encouraged the development of processes of social concertation. Unions, for instance, prefer centralized bargaining to decentralization as this helps them overcome their weaknesses at the company-level. Furthermore, there are relatively strong business organizations monopolizing the representation of the business community. These organizations are not inexorably opposed to unions and avoid ideological attacks on the labour movement: they have also proved willing to negotiate with unions in order to reach a social agreement.

The Portuguese concertation model has been characterized by several specific features that have resulted in a process very different from those elsewhere (for example, Sweden, Austria and the Netherlands). In Portugal, the social bargaining process has been identified by the primacy of political considerations over other objectives, strong state intervention, a unique institutional setting, specific goals related to the existing political and economic framework and the subordination of the trade unions' to the political parties.[62]

A key factor helping explain the evolution in the pattern of industrial relations in Portugal has been the nature of the

62 Royo (note 1), pp. 210–14.

transition to democracy. The revolutionary phases of the democratization process encouraged worker radicalization and amplified class antagonisms.[63] This created a legacy of mistrust among the actors and deepened the politicization of industrial relations. Portuguese labour was a major actor during the transition process and actively participated in the development of the pro-labour constitution of 1976.[64] The consequence of this has been that successive democratic governments have faced constraints when trying to reform employment laws to make them more favourable to business (for example, in 1987 the Constitutional Court declared labour reforms that had been approved by the PSD government to be unconstitutional), consequently, the employers' point of view has never had a hegemonic influence and they were aware they had to negotiate with labour in order to reform employment laws.

One of the major features facilitating the development and institutionalization of social concertation in Portugal was the establishment of the CPCS in 1983 by the Centre Bloc government. This body was charged with forging consensus between the social partners in order to facilitate concertation. Its main role is to formalize participation mechanisms, guarantee the transparency of the bargaining process and ensure the opinions of the social partners are considered in legislative process that may affect them. The CPCS has been able to moderate the CGTP's opposition to

63 Barreto and Naumann (note 4). Other scholars have argued the Spanish model seems to confirm a coalition of "intra-regime soft-liners" and "extra-regime soft-liners" results in a less consensual model of industrial relations in which the role of unions is diminished because they are not necessary for the consolidation of that coalition's goals. In contrast, in Portugal "extra-regime soft-liners" played a central role in the democratization process, resulting in a more inclusive system of industrial relations because they needed the support of organized labour for the consolidation of their programme. Nataf (note 7), p. 210.

64 R. Durán Muñoz, *Acciones colectivas y transiciones a la democracia: España y Portugal, 1974–1977* (Madrid: Centro de Estudios Avanzados en Ciencias Sociales, 1997).

central bargaining and has encouraged collaboration between the two union confederations.

No Portuguese government has been able to forge a constitutional majority with which it can impose its views: the PSD never obtained a majority sufficiently large that would allow them to rewrite the country's constitution. This has resulted in the need for political leaders to forge alliances with other social actors in order to reform the system. Institutional factors also help account for outcomes. The Portuguese political system is presidential, and while the president does not enjoy the same political power as the presidents of either France or the United States, he has been able to block government proposals he does not support. One of the major features of the Portuguese system is that it gives the president the authority to refer controversial legislation to the constitutional court. This balance is reinforced when the president comes from a different party from the government. During the latter half of the 1980s, while the PSD was in office, Mário Soares was elected president with the support of the PS and PCP. Once in office, he was able to restrain the PSD's impetus for reform and safeguard workers' rights. In 1986 he stopped the PSD's employment reform law by referring it to the constitutional court where it was declared unconstitutional. In total, he used his power of referral no less than 33 times, forcing the PSD to redraft its legislation on 22 occasions.[65]

The country's political parties continue to play a crucial role within the unions (and vice versa). Union representatives are often found on party lists for election to parliament, and party officials serve on union executive committees. This inter-relationship has played a critical role in the process of concertation, since it has allowed political parties (particularly the PSD and PS) to

65 Nataf (note 7), p. 191.

influence unions (particularly the UGT). The UGT consists of unions controlled by both the PS and the PSD (in 1981 the PS controlled 20 unions and the PSD 24). The union's executive is organized along party lines, with both parties agreeing the union should be involved in national dialogue on economic policy. Because of this, the UGT eschews class-conflict and prefers consensus and negotiation to confrontation.[66]

Conclusions:
The Europeanization of Interest Groups?

The European integration process has exerted a significant influence over the realm of industrial relations, both through the implementation of the *acquis communautaire* and European regulation of social affairs and by promoting elite socialization and the development of trans-national networks that have proved vital for strengthening interest groups (which receive substantive support from their European counterparts). The development of economic interests and networks at the European level has also strengthened support from the economic actors for democracy as well as for the European economic and social model. However, the most important effect of Europeanization has been to foster the opening of the Portuguese economy to competition, which has led to privatizations, downsizing and the internal restructuring of economic sectors and economic liberalization. These developments have generated pressures and have had significant influence on the social partners, thereby contributing to the emergence of new industrial relations patterns.

Nevertheless, the legacies of authoritarianism and experiences of the revolutionary period have hindered efforts to

66 Nataf (note 7), p. 143.

institutionalize modern and stable industrial relations based on trust. Indeed, Portuguese industrial relations are still marked by the heritage of authoritarian corporatism and the specific characteristics of the democratic transition: in particular, revolutionary mass mobilization encouraged radicalization and class antagonism and resulted in state intervention and regulation.[67] The absence of trust is rooted in the turmoil of the revolutionary period that was linked to the goal of eliminating capitalism and the introduction of legislation biased towards the workers. These developments shifted the balance of power between labour and capital, and as a consequence organized labour's political influence has been fairly strong in comparison to that exercised by organized business. The class conflict was further aggravated by the split between communists and socialists which, as we have seen, led to the labour movement's fragmentation. As a result, differences in strategy, structure and practices impede the development of closer relations between the unions. The consequences of this—ideological division, political polarization, fragmented labour and business movements, a rigid labour market (with limited scope for redundancies and a strict definition of what constitutes fair dismissal), antagonistic relationships between labour and capital and a high degree of mobilization and conflict—continue to be felt today and have mitigated the effects of Europeanization, blunting its impact on the behaviour and ideological outlook of actors and hindering the establishment of a model based on trust and cooperation.

The current state of affairs has some significant consequences. One of the main challenges for so-called under-organized economies is to develop a coordinating capacity among social partners enabling them to respond to international pressures and solve economic problems resulting from increased international

---

67   Naumann and Stoleroff (note 5), p. 547.

competition and market integration.[68] Unfortunately, in Portugal there have been limited improvements in technology, management and commercial strategies, and limited productivity growth. Portuguese competitiveness is still based on low wages; however, this is an unsustainable model in a globalized world in which Portugal faces increasing competition from new EU member states and the low-cost economies of East Asia.

The competitiveness challenge requires structural reforms and productivity growth, both of which demand higher investment in infrastructure, redoubled efforts to increase the quality of education, the rigorous promotion of competition in all areas and tax simplification. Portugal needs to shift from a low-cost model towards a high-value-added one based on adding value to the capital intensity of production. This will demand investment in capital technology, a new culture of entrepreneurship, human capital with strong skills and—more importantly—a more flexible industrial relations framework based on trust and cooperation. While changes in production regimes and occupational structure demand greater flexibility, increasing competition rewards institutional mechanisms that facilitate cooperation between social actors and tilts the balance of wage-setting towards the tradable sector of the economy; hence, the importance of social bargaining—which is key to promoting a shift from a low-cost model towards high-value-added one.

What are the Prospects for National Social Bargaining?

It is still not clear if current trends will persist in the future: whether they will consolidate the state's traditionally dominant

---

68 P. Hall and D. Soskice (eds), *Varieties of capitalism: The institutional foundations of comparative advantage* (New York, NY: Oxford University Press, 2001), pp. 1–70.

role in industrial relations, or if they will allow social actors to take the initiative and assert their autonomy. The success (or failure) of these initiatives will determine the consolidation of this approach. As we have seen, the return of national social bargaining has had positive consequences for the Portuguese economy and has contributed to sustained and rapid growth.

At the same time, the discussion above suggests the motivations that led social actors to return to national social bargaining are more structural than the goal of participation in the single European currency, and that they are likely to persist into the future. Given the difficulties government and employers have had in the past in controlling overall wage growth without support from unions, coupled with the erosion further fragmentation would have on the position of the main confederations, the social actors should have powerful incentives to continue this approach. The examination of the role played by the CES and the CPCS suggest a cooperative strategy based on social bargaining will be more durable the more the social actors are able to develop their capacity for strategic learning.

Other developments favour the continuation of these processes. Firstly, wage moderation is a key to closing the gap between Portugal and the richer EU countries (Portugal's per capita GDP is only 74 per cent of the EU average), to exploiting Europe-wide specialization, and to attracting investment from European partners (Portugal's average hourly manufacturing wage is still less than half that of Germany).

The abandonment of comprehensive macro-bargaining strategies—which cover every issue and culminated in macro-agreements—in favour of a new strategy based on different bargaining tables is more conducive to agreements. Portugal's social actors have adopted a more flexible approach through the parallel negotiation of various social concertation agreements—each of limited scope. This bargaining strategy is based on package deals that include labour market organization and flexibility in return for substantial social policy reforms.

The new pacts seek to maintain the balance between both flexibility and solidarity and equity and efficiency. They are part of a political exchange: social benefits and employment in exchange for flexibility and wage moderation.

In countries such as Portugal, where unilateral reforms have not been effective and have encountered significant resistance, governments are likely to continue using this strategy to gain legitimacy for unpopular employment and social reforms and overcome the social partners' institutional veto. In turn, the social partners are likely to accept this approach for as long as they participate in the policy-making process and receive compensation.

Finally, an additional incentive is the fact social bargaining helps prevent a negative spill-over from social policy into wage bargaining.[69]

With an industrial relations' settings deeply rooted in the law, and in which there is a strong tradition of state intervention, the challenge for Portugal is to build new institutional mechanisms that will provide the instruments needed for governments to adopt adequate supply-side policies and contain inflation, while maintaining sound fiscal policies and ensuring micro-actors have the necessary internal and external flexibility and lower costs enabling them to compete effectively in a globalized market.

Social bargaining is an adequate instrument for achieving these goals: it provides the social actors with processes through

69 A. Hassell and B. Ebbinghaus, "From means to ends: Linking wage moderation and social policy reform", in G. Fajertag and P. Pochet (eds), *Social pacts in Europe: New dynamics* (Brussels: ETUI, 2000), pp. 61–84.

which they can achieve the balance between efficiency and solidarity while also being able to overcome veto points.

Because monetary union subjects macro-economic policy in the Eurozone to a single monetary authority, the European Central Bank, monetary union results in further restrictions on domestic economic policy. Although some scholars have already predicted the end of centralized concertation schemes, new analyses are proving the importance incomes policy will have in the context of monetary union.[70]

Incomes policy, with its influence on both labour relations costs, seems to continue to be an adequate instrument that will enhance competitiveness and contribute towards the convergence objective being pursued by European economies. However, the benefits of centralized wage bargaining will hinge largely on the ability of union leaders to control overall wage growth in order to avoid monetary policy measures that will lead to increased levels of unemployment.[71] Monetary union will result in the decentralization of wage bargaining throughout the EU because the most encompassing union organizations will be less inclusive, and therefore may have less incentive to internalize inflationary pressures caused by wage increases.[72]

70 T. Iversen, *Contested economic institutions: The politics of macroeconomics and wage-bargaining in organized capitalism* (New York, NY: Cambridge University Press, 1999).

71 S. Perez, "Yet the century? The return to national social bargaining in Italy and Spain, and some possible implications", paper presented to the American Political Science Association, Boston (1998), p. 22; P. Hall and R. Franzese, "Mixed signals: Central bank independence, coordinated wage bargaining and European Monetary Union", *International Organization*, 52, 3 (1998), pp. 505–35.

72 The United Kingdom's industrial relations services' publication, *Towards a Euro wage?*, suggests the euro will push bargaining systems both ways—towards centralization and decentralization—depending on the region, economic sector and company. *Financial Times* (13 October 1998), p. 3. In a speech in London, European Central Bank board member Sirkka Hamalainen stated labour flexibility has improved and that wage settlements have become more moderate since the introduction of the single currency. She claimed "there is evidence of a very significant change in labour market behaviour

The risk will be that, in the context of monetary union—in which wage bargaining is relatively fragmented although there is a single monetary authority for the area—wage bargainers will be less responsive to threats from central bank. Nevertheless, since unit labour costs will remain a critical factor in improving competitiveness, there will be strong pressure on governments, employers and unions to pursue national social bargaining.

in the euro area countries, particularly in the field of wage negotiations … discipline has greatly improved in that field, with wage demands apparently assuming a permanently lower level of inflation and adjusting faster to cyclical conditions than was the case prior to the introduction of the euro", *Financial Times* (26 February 2002), p. 4.

7 | European Integration and Party Attachments: The Portuguese Case as an Example for New Democracies

André Freire

Introduction

The 2004 European Parliament elections marked a major change in the European Union's (EU) existence: due to the enlargement, ten new member states participated in those elections. Of those countries, eight are consolidating democracies that until around the beginning of the 1990s were under authoritarian communist rule (Latvia, Lithuania, Estonia, Poland, Czech Republic, Slovakia, Hungary and Slovenia).[1] Thus, they had their first European Parliament elections around 14 years after their first democratic elections. The southern European democracies that are also members of the EU (Greece, Portugal and Spain) share some characteristics with the eight post-communist democracies that might be relevant for the study of European Parliament elections. First, they began their transitions to democracy in the mid-1970s. Consequently, they share an authoritarian heritage with the new consolidating democracies of east and central Europe. Second, they held their first European elections shortly after their first national democratic elections. From 1981–87 until 2009, six (Portugal and Spain) or seven (Greece) European Parliament elections took

---

1 In 2007 two other post-communist countries (Bulgaria and Romania) entered the EU.

place in the new southern European democracies. We derive our research questions bearing these characteristics in mind.

The theoretical framework of the paper is mainly the perspective that was first presented by Reif and Schmitt (1980) following the first European Parliament elections in 1979, that is, the so-called second-order elections model. First-order elections are those where there is much at stake, that is, the control of executive power.[2] Due to their second-order nature, European Parliament elections are usually contended by the same actors, emphasizing mainly the same (national) issues and de-emphasizing European issues. Thus, voting behaviour is basically structured by the same contextual supply-side factors as in first-order national elections (in the present paper, and especially for the Portuguese case, these are the national legislative elections to the lower and single chamber).

However, not all contextual constraints active in first-order elections are active in European Parliament elections: there are usually no constraints in terms of government formation, furthermore, since the European Parliament elections have no major consequences for national (or European) politics, electors are more free to "vote with their heart" than in first-order elections, where they more often "vote with their head". Basically, there are three major modes of voting in European Parliament elections: "voting with the head", "voting with the heart" and "voting with the boot".[3]

2   C. van der Eijk and M. Franklin (eds), *Choosing Europe? The European electorate and national politics in the face of the Union* (Ann Arbor, MI: Michigan University Press, 1996); M. Marsh, "Testing the second-order election model after four European elections", *British Journal of Political Science* 28 (1998) pp. 591–607; and W. van der Brug and C. van der Eijk (eds), *European elections and domestic politics: Lessons from the past and scenarios for the future* (Notre Dame, IN: University of Notre Dame Press, 2007).

3   M. Franklin, "The fading power of national politics to structure voting behaviour in elections to the European Parliament", paper presented at the Conference on

Voting with the head is when voters take account of strategic considerations (so as to not waste votes on parties that are unlikely to have a say in government formation and to avoid voting for those parties that might have a destabilizing effect upon the parliament), voting with the heart is to vote for the preferred party without taking into account any strategic considerations while voting with the boot is often protest voting against the incumbent government, the political class, the programmes and/or the candidates of the parties voters would normally vote for, or to indicate support for a particular policy.[4]

In European Parliament elections, most voters vote with the head (mirroring their voting behaviour in first-order elections).[5] In these elections the number of those who vote with their heart or with their boot varies according to many factors, especially the timing of the national electoral cycle. Second-order elections provide opportunities for voters defect the parties they would normally vote for in first-order elections.[6]

Franklin envisages two major possible results of those opportunities for defection in European Parliament elections. First, "the experience of voting differently will affect socialization across the board and delay or prevent the acquisition of strong national partisanships".[7] This first effect might be especially disturbing for new democracies, creating major difficulties for the stabilization of the political and party systems by delaying or even preventing the establishment of stable patterns of voting behaviour. Second,

the 2004 European Elections, Central European University, Budapest, May 21 (2005), pp. 4–6. Available at www.ees-homepage.net/papers.

4   Franklin (note 3), p. 6.
5   Franklin (note 3).
6   Franklin (note 3).
7   Franklin (note 3), p. 7.

"it is possible that the different socializing experiences of these young voters will affect only their behaviour in European Parliament elections, building awareness that European Parliament elections are different even while allowing them to acquire just as strong a partisanship in national elections as earlier cohorts of voters did".[8]

A recent study focused on volatility measures based on aggregate data showed only small differences between first-order and European Parliament elections,[9] but we know volatility indices based on aggregate data are only very crude measures of the electoral fluxes between elections.

Considering Portugal as one example of the new (southern European) democracies, this chapter's objective is to analyse the impact of voting behaviour in elections to the European Parliament on the anchors of partisanship in Portugal (as an example of a new democracy). After some contextual introduction about the nature and characteristics of political institutions in Portugal, namely the electoral systems across the two different types of elections, we evaluate the specificity of voting behaviour in European Parliament elections, vis-à-vis voting behaviour in first-order contests, namely in terms of the extent to which the opportunities for defection are used by voters.

After those analyses, we evaluate the impact of voting behaviour in European Parliament elections on the anchors of partisanship (in new democracies). The strength of the anchors of partisanship will be assessed not only in terms of voting behaviour, but also in terms of the levels of party identification among the Portuguese

8   Franklin (note 3).

9   D. Caramani, "Is there a European electorate and what does it look like? Evidence from electoral volatility measures, 1976–2004", *West European Politics* 29, 1 (2006), pp. 1–27.

adult population immediately before the first European election and until 2009.

Due to their second-order nature,[10] European Parliament elections provide opportunities for defection without major consequences for the (national) political system; however, in new democracies—especially in the first decades of the new regimes—this can be disturbing for the consolidation of ties between electors and political parties and, consequently, for the stabilization of the party system. By studying Portugal in its first three decades of democracy we can learn some lessons about the impact of European Parliament elections upon the stabilization of the anchors of partisanship in new democracies, which may be helpful for post-communist member states. Thus, we will analyse the impact of voting behaviour in European Parliament elections upon the anchors of partisanship at the national level in Portugal (as an example of the new southern European democracies), and try to extract some lessons for the new EU members. However, some attention will also be given to the 2009 European Parliament elections in Portugal.

The 13 June 2009 European Parliament elections were especially interesting for the Portuguese media, politicians and citizens because they took place shortly before the legislative and local elections of 27 September and 11 October 2009, respectively. Because of this proximity, elections to the European Parliament were seen as a kind of primary for the forthcoming national elections. This also gave them special significance in terms of electoral

10 In fact, if we consider turnout rates, European elections can even be considered third-order elections. Let us consider only the example of the three recent southern European democracies. Between 1987 and 2004 the average turnout in local elections (Greece 72.33 per cent, Portugal 61.5 per cent, Spain 66.7 per cent) was much higher than the average turnout in European elections (Greece 68.22 per cent, Portugal 47.7 per cent, Spain 58.1 per cent), especially in Portugal and Spain where there is no compulsory voting, which allows us to consider the latter as third-order elections.

behaviour research concerning second-order elections. Here we also reflect on these issues, not only by looking at the 2009 European elections from a longitudinal perspective, but also by comparing the result with those of the national elections.

Considering what has been said above, it should now be clear why we are concentrating on the long-term interrelations between voting behaviour in national and European elections in Portugal: because we are especially interested in the impact of voting behaviour in these second-order elections on the long-term consolidation of partisanship in new democracies.

The existence (or absence) of a significant long-term impact of voting behaviour in European elections upon the anchors of partisanship can be of special interest for the new post-communist democracies in terms of the lessons for party system stabilization.

These lessons cannot be learned by studying the short-term interrelations between voting behaviour in national and European elections in the new post-communist democracies because we are talking about long-term impacts.[11] Therefore, the findings of this chapter are based mainly on longitudinal data.

This method of statistical analysis was chosen because the main aim of our research is to study data with repeated measurements on the same units over the period of study. Moreover, the second-order elections model makes no predictions in terms of the long-term interrelations between voting behaviour in national and European elections,[12] and that is yet another reason to consider our study innovative vis-à-vis previous studies.

    11 H. Schmitt, "The European Parliament elections of June 2004: Still second-order?" Available at www.ees-homepage.net/papers.

    12 K. Reif and H. Schmitt, "Nine second-order national elections: A conceptual framework for the analysis of European election results", *European Journal of Political Research* 8, 1 (1980), pp. 3–44.

There is a recent study that analyses European Parliament elections (vis-à-vis first-order elections) and uses a longitudinal perspective, but its scope is different from ours because it only analyses electoral volatility.[13] Finally, we should bear in mind that while this chapter will concentrate on the Portuguese case, whenever relevant it will also report the corresponding data from Greece and Spain.[14] Moreover, the conclusions will be built on the results from Greece, Spain and Portugal.

The Role of Elections in the Portuguese Political System

Before Portugal's relatively bloodless Carnation Revolution of 25 April 1974, free and fair elections with universal suffrage and a competitive party system were unheard of there. Portugal's transition to democracy was initiated by a coup led by junior military officers who committed themselves to holding free elections one year from the date of coup. The elections to the constituent assembly were held on 25 April 1975, followed by the first free constitutional parliamentary elections on 25 April 1976.

Portugal's political system is semi-presidential,[15] and thus the only two institutions with national electoral legitimacy and a responsibility for forming government are the president and parliament. The head of state is the directly-elected president, but this officeholder must share power with the head of government

13 Caramani (note 9).

14 These cases are analysed more thoroughly in A. Freire and E. Teperoglou, "European elections and national politics: Lessons from the 'new' southern European democracies", *Journal of Elections, Public Opinion and Parties* 17, 1 (2007), pp. 101–22 and A. Freire and E. Teperoglou, "Eleições europeias e política nacional: Lições das 'novas' democracias do sul da Europa", *Perspectivas: Portuguese Journal of Political Science and International Relations* 2 (2007), pp. 29–54.

15 M. Duverger, "A new political system model: Semi-presidential government", in A. Lijphart (ed.) *Parliamentary versus presidential government* (Oxford: Oxford University Press, 1980), pp. 142–9.

(prime minister) who is responsible to parliament. Although the president had more significant powers from 1976–82, leading to an unclear presidential-parliamentary balance of power, the 1982 constitutional revision substantially reduced some of these powers, making the system more "premier-presidential".[16] The presidential term is five years with a maximum of two terms. Since its transition to democracy began in 1974, Portugal has had six presidential elections, only one of which required a second round run-off.

The legislative branch, parliament, is unicameral and composed of 230 members elected in 22 multimember constituencies (the electoral systems used in European and legislative elections are presented below). Deputies serve four-year terms in office. Parliamentary elections ultimately determine which party will form the government, who will become prime minister and, thus, who will share executive power with the president. These are clearly the most important elections in the political system.

Less important elections (in terms of their contribution to the functioning of the national political system) also take place in Portugal at the local, regional and European levels. Local and regional level elections under democratic rules began in 1976, following the promulgation of Portugal's new constitution. The constitution provided for three distinct levels of local governance (*autarquias locais*) according to their respective territorial delimitations—the ward (*freguesia*), the county-level municipality (*concelho*) and the special administrative regions of the Azores and Madeira.

Elections to the European Parliament began in Portugal and Spain in June 1987, following their accession to the European Community in 1986. Voters have gone to the polls five times for European elections, and their importance for national politics is

16 M. Shugart and J. Carey, *Presidents and assemblies: Constitutional design and electoral dynamics* (Cambridge: Cambridge University Press, 1992).

the same as elsewhere in the EU: they are of secondary importance to the functioning of the political system, both in terms of the constitutional order and (usually) in terms of their political consequences.

The Electoral Systems in Legislative and European Parliament Elections

Except for the presidential contests, the electoral systems used across different types of Portuguese elections are quite similar.[17] Both legislative and European elections are contested under the d'Hondt system of proportional representation and closed lists. Since 1975 the only significant change in the electoral system for legislative elections was the reduction in the number of deputies from 250 to 230 for the 1991 election.

This change resulted in a minor reduction in the average district magnitude: from 11.4 seats per district between 1975 and 1987, to 10.5 from 1991 onwards.[18] This system benefits large parties the most (those receiving more than 25 per cent of the vote), is relatively fair to medium sized parties (those with 15–25 per cent of the vote) and can even allow for the entry of very small parties (those with around 1.5–3 per cent of the vote) due to the very large district magnitude of the Lisbon and Oporto constituencies.

As for European elections, the state consists of one single constituency returning 24 Members of the European Parliament (MEP) in 2004 (24 seats from 1987–89 and 2004, and 25 seats from 1994–99). However, although still maintaining a nation-

17 A. Freire, "Second-order elections and electoral cycles in democratic Portugal", *South European Society and Politics* 9, 3 (2004), pp. 54–79.

18 However, it should be noted the range of district magnitudes is very high. For further details, see F. F. Lopes and A. Freire, *Partidos políticos e sistemas eleitorais: Uma introdução* (Lisbon: Celta, 2002), especially pp. 135–43.

wide constituency, the number of Portugal's seats in the European Parliament was reduced to 22 between the 2004 and 2009 European elections. European elections are conducted under proportional representation with closed lists. Unlike in the national elections there is no legal threshold. It can be said the electoral system used for European elections is not as fair to small- and medium-sized parties as the parliamentary electoral system because of the absence of the two large city constituencies of Lisbon and Oporto in the European contest. However, average district magnitude in legislative elections is not as high as in European elections. Except for the small parties with urban constituencies concentrated in Lisbon and Oporto, the benefit introduced by legislative elections in terms of district magnitude is not entirely clear.

Considering the characteristics of the electoral systems in Greek and Spanish legislative elections (which are much more disproportional than in Portugal) and European elections (which are basically similar to those of Portugal), we can say that in Greece small and medium-small parties have a much greater chance of getting elected in European elections than they have in legislative elections.[19]

For the Spanish case the latter proposition is true only for the small and medium-sized parties with geographically dispersed votes (Communist Party of Spain/United Left [PCE/IU—Partido Comunista de España/Izquierda Unida] and the Democratic and Social Centre [CDS—Centro Democrático y Social). However, for the regionalist parties that benefited most from the geographic concentration of their vote in national elections, it is much more difficult to achieve representation in the European

19 Freire and Teperoglou "European elections" (note 14) and Freire and Teperglou "Eleições europeias" (note 14).

Parliament, which is why these parties usually run as a coalition for the European elections.[20]

The Party Systems in Legislative and European Parliament Elections

Portuguese democratic politics has been dominated by four parties: the centre-left Socialist Party (PS—Partido Socialista), the centre-right Social Democratic Party (PSD—Partido Social Democrata), the orthodox Portuguese Communist Party (PCP—Partido Comunista Português) and the right-wing Democratic Social Centre-Popular Party (CDS-PP—Centro Democrático e Social-Partido Popular).[21] Additionally, small and micro parties from both the left and the right have persisted in Portuguese politics.

There has been a fundamental transformation of the Portuguese party system in a majoritarian direction since 1987. As we can see in Table 7.1, since the end of the 1980s there has been a clear bipartisan trend in legislative elections, although this trend was reversed in the 2009 elections. These trends can be detected in Table 7.1 by observing the vote for the two major parties (the sum of the vote percentages of PS and PSD in each election) and by analysing the effective number of parties (ENEP: electoral—votes; ENPP: parliamentary—seats), especially at the parliamentary level (ENPP). In both cases, across time and since

20 G. Colomé, "Espagne", in Y. Déloye (ed.), *Dictionnaire des élections européennes* (Paris: Economica, 2005) pp. 238–42 and R. Espindola and F. Garcia, "Spain", in J. Lodge (ed.), *The 2004 elections to the European Parliament* (Houndmills: Palgrave Macmillan, 2005), pp. 230–8.

21 T. C. Bruneau, P. N. Diamandouros, R. Gunther, A. Lijphart, L. Morlino and R. S. Brooks, "Democracy, southern European style", in P. N. Diamandouros and R. Gunther (eds), *Parties, politics and democracy in new southern Europe* (Baltimore, MD: The Johns Hopkins University Press, 2001), pp. 16–83.

Table 7.1

Disproportionality, ENEP and ENPP

(Parties in Legislative Elections: Portugal)

	Disproportionality (least squares index)*	ENEP**	ENPP***
1975	5.70	3.66	2.93
1976	3.68	3.99	3.43
1979	3.74	4.65	3.92
1980	3.93	4.60	4.01
1983	3.04	3.74	3.35
1985	3.63	4.77	4.18
1987	6.12	2.98	2.36
1991	6.09	2.83	2.23
1995	4.60	3.09	3.06
1999	4.90	3.06	2.61
2002	4.64	3.15	2.57
2005	5.75	3.33	2.56
2009	5.64	4.08	3.25

Source: Author's calculations from data in www.cne.pt.

Notes:

* Least squares index = $\sqrt{(\Sigma (Si - Vi)^2/2)}$. Si and Vi — percentage of seats and votes for each party, respectively. See M. Gallagher, "Proportionality, disproportionality and electoral systems", in *Electoral Studies*, 10, 1 (2009), pp. 33–51.

** ENEP = $1 / \Sigma Vi^2$, where Vi represents the proportion of votes for party "i".

1. Effective number of electoral (ENEP) and parliamentary (ENPP) parties. Data elaborated by author using the formula proposed by M. Laakso and R. Taagepera, "Effective number of parties: A measure with application to West Europe", *Comparative Political Studies*, 12, 1 (1979), pp. 3–27.

*** ENPP = $1 / \Sigma Si^2$, where Si represents the proportion of seats for party "i", Laakso and Taagepera (1979), p. 4.

Table 7.2
Disproportionality, ENEP and ENPP
(Parties in European Elections: Portugal)

	Disproportionality (least squares index)*	ENEP**	ENPP***
1987	4.32	4.34	3.55
1989	5.60	4.35	3.39
1994	4.03	3.74	3.14
1999	5.35	3.33	2.68
2004	4.71	3.53	4.94
2009	5.41	4.96	3.79

SOURCE: Author's calculations from data in www.cne.pt.
NOTES: See Table 7.1.

Table 7.3
Disproportionality, ENEP and ENPP
(Parties in Local Elections: Portugal)

	Disproportionality (least squares index)*	ENEP**	ENPP***
1976	6.88	4.38	3.50
1979	6.16	4.10	3.54
1982	5.82	4.17	3.61
1985	6.38	4.17	3.42
1989	4.66	3.64	2.94
1993	4.92	3.42	2.89
1997	4.49	3.36	2.74
2001	5.23	3.70	2.90
2005	7.77	3.67	3.43
2009	5.54	3.43	2.76

SOURCE: Author's calculations from data in www.cne.pt.
NOTES: See Table 7.1.

1987, the format of the Portuguese party system is increasingly similar to a two-party system format. However, the 2009 legislative elections showed some significant change in the majoritarian trend (1987–2009). The winner (the PS) obtained the second-lowest share of the vote (36.6 per cent) since 1987 (the second lowest was in 2002, when the PSD obtained 40.2 per cent), and the two major parties together (65.7 per cent) had the lowest share of the vote since 1987 (the second lowest was 72.4 per cent in 1987). The increase in party system fragmentation benefited the medium/small parties, especially the CDS-PP: the ENEP (effective number of electoral parties) reached the highest level (4.09) since 1987 (the second highest level between 1987 and 2009 was 3.33 in 2005). At the parliamentary level (ENPP) things also changed significantly in 2009: the ENEP (3.25) reached the highest level since 1987 (the second highest was in 1999: 2.61).[22]

With the exception of the non-party cabinets president António Ramalho Eanes appointed during the late 1970s, the PS and PSD have always controlled government. This has been achieved either by the parties governing alone (PS: 1976–7, 1995–2002, 2005–9, 2009–11; PSD: 1985–95) or in coalition (PS-CDS: 1977–78; PSD-CDS-PPM: 1979–83; PS-PSD: 1983–85; PSD-CDS-PP: 2002–2005, 2011–present). The 1985 election is associated with several significant features, some of which only became clear at the 1987 realignment election and after.[23] Perhaps most

22 Freire and Teperoglou, "European elections" (note 14) and A. Freire, "A new era in democratic Portugal? the 2009 European, legislative and local elections", *South European Society and Politics* 15, 4 (2010), pp. 593–613.

23 Bruneau et al. (note 21), pp. 16–45; A. Freire, "Party system change in Portugal, 1974–2005: The role of social, political and ideological factors", *Portuguese Journal of Social Science* 4, 2 (2005), pp. 21–40; A. Freire, "Mudança do sistema partidário em Portugal, 1974–2009: O papel dos factores políticos, sociais e ideológicos", in M. A. Cruz, *Eleições e sistemas eleitorais: Perspectivas históricas e políticas* (Oporto: Universidade do Porto, 2009), pp. 215–62.

significant was the concentration of the vote in two major parties: a majoritarian trend in the political system.[24] The change from "consensual" to "majoritarian" democracy has several features: from a fragmented to a kind of bipartisan party system, from coalition (or minority) and unstable governments to single party majorities (most of the time) and rather stable governments and from a strong parliament (and president) to a strong government (and prime minister).[25]

Another major change associated with the majoritarian trend is that since 1987 cabinet stability has substantially improved.[26] During this period only one PS government (1999–2002) and the PSD-PP coalition (2002–5) did not complete their terms. On 30 November 2004, following a succession of problems with the new cabinet's performance, the president announced his intention to call elections in February 2005, which the PS won with its first ever majority. A long legislature (54 months) followed with the PS leading a single-party majority government. It was this legislature—the tenth—that was under scrutiny in the 2009 election cycle.[27]

Did the developments in the party system that occurred in legislative elections occur in European (and local) elections? Tables 7.2 and 7.3 shows the trends in the "effective number of electoral parties" in Portuguese European and local elections.[28] Comparing Portuguese legislative and European Parliament elec-

24 Freire and Teperoglou "European elections" (note 14); Bruneau et al. (note 21).

25 Freire (note 23); Bruneau et al. (note 21); Freire and Teperoglou "European elections" (note 14); Freire (note 22).

26 Freire (note 23); Freire, "Mudança do sistema" (note 23); Bruneau et al. (note 21).

27 Due to a legislative change that pointed to the need for national government mandates/terms to end by September so the new government could prepare its budget.

28 To trace the evolution of each of the four main Portuguese parties and compare the performance of large and medium-small parties across different types of elections in both countries, we used the same rules concerning the decomposition of the votes for Portuguese coalitions as those presented in Freire (note 18).

tions in terms of the trends in the "effective number of electoral parties" (ENEP) (Table 7.2), we can see there is a clear synchronicity. In both types of elections there was a majoritarian drive between 1987 and 2005, with a significant reduction in the effective number of parties. Moreover, what seems to be a very slight reversal of trends in recent legislative elections (1999–2005) is also mirrored in recent European contests (1999–2004).

Additionally, the strong reversal of trends in the election of 27 September 2009 was already anticipated in the 13 June 2009, European elections: a return to the party system format characteristic of the consensual era of Portuguese politics (1975–87). Furthermore, we can see that European elections seem to be losing their distinctive character vis-à-vis first-order ones. Still, in the medium- to long-term, first-order elections seem to be contaminating the European contests, a feature not predicted by the second-order elections theory, since this model makes no longitudinal predictions.[29] However, the 2009 also showed the oppositive "influence": changes in the party system format begun first in European elections (13 June 2009) and were mirrored in the legislative elections (27 September 2009). Thus, party system change is clearly an element of continuity between the 2009 European and legislative elections.

The majoritarian trend in the Portuguese party system at the level of legislative elections, which is visible in the concentration of votes for the two major parties and in the decline in the "effective number of electoral parties", was also mirrored both in the European and local elections, albeit with a delay (see Tables 7.2 and 7.3). This trend first became apparent at the national level,

29 For further details, as well as for a systematic comparison of this data for the Portuguese case with Greece and Spain, where similar conclusions were found for Spain but not for Greece (due to the presence of a two-party system format right since the 1970s), see Freire and Teperoglou "European elections" (note 14).

before spilling over to both the European and local levels. And all this took place without any significant change to the electoral system—only changes in the patterns of electoral behaviour.

What we see in the 2009 European elections is a sharp inversion of that trend. In the 2009 European elections the ENEP index (which considers the number of parties weighted by their respective electoral strength) reached 4.96, its highest figure since 1987 and well above its second-highest level of 4.35 achieved in 1989: between 1994 and 2004 the ENEP index was always below 3.75. This sharp inversion of the majoritarian trend was replicated in the September 2009 legislative elections in which the ENEP index reached 4.08, its highest level since 1987, and while lower than the figure obtained in the European elections it was nevertheless higher than that found in the "consensual period" elections of 1975, 1976 and 1983 (which were 3.66, 3.99 and 3.74, respectively) (see Table 7.1). However, in the 2009 local elections the ENEP index actually fell to 3.43 from the 3.67 obtained in 2005 (Table 7.3).

The reasons for this latter deviation in the local elections are several and beyond the scope of the present paper.[30] Nevertheless, several elements can be outlined in an attempt to understand why the sharp inversion of the majoritarian trend was not followed in the 2009 local elections. First, we should bear in mind local elections are more disproportional: average values for the complete period are 4.7 per cent (legislative, 1975–2009), 4.9 per cent (European, 1987–2009) and 5.80 per cent (local, 1976–2009) (for the full distributions see Tables 6.1, 6.2 and 6.3). One of the main reasons for this is the average district magnitude, which is much lower in local than in European or legislative elections. Second, in local elections there are 308 competitions: logistically very demanding

30 For those interested see Freire and Teperoglou, "European elections" (note 14) and Freire (note 22).

for small parties. Third, national factors have much less weight in local elections. Fourth, incumbent government punishment was reduced in the 2009 local elections due to the fact the legislative contest took place shortly before.[31]

Although the spill-over of the majoritarian trend from legislative to European elections was not predicted by the second-order elections model, we believe it is a phenomenon that can nevertheless be accommodated in that theoretical framework. We should bear in mind first-order elections are more important than European elections in terms of financial state resources, mass media visibility and organization structure.[32] Therefore, if some parties lose their force on the national level, this will tend to contaminate other levels of power.

Let us pass to the differential performance of political parties (across types of elections) according to their size.[33] The first hypothesis to be tested is whether or not on average, small- (Left Bloc [BE—Bloco de Esquerda] before 2009, among others) and medium-sized parties (PCP, CDS-PP, and BE since 2009) have always performed better (that is, they received higher percentages of votes) in European than in legislative elections.[34] The second hypothesis is to discover if on average the large parties (PS and PSD) have always performed better in legislative than in European elections.

31 For further information, see Freire (note 22).

32 Eijk and Franklin (note 2); Y. Déloye (note 20); J. M. Magone, "Portugal", in Lodge (note 20), pp. 210–7; Espindola and Garcia (note 20); Kavakas, D. (2005), "Greece", in Lodge (note 20).

33 Reif and Schmitt (note 12); Marsh (note2); Eijk and Franklin (note 2).

34 Although in 2009 the BE changed category in terms of its size, for the sake of longitudinal comparisons we kept it in the small parties category.

TABLE 7.4
Political Parties' Average Vote Percentages by Decade in Legislative, European and Local Elections (1980–2009, %)

Parties	Election type	1980s	1990s	2000s	2009	1980s–2000s
PS+PSD (large parties)	Legislative	61.1	77.9	72.3	**65.7**	70.4
	European	60.1	71.7	65.5	**58.3**	65.8
	Local	63.4	74.2	74.9	**74.4**	70.8
PCP+CDS (medium parties	Legislative	26.5	16.1	16.3	**18.4**	19.3
	European	27.7	21.1	17.8	**19.1**	22.2
	Local	29.5	20.5	15.5	**14.7**	21.8
PRD (medium parties)	Legislative	11.2	0.6	–	–	6.1
	European	4.4	0.2	–	–	2.3
	Local	2.8	–	–	–	2.8
Others: left and right (small parties)	Legislative	4.1	3.6	8.8	**13.4**	5.5
	European	6.6	4.0	16.7	**16.0**	9.1
	Local	1.7	3.3	3.3	**3.6**	2.8

SOURCES: A. Freire, "The 2009 European elections in Portugal: Primaries or simply second order?", *Portuguese Journal of Social Science* 9, 1 (2010), pp. 71–88, using data elaborated from www.cne.pt and www.dgai.mai.pt.
NOTE: about the procedures used to disaggregate coalitions, see A. Freire, "Second-order elections and electoral cycles in democratic Portugal", *South European Society and Politics* 9, 3 (2004), pp. 54–79; and A. Freire and E. Teperoglou, "European elections and national politics: Lessons from the 'new' southern European democracies", *Journal of Elections, Public Opinion and Parties* 17, 1 (2007), pp. 101–22.

In terms of the performance of different types of political parties, according to their size, theories about second-order elections always received empirical support (Table 7.4).[35] Some qualifications are due, however.

In Table 7.4 we can see the PS and PSD always perform better in legislative than in European elections, but this differential performance was more pronounced in the 2000s (+6.8) and much more pronounced in the 2009 elections (+7.4) (legislative versus European) than in the 1990s (+6.2). The elections of the 1980s are not completely comparable with those of the 1990s and 2000s, particularly because of the presence of the short-term flash party, the Democratic Renewal Party (PRD—Partido Renovador Democrático) in the 1980s. On the contrary, the two mid-sized parties (PCP and CDS-PP) always performed better in European than in legislative elections, but this differential performance was much less pronounced in the last decade.

Finally, the very small parties (both from the left and the right) always performed better in European than in legislative elections, but this differential performance was especially pronounced in the last decade. Thus, in the last decade the losses of the largest parties (from legislative to European elections) mainly benefited the very small parties. This situation is largely due to the BE's extraordinary result obtaining 10.7 per cent of the votes to become the third party and entering the group of middle-sized parties, but also to the growth of the very small parties in general. This situation was replicated at the last legislative elections, although to a minor extent: the BE was the party with the highest growth vis-à-vis the

35 The appropriate tests (t-test for paired samples) revealed that the differences in party performance are always significant. For further details, as well as for a systematic comparison of this data for the Portuguese case with Greece and Spain, where similar conclusions were found for Greece but not for Spain (due to the regionalist/nationalist parties), see Freire and Teperoglou "European elections" (note 14).

2005 legislative elections, and there was also some growth in the other medium/small and micro parties.

Except for the small parties, local elections used to be similar to European elections: better for medium-sized parties and worse for the largest parties (than in the legislative), but this was not the case in the 2000s, nor in the 2009 local elections. Overall, these local elections were rather bipartisan (as in the rest of the decade), and thus the largest parties performed better here than in either the legislative or in the European elections. The reverse is true for both medium and small parties, but especially for the latter. Again, the reasons for this latter deviation in the local elections are several and beyond the scope of this chapter.

The Long-Term Impact of Voting Modes upon the Anchors of Partisanship

As we noted above, there are three major modes of voting in European elections: voting with the head, voting with the heart and voting with the boot. In European elections, most voters vote with the head.[36] However, European elections provide opportunities for voters to defect from the parties they would normally vote for in legislative contests (usually either by voting with the heart or by voting with the boot).

Franklin envisages two possible effects of those opportunities for defection in European elections. First, the use of opportunities for defection in European elections will affect the socialization of young voters—both in European and legislative elections, and this will delay or prevent the acquisition of strong national partisanships. This effect across the board might create major difficulties for the stabilization of the political and party systems in

36 Franklin (note 3), p. 6.

new democracies by delaying (or even preventing) the establishment of stable patterns of voting behaviour. Second, the use of the opportunities for defection by young voters will affect their behaviour only in European elections, thus allowing them to acquire "just as strong a partisanship in national elections as earlier cohorts of voters did".[37]

Through the differential performance of the parties according to their size in first-order and European elections, we have already seen electors in the recent southern European democracies do— at least apparently—use the opportunity for defection in European elections, especially in the cases of Greece and Portugal. Of course, even leaving aside differential turnout (which might have a significant impact upon the performance of the different types of parties), those are at best only crude measures of defection, since they cannot take into account the vote transfers (on the individual level) cancelling each other out (and therefore not visible at the aggregate level).

Consequently, we need to evaluate the level of disloyal electoral behaviour in European elections through the use of individual-level data.

Analysing the level of "quasi-switching" is one way to conduct such an evaluation (it is measured by comparing the vote recall in European Parliament elections with the voting intention in a hypothetical and concurrent national election). "To the extent that such voters (the defectors in European elections) vote differently than they would have done in a concurrent national election they have been characterized as being engaged in 'quasi-switching'." The expectation is the following: "we should observe increasing levels of quasi-switching as the passage of time allows voters to leave the electorate (through death and infirmity) who have

37 Franklin (note 3), p. 7.

learned a more rigid habit of voting, and as the number of voters who experienced European Parliament elections during their formative years increase".[38]

According to the data processed by Franklin,[39] and considering only those who voted in European Parliament elections, the levels of quasi-switching for 1989, 1994, 1999 and 2004 are the following: Greece—8.1, 12.4, 9.6 and 8.6 per cent; Portugal—9.7, 12.7, 7.5 and 42.8 per cent; Spain—22.2, 12.5, 15.5 and 10.8 per cent. Except for Portugal, which has a surprisingly high level in 2004, there is no

Table 7.5
Electoral Volatility in European Elections

	Total volatility*	Inter-bloc volatility**
1987	–	–
1989	11.25	6.45
1994	9.50	1.40
1999	8.95	7.55
2004	7.20	4.39
2009	18.35	9.13

Source: A. Freire, "The 2009 European elections in Portugal: Primaries or simply second order?", *Portuguese Journal of Social Science*, 9, 1 (2010), pp. 71–88.

Notes:

* Total volatility (TV) = (|PiV |+ |PjV|+ |PkV|+ |PlV|...+|PnV|)/2, where PiV represents the change, in absolute terms, in the aggregate vote for a party between two consecutive elections, in S. Bartolini and P. Mair, *Identity, competition and electoral availability: The stabilization of European electorates, 1885–1985* (Cambridge: Cambridge University Press, 1990), p. 20.

** Inter-bloc Volatility (BV) = (|P(iV + jV + kV)|+ |P(lV + mV + nV)|)/2, where P(iV + jV + kV) represents the net change, in absolute terms, in the aggregate vote for parties i, j and k—all of which come from the same bloc—between two consecutive elections, in S. Bartolini and P. Mair, p. 22.

38 Franklin (note 3).

39 Franklin (note 3), p. 9.

Table 7.6
Electoral Volatility in Legislative Elections

	Total volatility*	Inter-bloc volatility**
1975	–	–
1976	8.60	5.00
1979	8.00	0.50
1980	4.00	2.10
1983	9.90	4.20
1985	21.30	0.20
1987	22.30	13.60
1995	19.40	6.90
1999	2.60	2.10
2002	8.85	7.85
2005	12.90	12.10
2009	8.92	4.25

Source: See Table 7.5.
Notes: See Table 7.5

general increase in the level of quasi-switching, and there are no linear trends in this respect.

Thus, while the level of quasi-switching seems to be dependent upon political conjunctures the individual-level data regarding quasi-switching does reveal some propensity of voters to defect in national legislative elections. Moreover, quasi-switching can be said to be only an underestimation of disloyal electoral behaviour: voters do not experience the same level of constraints in a hypothetical national election as in a real one.

Has that apparently disloyal electoral behaviour had any impact upon legislative electoral behaviour? If so, did it have major consequences in terms of the stabilization of the political and

TABLE 7.7
Electoral Volatility in Local Elections

	Total volatility*	Inter-bloc volatility**
1976	–	–
1979	8.60	5.00
1982	8.00	0.50
1985	4.00	2.10
1989	9.90	4.20
1993	21.30	0.20
1997	22.30	13.60
2001	19.40	6.90
2005	2.60	2.10
2009	8.85	7.85

SOURCE: See Table 7.5.
NOTES: See Table 7.5

party systems in Portugal (and the new southern European democracies) by delaying or even preventing the establishment of stable patterns of voting behaviour?

To answer these questions, we will use both aggregate measures of electoral volatility and indicators of the level of social and ideological anchoring of partisanship on the individual level.

On the aggregate level, the concepts of total and inter-bloc electoral volatility will be used.[40] Considering second-order elections may be used by voters to express their discontent with the incumbent government, and considering these elections have no direct consequences for national government formation, it is possible for voters to feel more able to change their voting options in

40 S. Bartolini and P. Mair, *Identity, competition and electoral availability: The stabilization of European electorates, 1885–1985* (Cambridge: Cambridge University Press, 1990), pp. 17–52, 313–4.

second-order than in first-order elections. We expect this might happen both in terms of vote swings within the same ideological quadrant (within-bloc volatility) and between the left–right boundary (inter-bloc volatility). Note that the sum of within- and inter-bloc volatility gives us total volatility.

The results in the case of Portugal (1975-2009) were deceiving (see Tables 6.5, 6.6 and 6.7). With minor exceptions, total volatility usually plays a larger role in legislative elections than in both local and European Parliament elections—sometimes much larger; as for within-bloc volatility, the findings were also negative, although here the picture is more mixed.[41]

For Greece and Spain, considering the average of total volatility in national and European Parliament elections for the entire period (1981–87 and 2004), Caramani found total volatility was higher in national than in European elections,[42] although the differences are rather small (the opposite was found by the author for the 12 EU member states: higher total volatility was usually found in European than in national elections, except in Finland, Luxembourg and the Netherlands where the reverse was true). In the Portuguese case average total volatility was much higher in national than in European elections.[43]

In a general comparative and longitudinal perspective, at the national level Greece, Portugal and Spain do exhibit some of the most volatile elections of the Western European countries between 1945 and 2002.[44] This is, of course, an indicator of their

41 Freire (note 17).

42 Caramani (note 9), p. 5.

43 Caramani (note 9).

44 R. Gunther, "As eleições portuguesas em perspectiva comparada: Partidos e comportamento eleitoral na Europa do sul", in A. Freire, M.C. Lobo and P. Magalhães (eds), *Portugal a votos: As eleições legislativas de 2002* (Lisbon: Imprensa de Ciências Sociais, 2004), p. 39.

TABLE 7.8
2009 European and Legislative Elections: Social Structure, Church Attendance, Left–Right Self-Placement and Vote
(logistic regressions)

Independent variables	Dependent variable: Past vote (recall) in elections	
	2009 Legislative	2009 European
Self-placement on left–right scale	0.566***	0.876***
Education	0.413***	0.032
Subjective social class	-0.087	0.281
Church attendance	0.196*	0.325***
Pseudo R² (Nagelkerke)	0.420	0.609
N	674	1000
Valid N	492	399

SOURCES: data elaborated by the author from the *European Election Study* (EES) 2009, and the *Portuguese National Election Study* (2009). See also www.piredeu.eu and www.ics.ul.pt.

NOTES: Dependent variables are vote in European or legislative election recoded as left (0) and right (1). The positioning of the parties in terms of left and right was done using electors' perceptions of parties' locations on the left-right scale. Independent variables: (a) self-placement on a left (1) right (10) scale; (b) education—age when voter stopped studying (years old); (c) subjective social class—(1), "working class"; (5) "upper class"; (d) church attendance—"never" (1) to "several times a week" (5); (e) PNES—the same independent variables but sometimes with different operational definitions were used (f) *** $p < 0.01$, ** $p < 0.05$, * $p < 0.1$; (g) due to differential turnout, only those who also voted in European elections were included for the legislative elections.

character as recent democratic regimes, within which patterns of electoral behaviour were not yet stabilized. However, after analysing electoral volatility in each election since the first democratic contest until 2002,[45] we can say European elections have had only

45 Gunther (note 44), p. 40.

a minor effect, if any, upon electoral behaviour instability, and thus on the stabilization of each one of the three party systems.

In terms of total volatility, the highest levels of volatility occurred before the first European elections took place (and also concurrently in the Greek and the Portuguese cases: 1981 and 1987, respectively). In terms of within-bloc volatility the picture, while more mixed, is basically similar. In any case, the major changes in the party systems took place before (or concurrently with) the first European elections, and were related to changes in the supply-side of politics: Greece in 1981 (the collapse of the Union of the Democratic Centre [EDIK] and the ascension of the Panhellenic Socialist Movement [PASOK]); Portugal in 1985 and 1987 (the rise and fall of the PRD and the rise of the PSD) and in Spain in 1982 (with the collapse of the Union of the Democratic Centre [UCD—Unión de Centro Democrático] and the rise of the Spanish Socialist Workers' Party [PSOE—Partido Socialista Obrero Español]).

Aggregate volatility is a crude measure of electoral change, in that it may sometimes represent understated values for shifts in individual-level political preferences: there may be many voting shifts that cancel each other out. That is why we will test to see whether the social and ideological anchors of partisanship are weaker in second-order than in first-order elections, thus indicating the greater probability of vote shifts between left and right in second-order elections. Because we want to test the electors' propensity to cross the left–right divide, in Table 7.8, we use the vote for parties of the left (0) and the right (1) as our dependent variable in each type of election. The independent variables are: (1) several indicators of the social anchors of partisanship (see notes in Table 7.8) and (2) left–right self-placement. Since the dependent variable is a dichotomy, we will be using logistic regressions.

The results in Table 7.8 show the vote in the 2009 legislative elections was less anchored in ideological and social factors than the 2009 European elections. Similar tests for Greece and Spain and Portugal (for the 2004 elections) were presented elsewhere.[46] The latter reveal sometimes the vote is more anchored in European than in legislative elections (Greece); however, sometimes the reverse is true (Portugal and Spain). Only for Greece and Portugal, the same comparisons between legislative and European Parliament elections for an extensive period (1985-87 and 2004 respectively for Greece and Portugal) lead to the conclusion that "the individual-level evidence allows us to infer that sometimes people are more prone to change their vote across party/ideological blocs in European elections than in legislative ones; on other occasions the reverse is true. Therefore it can be ascertained the phenomena is mainly dependent upon the political conjuncture".[47] Thus, the more recent 2009 data again reinforces this conclusion.

As a result, we must conclude the levels of defection are not necessarily higher in European than they are in legislative elections, because the levels of defection are dependent upon the political conjuncture in any type of election and the highest levels of defection regarding legislative elections in Portugal (and also in the other two recent southern European) democracies began before (or concurrently with) the first elections to the European Parliament. Consequently, the latter elections could not have had any significant effect upon that disloyal electoral behaviour on the national level. We must also conclude European elections have had only a minor effect upon the instability of legislative electoral

46 Freire and Teperoglou "European elections" (note 14).

47 A. Freire and E. Teperoglou, "European elections and electoral cycles in Greece and Portugal, 1981/87–2004", paper presented to the European Parliament Elections 2004 conference, Budapest, 21–22 May 2005. Available at www.europeanelectionstudies.net/Papers/Paper_Draft_Budapest_May-10-2005_Freire_Teperoglou.pdf.

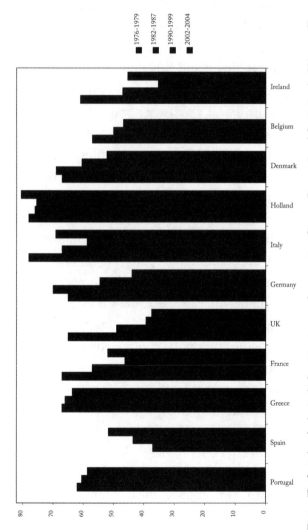

FIGURE 7.1
Party Identification in Europe
(1976–2004, average % by decade)

SOURCE: A. Freire, "Left-right ideological identities in new democracies: Greece, Portugal and Spain in the Western European context", *Pôle Stud: Revue de Science Politique de l'Europe Méridionale*, 25, II (2006), pp. 153–73.

behaviour and thus, had only a minor effect on the stabilization of the party systems in each of the three countries.

A more direct indicator of the level of party attachments in a country is that of the percentage of citizens who identify with any political party (party identification). In Figure 7.1 we present data comparing the levels of party identification in the three recent southern European democracies and in eight long-established European democracies between the 1970s (or 1980s, according to data availability) and 2004. There we can see there is a generalized downward trend in terms of party identification among the European electorates except in Spain and the Netherlands. However, the causes for this quasi-generalized downward trend have been traced elsewhere, and have not been connected with defection rates at European elections (although this hypothesis was not tested).[48] Moreover, both Portugal and Greece do show some of the smaller downward trends in party identification across Europe, so low they are neither statistically significant nor relevant: we would be better talking about stabilization rather than decline in these two cases.[49]

Thus, at least for the three southern European democracies, the decline in party identification cannot be derived from defection rates at European elections because either there is no decline in party identification (Spain) or the decline is small (Greece and Portugal) and is more properly classified as stabilization.

The reversion of the trend (away from majoritarian politics) we found both in the 2009 European and legislative elections but

48 H. Schmitt and S. Holmberg, "Political parties in decline?" in H.-D. Klinge-mann and D. Fuchs (eds) *Citizens and the state* (Oxford: Oxford University Press, 1995, 1998), pp. 95–133; R. J. Dalton and M. P. Wattenberg, *Parties without partisans: Political change in advanced industrial democracies* (Oxford: Oxford University Press, 2000).

49 A. Freire, "Left–right ideological identities in new democracies: Greece, Portu-gal and Spain in the Western European context", *Pôle Sud: Revue de Science Politique de l'Europe Méridionale* 25, II (2006), pp. 153–73.

TABLE 7.9.1
Party Attachments in Portugal (1994–2009, %)

Party identification	Years				
	1994	1999	2004	2008	2009
Yes	71.4	57.2	65.7	58.1	66.0
No, don't know, no reply	28.6	42.8	34.3	41.9	34.0
N	100	100	100	100	100
N absolute	1000	500	1000	1350	100

SOURCES: *Eurobarometer* 41.1 (1994) (1994 mass survey); *European Election Study* 1999; 2004; 2009 (1999, 2004 and 2009 mass surveys); A. Freire, J. M. L. Viegas and F. Seiceira (eds), *Representação política: O caso português em perspectiva comparada* (Lisbon: Sexante, 2009).

NOTES: 1) PID—Party Identification; 2) basically, the same question wording was applied in each one of the five surveys ("Do you consider yourself to be close to any particular party?").

TABLE 7.9.2
Party Attachments by party in Portugal (1994-2009, %)

Party identification	Years				
	1994	1999	2004	2008	2009
BE	–	0.8	6.0	4.8	13.5
CDU/PP	8.9	4.9	4.6	10.2	11.9
PS	48.3	53.0	47.5	44.2	29.7
PSD	36.6	34.5	37.0	37.1	40.1
CDS-PP	5.4	6.3	4.0	2.3	4.5
Others	0.8	0.5	1.1	1.4	0.2
N	100	100	100	100	100
N absolute	646	286	657	785	660

SOURCE: See Table 7.9.1.
NOTES: See Table 7.9.1.

not in that year's local elections, are at least partially due to the more severe institutional barriers in the latter elections. Nevertheless, this raises some doubts about the existence of a trend away from majoritarian politics in the 2009 Portuguese election cycle. Of course, we need to wait for more elections to clarify this doubt, namely to know if the "new era in Portuguese politics" we are sure arrived with the 2009 European and legislative elections is here to stay or if it is only a short-term episode in Portuguese democracy.[50] However, data on party identification can also help us in this task.

On the one hand, data on the distribution of party attachments presented in Table 7.9.2 also points to a trend away from majoritarian politics in 2009: the joint percentage of PS and PSD oscillated between 84 (in 1994 and 2004) and 87 per cent (1999) in the first period; but since 2008 there has been a reduction in the concentration of party attachments in the two major parties: 81 per cent (2008) and 69 per cent (2009) (see Table 7.9.2). The decline in party identification with the two major parties is due mainly to the growth of identification with the radical left taken together (PCP and BE): from 5.7 per cent in 1994 to 25.4 per cent in 2009 (and with 10.6 and 15 in 2004 and 2008). And this is also why the decline in party attachments is hurting the PS above all (from 48.3 in 1994 to 29.7 in 2009), and not the PSD (which in fact increased its respective level of party identification: from 36.6 in 1994 to 40.1 in 2009) (see Table 7.9.2).

On the other hand, while the overall level of party attachment (i.e. the total number/percentage of people identifying with any party) declined between 1994 (71.4 per cent) and 2009 (66.0 per cent), there are significant ups and downs (i.e. a trendless fluctuation) in the entire period (1994–2009) while between 2004

50 Freire (note 22).

and 2009 the number of party identifiers increased (see Table 7.9.1).

In any case, for three main reasons the developments in the overall level of Portuguese party attachments between 1994 and 2009 shown in Tables 6.9.1 and 6.9.2 can hardly be said to be a result of the second-order nature of European elections on the formation of the partisan identities of Portuguese citizens. First, because these changes occurred around 30 years after the transition to democracy in Portugal, and after five elections to the European Parliament: thus, they can hardly be said to be the result of the impact of the European Parliament upon the early formation of Portuguese citizens' partisan attachments. Second, because the decline in the overall level of partisan attachments in 2009 is mainly a result of changes that occurred on the left of the ideological spectrum (decline in the number of PS identifiers, growth in the number of radical-left identifiers). Third, because these latter changes are mainly the result of specific political circumstances between 2005 and 2009, which had an impact on both the European and the legislative elections.

The 2009 European elections were marked by some interesting features. First, the incumbent PS government received the greatest punishment ever in European elections. This element was in part due to the severe economic crisis, which was also present in other European countries (the severe punishment of the incumbents, especially those from the centre-left camp). Second, the PSD's victory and the PS's punishment were not predicted by the polls. Third, the near extinction of the CDS-PP predicted by many polls was not confirmed by the final results. Fourth, the radical-left parties, BE and PCP, received a very large proportion of the vote (21.3 per cent). Fifth, the BE more than doubled its vote percentage (from 5.1 per cent in 2004 to 10.7 per cent in

2009) and was one of the major winners of this European Parliament election. Sixth, the PS and PSD together received the lowest vote percentage in European elections since 1987 (58.2 per cent).[51] As we have seen, data on the distribution of party identification 1994–2009 also points to a trend away from majoritarian politics: a decline in the percentage of party identifiers with the two major parties, due mainly to a decline in PS identifiers and to an increase in radical-left identifiers.

Two of the most curious factors in the 2009 European election—the punishment of the incumbent government and the change in party system format (away from the majoritarian format in place since 1987)—were at least partly mirrored in that year's legislative elections (more the latter element than the former), thus showing that European elections did function as a kind of primary for the national election.

On the other hand, the results of the European election were not fully replicated in the ensuing legislative election: the level of incumbent punishment was much lower—the winning party (the PS) was different. Thus, in this particular respect the European elections did not function as primaries for the national elections that followed.[52]

Conclusions

On 25 April 1974, Portugal initiated the so-called "third-wave" of world-wide democratization. Greece (November 1974) and Spain (1975) soon joined that trend. Thus, the three countries share an authoritarian heritage that is much longer in the cases of Portugal and Spain than in the case of Greece. Moreover, between

51 Freire (note 22).
52 Freire (note 22).

seven and ten years after their first democratic elections, each of these countries held their first election to the European Parliament. Thus our main research question was the following: what lessons can be learned from the longitudinal (1981–87 and 2009) and comparative study of European elections in the recent southern European democracies regarding the interrelations of voting behaviour in first- and second-order elections, both for consolidating and established democracies?

More specifically, what lessons can the eight post-communist democracies that joined the EU in 2004 learn from this study? Most of all, we sought to evaluate the impact of voting behaviour in European elections upon the stabilization of partisanship anchors of in new democracies.

In these democracies, especially during the first decades of their new regimes, this can be upsetting for the consolidation of partisanship anchors and, consequently, for the stabilization of the party system. Thus, by studying Portugal (although mainly as an example of the "new" southern European democracies), in its first three decades of democracy, we wanted to learn some lessons about the impact of European elections upon the stabilization of partisanship anchors in new democracies that might be helpful for the post-communist member states.

Additionally, the second-order elections' model makes no predictions in terms of the long-term interrelations between voting behaviour in national and European elections, and that is yet another reason to consider our study innovative. Moreover, to our knowledge the only longitudinal study on this subject focused only on volatility measures at the aggregate level.[53]

Several conclusions are worth mentioning in terms of the short- and long-term impacts of national factors upon voting

53 Caramani (note 9).

behaviour in European elections. First, with the partial exception of Spain, political parties perform differently in legislative and European elections: the large parties perform better in first-order than in European elections, while for the medium, medium-small and small parties, the reverse is true.

Schmitt found a different picture for the eight post-communist consolidating democracies that participated in European elections for the first time in 2004: the party system format was not significantly different in legislative and European elections.[54] What are the reasons for these differences between the post-communist consolidating democracies and the group consisting Greece, Portugal and Spain?

The first point is that we must be cautious in making this comparison, because there has only been one European election for the former set of countries. Bearing this in mind, we can point to the different level of party system institutionalization in southern Europe and in central eastern Europe (even if the situation in central eastern Europe is not homogeneous, with some systems much more stabilized than others) as an explanation that needs to be further developed in future studies: by the time of the first European election, levels of party system institutionalization were significantly higher in the former set of countries than in the latter.

Perhaps the first major lesson from the study of Portugal regarding the impact of national factors upon European voting behaviour is that such an impact has both a short-term and a long-term nature. Comparing legislative and European elections in terms of the trends of the ENEP we concluded that for both Portugal and Spain the majoritarian drive in the party system during legislative elections—in force since the end of the 1980s

54 Schmitt (note 11).

and the beginning of the 1990s—is mirrored in the European contests.

Furthermore, European elections seem to be losing their distinctive character vis-à-vis first-order elections: the differences in the ENEP are fading in both countries. Although the spillover of the majoritarian trend from legislative to European elections we observed in Portugal and Spain was not predicted by the second-order election model, that phenomenon can nevertheless be accommodated in that theoretical framework: if some parties lose their force in the more important political arena (the national level), this will tend to contaminate other levels of power (European). Thus, we believe future studies of second-order elections should investigate the long-term impact of national factors upon European elections in more countries, particularly in terms of party system format.

These results are somehow parallel/similar to those encountered by Caramani, who found that, except for some cases with "higher differentials" (Denmark, France, Austria, Sweden, the United Kingdom, Germany and Ireland), the levels of volatility between European and national elections ("mixed volatility") vis-à-vis volatility in national elections, are relatively small.[55]

All these results suggest a major problem with the second-order elections' model is that it is trying to explain differentials in voting behaviour between national and European elections but, except in some countries, such differentials are usually small. Thus, in future studies, we should perhaps focus more on explaining the absence of major differences between voting in European Parliament and national elections.

The second major lesson is especially relevant for consolidating democracies. It relates to the long-term impact of voting

55 Caramani (note 9).

behaviour in European elections upon partisanship anchors in national electoral politics and is related to the chapter's four major conclusions. First, the levels of defection are not necessarily higher in European than in legislative elections, because they are dependent upon the political conjunctures. Second, the highest levels of defection in legislative elections (in Greece, Portugal and Spain) began before (or concurrently with) the first European elections, consequently, the latter elections could not have had any significant effect upon that disloyal electoral behaviour on the national level. Third, European elections have had only a minor effect upon the instability of legislative electoral behaviour, and thus they have had only a minor effect upon the stabilization of the political and party systems in each of these three countries. Fourth, at least in the three recent southern European democracies, the decline in party identification cannot be derived from defection rates at European elections because either there is no decline in party identification (Spain) or the decline is small (Greece and Portugal), and more properly classified as stabilization.

Both the similarity in party system format between national and European elections and the lack of any impact of defection rates in European elections on partisanship anchors in the recent southern European democracies can be due to reduced levels of Euroscepticism being voiced in the European arena.[56]

Things might be different in at least some of the new eastern member states where Euroscepticism is more widespread.[57] In fact, in Table 7.10 we see that, on average, central and eastern

56 C. van der Eijk and M. N. Franklin, "Potential for contestation on European matters at national elections in Europe", in G. Marks and M. R. Steenbergen (eds), *European integration and political conflict* (Cambridge: Cambridge University Press, 2004), pp. 32–50.

57 P. Taggart and A. Szczerbiak, "Contemporary Euroskepticism in the party systems of European Union candidate states of central and eastern Europe", *European Journal of Political Research* 43, 1 (2004), pp. 1–27.

TABLE 7.10

Polarisation of left-right and anti/pro European Union party positions

Country	Left-Right Scale			Anti-/Pro-Europe Scale		
	Median difference. Two main parties	Median difference. Extreme parties	Weighted sum of Differences	Median difference. Two main parties	Median difference. Extreme parties	Weighted sum of Differences
Austria	2.0	5.0	2.28	1.0	0.0	1.24
Cyprus	8.0	8.0	8.98	3.0	3.0	2.15
Denmark	3.0	7.0	2.67	0.0	1.0	3.37
Finland	4.0	6.0	3.76	0.0	3.0	0.16
France	3.0	9.0	2.37	0.0	1.0	0.98
Germany	3.0	6.0	2.59	1.0	1.0	0.11
Greece	3.0	8.0	3.40	1.0	2.0	0.72
Ireland	4.0	4.0	3.25	2.0	2.0	1.04
Italy	5.0	8.0	4.01	1.0	1.0	1.62

Luxembourg	2.0	2.0	2.0	2.32	0.70
Netherlands	3.0	6.0	1.0	2.65	2.32
Portugal	2.0	6.0	1.0	5.81	0.88
Spain	5.0	6.0	2.0	6.95	1.25
UK	2.0	3.0	0.0	1.91	0.00
Average west	**3.3**	**5.7**	**1.0**	**3.60**	**1.20**
Czech Rep.	8.0	8.0	2.0	8.05	2.01
Estonia	2.0	3.0	1.0	1.87	1.38
Hungary	6.0	6.0	1.0	9.80	1.63
Latvia	6.0	6.0	2.0	4.86	1.62
Slovakia	5.0	5.0	3.0	3.41	2.04
Slovenia	4.5	4.5	1.0	4.10	0.91
Poland	2.0	7.0	5.0	2.46	3.25
Average east	**4.8**	**5.6**	**2.1**	**4.90**	**1.80**

SOURCE: A. Freire, M. C. Lobo and P. Magalhães, "The clarity of policy alternatives: Left-right and the European Parliament vote in 2004", *The Journal of European Integration* 31, 5 (2009), pp. 665–83

European societies are more polarized than Western societies, both in terms of the left–right divide and in terms of European issues—although the differences are more marked in terms of the latter. One basic lesson for the eight post-communist con- solidating democracies is the following: due to their second-order nature,[58] European elections do not seem to have much of an ef- fect upon disloyal behaviour in legislative elections, or upon the disturbance of the stability or the institutionalization of the po- litical and party systems in new democracies.

However, these effects were explored both in Portugal and in other two recent democracies that, by the time of their first Eu- ropean elections had already had a nearly fully-stabilized party system. The effects of European voting behaviour upon legislative elections might be different in polities in which the party system is not yet (fully) stabilized (as it is the case at least in some of the countries in central and Eastern Europe).

Moreover, when there is more polarization around European issues, as it is the case at least in some of the countries in central and Eastern Europe, it is more likely what happens at the Euro- pean level can contaminate the party systems at the national level and, consequently, Europeanization is more likely to influence national party politics in these cases. Thus, further research into these issues will still be required—and the new post-communist member states will provide a good laboratory for that.

---

58 There is a major difference between the first European Parliament elections that took place in Greece (81.5 per cent with compulsory voting), Portugal (51.28 per cent for the second European Parliament elections in the country because the first were concurrent with national legislative elections) and Spain (68.52 per cent) vis-à-vis the 2004 European Parliament elections in the eight post-communist countries (which had an average turnout of 31 per cent)—a much higher turnout in the former three countries than in the latter. However, turnout is not a topic analysed in this chapter and therefore the explanation for this difference is a matter for future research.

8 | The Support for European Integration in Portugal: Dimensions and Trends

Pedro Magalhães

Introduction

The study of the attitudes of European citizens in relation to European integration can benefit from the use of a singularly vast amount of data, particularly those provided by the regular and frequent *Eurobarometer* surveys funded by the European Commission.

These surveys have been conducted in Portugal since 1980.[1] Analysis of those results by scholars interested in the intensity, tendencies and causes of support for the integration process from the 1980s to the present have arrived at three fundamental conclusions in respect of Portugal:

1. Portuguese public opinion is characterized, at least since the country's accession to the European Union (EU), by strong levels of support for European integration.[2]

2. Despite a fall in the level of this support since 1992—part of a general European trend—support for integration

---

1   *Eurobarometer* 14 (January 1980).

2   M. Bacalhau, *Atitudes, opiniões e comportamentos políticos dos portugueses (1973–93)* (Lisbon: Author, 1994) and M. C. Lobo, "Portuguese attitudes towards EU membership: Social and political perspectives", in S. Royo and P. C. Manuel (eds), *Spain and Portugal in the European Union: The first 15 years* (London: Frank Cass, 2003), pp.97–118.

continues at a very high level, both in absolute and in comparative terms.[3]

3. This support is based on principally "instrumental" criteria, however. That is to say, it is based more on a perception of the benefits of integration for the country and specific social groups than the consequence of an "affective" relationship with either the European political system or its institutions.[4]

These conclusions result from the analysis of two indicators regularly present in the *Eurobarometer* surveys. The first measures the opinions of individuals on whether their country has "benefited or not" from being a member of the EU (*benefit*). The second, rather than explicitly seeking a cost-benefit assessment of integration, measures the opinions of individuals on whether their country belonging to the EU is "a good thing, a bad thing or neither one nor the other" (*membership*). These indicators provide us with the longest running data series in the *Eurobarometer* surveys.[5]

Analyses made in Portugal from the results of the application of these questions in opinion polls tend to begin with the assumption that each one measures dimensions that are fundamentally distinct from the attitudes of the individuals. From this perspective, the benefit indicator will capture "a utilitarian view of integration", "soliciting a retrospective analysis of the advantages and

3   Lobo (note 2) and A. C. Pinto and M. C. Lobo, "Forging a positive but instrumental view: Portuguese attitudes towards the EU, 1986–2002", in A. Dulphy and C. Manigand (eds) *Public opinion and Europe: national identity in European perspective* (Paris: Peter Lang, 2004), pp. 165–81.

4   Lobo (note 2); Pinto and Lobo (note 3).

5   Data relating to membership has been collected in a total of 51 Portuguese surveys, from *Eurobarometer* 14 (note 1) to *Eurobarometer* 64 (November 2005), which is the last survey available at the time of writing. There have been 40 surveys with questions relating to benefit, from *Eurobarometer* 25 (March 1986), also to *Eurobarometer* 64.

disadvantages of belonging to the EU".[6] In other words we are in the domain that is normally designated as "specific support" for a political system, related to "the satisfaction that the members of a system feel who obtain from the outputs and perceived performances of the political authorities".[7] Similarly, some of the first studies of political attitudes towards the EU identified the existence of a "utilitarian response base", connected to the "support based in a relatively firm perceived interest" on the citizens' part,[8] captured precisely as recourse to the indicator measuring the citizens' perceptions of the benefits resulting from European integration.

Conversely, in existing studies of the Portuguese case, the indicator membership has been treated as capturing an "affective and diffuse vision" of integration. At the root of this assumption, the fact the percentage of people who believe Portugal has benefited from its membership of the EU has been consistently higher than the percentage of those who believe EU membership "is a good thing" has been interpreted as indicating that, in the Portuguese case, the "consensus" on integration is based on a "narrow and instrumental view of the benefits of belonging to the EU".[9]

However, there are some potential problems with this type of analysis. On the one hand, the direct comparison of the proportion of respondents who believe Portugal has benefited from its membership of the EU and those who state belonging to the EU is a good thing, neglects the fact the two indicators are not

6   Lobo (note 2), p. 102.

7   D. Easton, "A reassessment of the concept of political support", *British Journal of Political Science* 5, 4 (1975), p. 437.

8   L. N. Lindberg and S. A. Scheingold, *Europe's would-be polity: Patterns of change in the European Community* (Eaglewood Cliffs, NJ: Prentice-Hall, 1970), p. 40.

9   Pinto and Lobo (note 3), p. 173.

strictly comparable: while the former solicits a dichotomous response ("benefited" or "not benefited"), the latter allows a third response ("neither one thing nor the other"), which makes their direct comparison a questionable exercise. On the other hand, the assumption that the former yields an instrumental dimension or a cost-benefit relationship in the individual's attitudes, while the latter gives a distinct dimension of diffuse support and affection— not contingent in relation to the costs and benefits produced by integration— is also questionable from an empirical viewpoint.

In fact, there are good reasons to believe the membership indicator is just one more indicator of utilitarian support. Recent analyses of the dimensionality of the European citizens' attitudes towards the EU have come to confirm the membership and benefit indicators are, in fact, measures of the same latent variable. For example, Lubbers and Scheepers demonstrate the instrumental support or scepticism with respect to the EU, connected to perceptions of the costs and benefits resulting from the integration process (measured by either the membership or the benefit indicator) must be clearly distinguished from political support or scepticism in relation to the EU, which is connected to the extent citizens accept the sharing of political authority between the nation state and the EU as a political system.[10] Similarly, Chierici shows that indicators of specific support, such as membership or benefit, must be clearly distinguished from indicators of diffuse support for the EU as a political community, among which are included the individual's attitudes regarding the sharing of sovereignty between the nation state and the European political system.[11] Even authors less concerned with establishing distinctions

10 M. Lubbers and P. Scheepers, "Political versus instrumental Euro-scepticism", *European Union Politics* 6, 2 (2005), pp.223–42.

11 C. Chierici, "Is there a European public opinion? Public support for the

between these political and instrumental dimensions of attitudes towards the EU have noted that the questions on individuals' positions with respect to the sharing of powers with European institutions in the creation of public policy are those that capture a dimension of political attitudes relating to the legitimacy of the EU as a political system, which is largely independent of the assessment of its actual performance and the costs it incurs or benefits it distributes.

Thus, this chapter has two aims. First, to investigate up to what point the distinction between instrumental support and political support is empirically sustainable in the Portuguese case; and second, in the light of this, to reassess some of the main conclusions concerning the intensity, evolution and basis of the support for Europe in Portugal.

Instrumental Support and Political Support

One possible way to assess to what point Portuguese support for the EU is in fact multidimensional—and which indicators will give us access to these possible different dimensions—consists in an examination of the data that already exists at the individual level. Table 8.1 shows the results of the factor analysis of a series of variables available in the *Eurobarometer Trend File 1970–2002*, limited in this case to the surveys conducted in Portugal from the 1980s. Included in this analysis are the membership and belonging indicators that, as we have already seen, have been used in previous studies of the Portuguese case as indicators of specific and

European Union, theoretical concepts and empirical measurements", paper presented to POLIS (Paris, 2005). Chierici added a third dimension, that of diffuse support for European political institutions (measurable through indicators of the confidence citizens have in institutions such as the European Commission or the European Parliament). However, since there are many fewer surveys of these dimensions than those measuring scales of instrumental and political support, we will not discuss this third dimension.

of diffuse support, respectively. Also included are the answers to questions put to the same individuals to ascertain their views on whether a decisions in a range of public policy areas ought to be taken by the Portuguese government or within the EU. The public policy areas included in this study are those available in the longest running series, between *Eurobarometer* 31 (March 1989) and *Eurobarometer* 57.1 (May 2002), viz: environment, foreign affairs, education, health and social security, scientific and technological research, monetary policy and social communications.[12] As can be seen from Table 8.1, the solution encountered suggests that, in Portugal, as is true of European public opinion in general,[13] while the measures benefit and membership form a single dimension (which we shall call instrumental support), this dimension is empirically distinct from another connected with the acceptance or rejection of the EU as a political authority with public policy decision-making powers (political support). In other words, those who tend to believe Portugal has benefited with integration also tend to believe membership of the EU is a good thing.[14] Similarly, the respondents' attitudes about the convenience of reserving decision-making power on a number of public policies to the Portuguese political authorities, or sharing it with the EU, tends to result in a single attitudinal dimension that is largely independent of perceptions of the benefits or the benevolence of Portugal's membership of the EU.

12 All of these variables were codified with three values, from the least to the greatest degree of support, as follows: Belonging (1 "bad", 2 "neither good nor bad", 3 "good"); benefits (1 "no benefits", 2 "Don't know/no reply", 3 "benefits"); with regards the different areas of public policy (1 "by the Portuguese government", 2 "Don't know/no reply", 3 "as a set within the EU").

13 Lubbers and Scheepers (note 10) and Chierici (note 11).

14 At the individual level, the correlation between the two variables is 0.59 (p < 0.001).

TABLE 8.1
Principal Axis Factor Analysis
(varimax rotation)

	Factor 1: Political	Factor 2: Instrumental
Health and social security	0.694	0.043
Education	0.654	0.018
Environment	0.637	0.130
Science	0.635	0.167
Communications	0.620	0.035
Monetary	0.553	0.213
Foreign affairs	0.515	0.215
Benefit	0.095	0.749
Membership	0.133	0.748
Explained variance	30.02%	13.79%

SOURCE: Author's own data.
N=24,002

The idea were are faced with two clearly distinct dimensions of the attitudes of individuals in relation to European integration gains additional support by testing, for each of them, some hypotheses about the factors which at the individual level determine the adoption of attitudes of greater or lesser support for European integration. The investigation on this theme converges in some of the following fundamental hypotheses.

Cognitive mobilization: according to Inglehart, elevated levels of interest and political information are necessary for the understanding of information concerning a process, such as European integration, which has a high level of abstraction.[15] In this way, we should expect that the greater the level of cognitive mobilization, the lesser will be the perception of threat and incomprehension

15 R. Inglehart, "Cognitive mobilization and European identity", *Comparative Politics* 3, 1 (1970), pp. 45–70.

felt by individuals in relation to integration and, consequently, the greater the support for integration will be.

Utilitarianism: according to some analysts, the process of European integration, in enabling the liberalization and mobilization of capital, goods and labour, produces differential benefits and costs for the citizens. Those with the greatest levels of human capital—education and skills—are much better equipped to adapt to the occupational competition promoted by the single market and consequently will generally be more supportive of integration.[16]

Systemic performance: Anderson advances the hypothesis that, despite being poorly informed about the process and consequences of European integration, citizens are able form opinions about it on the basis of simple heuristic rules allowing them to reach conclusions on complex matters. In particular, in order to assess the process of European integration and its consequences, individuals tend to resort to their degree of satisfaction with the performance of the political institutions or with the domestic economy, using these as reference points for a more distant and complex reality.[17]

From this point of view, the greater the degree of satisfaction with the operation of the domestic political institutions, the better the light under which the process of European integration is judged. This hypothesis is, moreover, the one research in Portugal has suggested as providing the best explanation for the relationship of the Portuguese with Europe. As Lobo argues, "satisfaction

16 M. Gabel and H. Palmer, "Understanding variation in public support for European integration", *European Journal of Political Research* 27, 1 (1995), pp. 3–19, and M. Gabel, *Interests and integration: Market liberalization, public opinion and European union* (Michigan, MI: University of Michigan Press, 1998).

17 C. J. Anderson, "When in doubt, use proxies: Attitudes towards domestic politics and support for European integration", *Comparative Political Studies* 31, 5 (1998), pp. 569–601.

with [national] democracy is the most important variable in explaining support for European integration".[18]

The comparative study of this theme has, however, raised some doubts about the generalization of this explanation. Sánchez-Cuenca, for example, suggests a hypothesis that is, *prima facie*, opposed to the previous one: support for the EU is likely to increase with *dissatisfaction* with the national political system.[19] In other words, when citizens have less confidence in their domestic political system—whether it is thought to be affected by inefficiency or corruption, for example—the greater will be their support for deeper European integration and the transfer of powers to the supra-national political system. Yet others suggest attitudes towards the EU political system are in-and-of-themselves consequential since in spite of information deficits individuals form independent opinions in relation to the performance of the European institutions in their own right, attitudes that end up being relevant for the rise or decline in support for European integration.[20]

National identity: an additional hypothesis concerning support for integration concerns feelings of national identity. Carey suggests the transfer of sovereignty involved in the integration process is particularly rejected by those individuals whose political identity is linked exclusively with the nation state rejecting the concurrent sense of belonging to a multi-national political community.[21] McLaren suggests these individuals are more likely

18   Lobo (note 2), p. 105.

19   L. Sánchez-Cuenca, "The political basis of support for European integration", *European Union Politics* 1, 2 (2000), pp. 147–71.

20   L. McLaren, "Explaining mass-level Euro-scepticism: Identity, interests and institutional distrust", paper presented to annual meeting of the American Political Science Association (Washington, DC, 1–4 September, 2005).

21   S. Carey, "Undivided loyalties: Is national identity an obstacle to European integration?", *European Union Politics* 3, 4 (2002), pp. 387–413.

to sense European integration as a threat to (the loss of) national identity, which leads them to exhibit lower levels of support for integration.[22]

Party preferences: The final hypothesis relates the support conceded to integration with party preferences. Studies, such as those carried out by Gabel or Anderson, suggest the proximity of individuals to the party or parties controlling the government of the day has a positive influence on support for the European integration process.[23] Given it is the national governments that are the main actors in the political decision-making process within the institutional architecture of the EU, citizens will project their assessments of the governing party into an evaluation of the entire integration process: the closer they are to the government, the more favourable they are to Europe.

However, not all studies on this line arrive at the same conclusion. For example, Roy argues the relationship between support for the party of government and support for integration is conditional and that during normal periods the effect of preferences for parties of government upon support for the EU is reduced, if not negative. The argument is that when citizens feel better represented by their national government they have few incentives to wish to see power being lost to European institutions through the process of integration.

Table 8.2 shows the result of the empirical test of these hypotheses in the Portuguese case. Two indices were constructed. The first, instrumental support, resulted in the calculation of an average for each individual of values for the membership and benefit variables, an index that which oscillates between one (minimum

22 L. McLaren, "Public support for the European Union: Cost-benefit analysis or perceived cultural threat?", *Journal of Politics* 64 (2002), pp. 551–66.

23 Gabel (note 16); Anderson (note 17).

support) and three (maximum support).[24] The second variable, political support, resulted in the calculation of the average of the variables measuring support for joint decision-making in the areas of environment, foreign affairs, education, health and social policy, scientific and technological research, monetary policy and social communication, which, as above, reached values between one (minimum support) and three (maximum support).[25]

The independent variables, the effects of which are being tested, are: an index of opinion leadership (which measures the frequency with which respondents discuss political topics and seek to persuade those around them), capturing the degree of individual cognitive mobilization; education (age at which the respondent ceased formal education) and occupation (-1, manual labourers and unemployed; 1, professionals and executives; 0, others), measuring the level of educational capital and occupational abilities of the individuals; satisfaction with national democracy and satisfaction with democracy within the EU, which measures the performance of the Portuguese and European political systems as they are assessed by the respondents; exclusive national identity (1, exclusively Portuguese, 0, others), distinguishing those individuals who feel part of the national political community alone and all others; and intention to vote for the party of government (1, yes, 0, no), through which we can distinguish those individuals who support the activities of the national government and the others. Gender (1, female; 0, male), age and left-right ideological self-placement (1, more to the left; 10, more to the right) are used as control variables. The set of cases includes the results of the *Eurobarometer* surveys conducted during 1993, 1998, 1999, 2000 and 2001, the only years in which the surveys include information

24 Alpha value = 0.71.

25 Alpha value = 0.82.

TABLE 8.2

Explanatory Factors for Instrumental and Political Support

(linear regression coefficients, margin of error in parenthesis)

	Dependent variable: Instrumental support	Dependent variable: Political support
Gender (female)	-0.079*** (0.020)	-0.019 (0.019)
Age	-0.002*** (0.001)	-0.004*** (0.001)
Left–right self-positioning	0.007 (0.004)	-0.003 (0.005)
Opinion leadership	0.043*** (0.009)	0.041*** (0.011)
Education	0.014*** (0.004)	0.002 (0.004)
Occupation	0.033 (0.018)	0.061** (0.020)
Satisfaction with national democracy	0.043*** (0.009)	0.010 (0.011)
Satisfaction with European democracy	0.103*** (0.100)	0.053*** (0.011)
Exclusive national identity	-0.167*** (0.018)	-0.258*** (0.020)
Intention to vote for governing party	0.044* (0.021)	-0.001 (0.024)
Constant	0.801*** (0.062)	1.601*** (0.072)
N	4339	4339
R² adjusted	0.15	0.09

* p < 0.05; ** p < 0.01; *** p < 0.001
SOURCE: Author's own data

on all of the variables in the model. Thus, in order to capture and control temporal tendencies, taking into account the fact the database incorporates surveys conducted at different times, a set of dummies were introduced for each year (the coefficients of which are not presented). The results of the linear regression analysis are shown in Table 8.2

With respect to the control variables, it should be noted that both the instrumental support and (especially) the political support for integration tends to be greater the younger the respondent. Second, the gender differences only have an effect on instrumental support, with women exhibiting greater scepticism than men, when it comes to the benefits and advantages of European integration. Finally, the political views of the respondents do not seem to have any effect on either the instrumental or the political support for Europe.

In relation to the cognitive mobilization hypotheses, it can be seen that the variable used to test it behaved in similar manner in the two models: the effect is in the expected (positive) direction and has the same order of magnitude (with practically equal coefficients for the dependent variables measured on a scale with the same amplitude). This effect, however, is relatively reduced, with the coefficients standardized and not exceeding the value of 0.06 in both models. Equally limited is the explanatory power of the two variables—education and professional occupation—which test the utilitarian hypotheses at the individual level. In the model applied to the dependent variable "instrumental support", only education produced statistically significant effects (with occupation approaching statistical significance). However, despite being in the expected direction (more years of education, greater support), these effects are also limited when compared with those produced by other variables in the model. With respect to the model applied to the dependent variable "political support", only occupation produced statistically significant effects, despite the importance of the variable in this model —with a standardized beta coefficient of only 0.05— being even less than that produced in the previous one. In summary, the idea the attitudes of individuals in relation to Europe are determined by social attributes through which they receive the benefits of integration, despite receiving confirmation in respect of instrumental support and (less, as is to be expected) with respect to political support, is far from providing the best available explanation for that which moves Portuguese opinion in relation to Europe.

Much more successful are those explanations connected both to the subjective assessments of the performance of the political system and to political identities. In the Portuguese case, McLaren's hypotheses are immediately confirmed: despite the low levels of information about the integration process, the electors do not stop evaluating the performance of European institutions in a manner that has consequences for the support conceded to integration.[26] The satisfaction with democracy in the EU variable affects the level of support for integration in the expected direction, independently of levels of satisfaction with national democracy, and has an effect in both instrumental and political levels of support.

However, there are also very important differences between the two models. First, despite those whose political identities are connected exclusively with the nation state also being those least likely to support European integration, the effect of the identity variable is greater with respect to political support. Second, although the assessment of the operation of democracy in Portugal and support for the governing party of the day result in greater instrumental support for integration, neither one nor the other variable has any

26 McLaren (note 20).

effect on political support for integration. In other words, while the evaluation of the benefits the country receives as a result of integration is affected—understandably—by the assessments of the systemic performance of the EU, the national government and the national institutions, the willingness of citizens to share decision making-power within the EU is only affected by the assessment made of the European institutions within which this power is to be shared.

It can be said, then, there are some variables tending to affect support for integration, whether this support is instrumental or political. The younger, the more cognitively mobilized, the better the opinion of the functioning of EU democracy and the better the ability to consider oneself as European (as well as Portuguese) display greater levels of support for European integration. However, while instrumental support for integration is seriously conditioned by the assessment of the national political system's performance—used by individuals as a heuristic through which they weigh up the costs and benefits of integration—political support for integration is fundamentally conditioned by the political identity of the individuals and by their evaluation of the systemic performance of the EU—and only of the EU. In sum, instrumental and political support for integration are dimensions that despite being connected, are fundamentally different in their distribution among individuals and in their fundamental attitudinal correlates.

Tendencies of Support for the EU

How have Portuguese attitudes towards the EU evolved? The diagnostic made by the majority of analysts is convergent: during a first phase, from accession to the beginning of the 1990s, there

Figure 8.1
Evolution of the Net Difference between "Good" and "Bad"
Evaluations of EU Membership
(1980–2005)

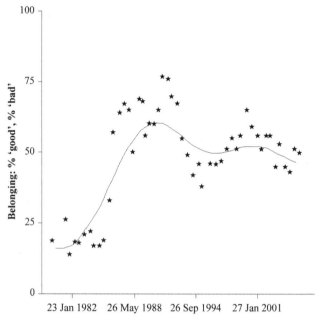

Source: Author's own data

was a strong increase in the perception of benefits and in support for EU membership.[27] Since then, it is argued, there has been a slight decrease in support for the EU, without, however, affecting the generalized consensus concerning integration.[28] However, what we have seen so far makes us suppose two things: on the one hand, this assessment deserves to be made not only at the level of instrumental support, but also at the level of political support for integration; and on the other, that the evolution of these two dimensions cannot be entirely coincident.

27 Bacalhau (note 2); Lobo (note 2).

28 Pinto and Lobo (note 3).

FIGURE 8.2
Evolution of the Net Difference between "Benefited" and "Not Benefited" Responses
(1985–2005)

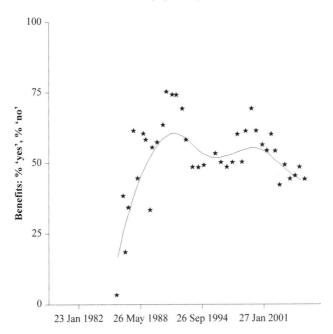

SOURCE: Author's own data

Figure 8.1 presents the evolution over time of the net differ-ence between the proportion of respondents in each *Eurobarom-eter* survey who have stated membership of the EU has been good and bad for Portugal, with a local regression curve adjusted to the data points.[29] As we can see, there is indeed a very rapid in-crease in the positive instrumental support for integration until the beginning of the 1990s, followed by a decline that, although interrupted around 2000, has become more accentuated in recent years. Predictably in the light of what has been said above, the evolution of the perception of the benefits of EU membership has

29 Between *Eurobarometer* 14 (note 1) and *Eurobarometer* 63 (May 2005).

TABLE 8.3
Trends in Instrumental Support Indicators
(linear regression coefficients; margin of error in parenthesis)

	Dependent variable: belonging (% "good"–% "bad")	*Dependent variable: benefits (% "yes"–% "no")*
Constant	4.848 (3.997)	-39.246** (12.840)
Years	6.064*** (0.561)	9.802*** (1.432)
Maastricht (0 before; 1 after)	-21.070** (6.101)	-16.681* (7.036)
Years since Maastricht	-7.821*** (1.335)	-11.862*** (1.864)
Monetary union (0 before; 1 after)	15.584*** (7.149)	15.578* (7.066)
Years since monetary union	-0.610 (1.823)	-1.703 (1.796)
N	50	39
R^2 adjusted	0.72	0.60

* $p < 0.05$; ** $p < 0.01$; *** $p < 0.001$
SOURCE: Author's own data

followed a course that is equal to that of the belonging variable (Figure 8.2). Furthermore, the decline in instrumental support for European integration recorded in Portugal since the beginning of the millennium has a particular importance: despite the proportion of those with positive opinions concerning integration being 40 per cent greater than those with negative opinions, in both cases the decline in instrumental support for integration has been such that in 2005 it reached its lowest value since 1986–7—the immediate post-accession years.

Table 8.3 shows the results of a more detailed analysis of the tendencies verified in relation to Portuguese instrumental

support for integration. We also test the effect of the two historically important dates: the signing of the Maastricht Treaty and
confirmation of the entry of monetary union, of which Portugal
was a founding member in 1999. It is almost entirely accepted the
signing of the Maastricht Treaty in February 1992 and the "no"
vote in Denmark's referendum in July of the same year signified a
turning point in the so-called permissive consensus with respect
to European integration, with public support for the process declining across Europe.

As for monetary union, it signified a qualitative leap in the
integration process, whether by making visible a remarkable level
of economic coordination between the member states, or by—
particularly in the Portuguese case—representing the manifest
triumph of the national political authorities in the prosecution
of the principal strategic economic policy objective of the second
half of the 1990s.

The results presented in Table 8.3 confirm the statistical significance of the tendencies we detected visually. Until 1992, the
balance in favour of the idea that Portugal's membership of the
EU was a good thing for Portugal grew in a statistically significant manner at the rate of six points each year (since 1980), and
almost ten per cent in the case of benefit. However, Maastricht
produced a double effect: in the short-term, an abrupt fall in instrumental support, and in the long-term, a decline at a rate of
almost two points per year. Although monetary union had a positive impact in the short-term, this positive impact was inferior
in magnitude to the negative impact of Maastricht and has not
produced any statistically significant long-term effect. In other
words, apart from the temporary jump brought by monetary union, instrumental support for integration amongst Portuguese has
declined constantly since 1992.

FIGURE 8.3

**Evolution of the Net Difference between "Within the EU"
and "By the Portuguese Government" Responses to the
Question about Decision-Making over Science Policy**

(1989–2003)

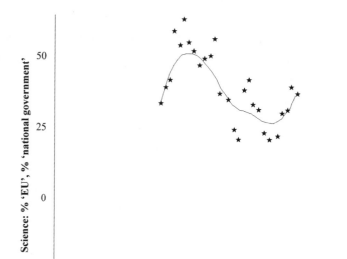

SOURCE: Author's own data

To what extent is this decline in support for integration also reflected in a decline of support for the sharing of decision-making power with European institutions? In order to answer this question, we have analysed four public policy areas: science, environment, education and health and social policy.

The first pair, science and environment, are themes traditionally described as belonging to a higher level of endogenous internationalization,[30] that is, they are intrinsically international

30 R. Sinnott, "Policy, subsidiarity and legitimacy", in O. Niedermayer and R. Sinnott (eds), *Public opinion and internationalised governance* (Oxford: Oxford University Press, 1995), pp. 246–76.

FIGURE 8.4
**Evolution of the Net Difference between "Within the EU"
and "By the Portuguese Government" Responses to the
Question about Decision-Making over Environmental Policy**
(1989–2003)

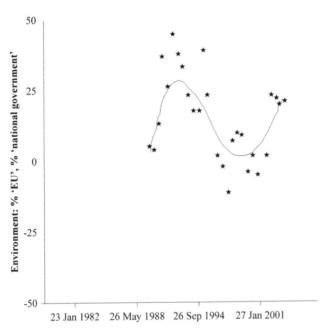

Source: Author's own data

areas of government in which supranational decision-making brings potential benefits of efficiency. Education and health and social policy, however, are areas traditionally reserved to national governments, because their alteration could have important distributive consequences or because they are closely identified with national culture.

Figure 8.3 and Figure 8.4 show the evolution of support given to the sharing of decision-making with the EU in the areas of science and the environment. In both cases, and for the entire period studied, the majority of Portuguese want these policies to be

TABLE 8.4

Trends in Political Support Indicators for Science and Environment

(linear regression coefficients, margin of error in parenthesis)

	Dependent variable: Science (% 'EU'- % 'national')	Dependent variable: Environment (% 'EU'- % 'national')
Constant	-81.177 (51.056)	-133.318 (68.338)
Years	11.790* (4.776)	13.996* (6.392)
Maastricht (0 before; 1 after)	-1.185 (7.826)	6.469 (10.475)
Years since Maastricht	-16.208** (4.872)	-20.406** (6.251)
Monetary union (0 before; 1 after)	-3.979 (6.351)	-1.682 (8.501)
Years since monetary union	6.113** (1.918)	11.779*** (2.567)
N	27	27
R² adjusted	0.64	0.57

* $p < 0.05$, ** $p < 0.01$, *** $p < 0.001$
SOURCE: Author's own data

established within the EU. Table 8.4 applies the previous model to the evolution of net support for the sharing of powers in the areas of science and the environment.

There are similarities in relation to the tendencies previously detected with respect to instrumental support; however, there are also very important differences. The similarities relate to the increase of support for the Europeanization of these policies during the years preceding the Maastricht Treaty, an increase at a rate similar to that in the case of the instrumental support indicators. Similarly, Maastricht had a long-term impact, with the level of

TABLE 8.5
Trends in Political Support Indicators for Education and Health and Social Policy
(linear regression coefficients, margin of error in parenthesis)

	Dependent variable: Education (% 'EU' - % 'national')	Dependent variable: Health and Social (% 'EU' - % 'national')
Constant	-81.321 (63.859)	-27.528 (92.283)
Years	5.579 (5.973)	1.849 (8.632)
Maastricht (0 before; 1 after)	2.450 (9.788)	15.921 (14.145)
Years since Maastricht	-10.360 (6.094)	-8.174 (8.806)
Monetary union (0 before; 1 after)	-2.925 (7.944)	6.251 (11.480)
Years since monetary union	10.684*** (2.339)	10.609** (3.467)
N	27	27
R^2 adjusted	0.48	0.30

* $p < 0.05$, ** $p < 0.01$, *** $p < 0.001$
SOURCE: Author's own data

political support decreasing since the treaty's implementation at a rate of around five per cent per annum in the case of science and seven per cent per annum in the case of environment. However, there are two crucial differences in comparison with instrumental support. On the one hand, political support in these two areas of governance was insensitive to the short-term impact of either the Maastricht Treaty or of monetary union. On the other hand, though, since the introduction of monetary union, political support has increased at a rate of two per cent per annum in the case of science, and seven per cent in the case of environment. In other words, unlike with instrumental support, monetary union appears to have had a long-term effect on political support that constitutes an inversion of the downward trend seen since Maastricht.

Table 8.5 shows the result of the same analysis, this time applied to policies traditionally considered as belonging to nation state: education and health and social policy. In this example, the trends of rising support up to Maastricht then falling support after, are not statistically significant. However, the long-term effect of monetary union is also visible. Since monetary union, support for sharing power with the EU in these two areas has increased in Portugal at an annual rate of five per cent for education and three per cent for health and social policy.

Conclusion

Existing research into Portuguese attitudes towards European integration has converged on the idea an instrumental consensus prevails among the general public: a large majority of citizens support integration, but based on the perception there is a cost-benefit relationship in the country's favour. Despite a small decline in the level of support since 1992, this general consensus is argued to have remained largely in place.

This chapter suggests these analyses have only captured part of that which is important to describe and explain in relation to Portuguese support for the EU. That part is what is here described as instrumental support, based upon an assessment of the relationship between the costs incurred and the benefits received through Portugal's membership of the EU. What is important to note, however, is that citizens seem to make this assessment by resorting to the information available and that can be processed concerning Portuguese reality: the performance of both the political institutions and the Portuguese government. Thus, since several studies have shown these performances have been assessed ever more negatively by the Portuguese—at least since the beginning of the 1990s—[31]it comes as no surprise the indicators of instrumental support for integration have also exhibited a structural tendency to decline since 1992. In fact, saying there is a consensus in Portugal on the benefits of integration may have become excessively optimistic: despite a majority of Portuguese continuing to see integration more as a source of benefits than of costs, the decline in instrumental support over recent years has resulted in levels of support that have reached their lowest point since the country's accession.

However, none of what has been said seems to prevent an apparent increase of another form of support for integration: defending or at least accepting the sharing of power between member states and the EU's institutions in the definition of public policies. This sort of political support is not been greatly affected at the individual level by the evaluation of national institutions. What counts instead is the assessment of the general performance of the EU as a political system, as well as feelings of national identity. In contrast with what happened with instrumental support, the available data suggests political support for integration has increased during recent years—particularly since the realization of monetary union—both in areas in which such support has always been relatively high (scientific and environmental policies) and in areas that traditionally have been reserved to the national government (education and health and social policies).

In conclusion, the nature of support for integration seems to be changing in Portugal, from a support fundamentally based in

31 A. Freire, "Desempenho da democracia e reformas políticas: O caso português em perspectiva comparada", *Sociologia: Problemas e Práticas* 43 (2003), pp. 133–60.

the perception of benefits accruing to the nation state towards a support based in the acceptance of the EU as a political community and political system. This destiny, however, is not inevitable. We have already seen some historic markers in the construction of Europe resulting in the inversion of previous tendencies (the Maastricht Treaty in the case of instrumental support and monetary union in the case of political support). Only time will tell to what extent more recent events—the failure to obtain approval for the European constitution and the French and Dutch referendums, for example—have produced comparable effects.

9 | Conclusion: Europeanization and Democratization in Portugal – Brothers-in-Arms or *Frères Ennemis?*

Maarten Peter Vink

The contributions in this volume tell the story of how Portugal's membership of the European Union has shaped political processes in Portugal since the country's accession to the European Economic Community (EEC) in 1986.[1] This story of adaptation to Europe, in particular the adaptation of democratic institutions—in other words, the story of the Europeanization of Portuguese democracy—is told from two main perspectives. On the one hand, there are chapters that focus on institutional adaptation (Jalali on government; Resende and Paulo on parliament; Piçarra and Coutinho on courts; Royo on interest groups), on the other, there are chapters that focus on adaptation of behaviour and attitudes (Ruivo et al on elites; Freire on voting behaviour; Magalhães on support for European integration). Seen together these contributions comprehensively capture the different facets of Europeanization, allowing the reader to understand the structural effects of what Teixeira in his introduction to this volume calls "the closing of the cycle of normalization of the Portuguese presence in the international system".

1   The author would like to thank Tiago Fernandes and Pedro Lains for their comments on an earlier draft of this chapter.

I would like, in this concluding chapter, to come back to the central theme of the book and discuss the broader implications of European integration for Portuguese democracy. In particular, my aim is to use the findings from the preceding chapters to discuss the question to what extent European integration has strengthened—or rather undermined—national democracy in Portugal. In other words, rather than summarizing the separate conclusions from the different contributions in this rich volume, I draw on the key findings of the book to discuss how the two related processes of Europeanization and democratization play out in the Portuguese context.

Two Contrasting Views

Reading through the different contributions of this volume, it is evident that the question of democratization and Europeanization pervades any discussion of Portugal's recent political history. A preliminary remark is that, as Teixeira notes, whereas Portugal did not join the EEC until 1986, it was already active in other international organizations, such as NATO, the Organization for European Economic Cooperation (OEEC) and the Organization for Economic Cooperation and Development (OECD), even before the 1974 revolution. Moreover, Portugal had been a member of the UK-led European Free Trade Association (EFTA) since 1960.[2] Hence, even under the authoritarian regime, Portugal had been relatively well integrated in an internationalizing Europe. One point to note is that while this might lead to the question about the effect of Europeanization or internationalization on regime change, this question is not explicitly discussed in this vol-

---

2   Teixeira, chapter 1; see also N. Andrese Leitão, "Portugal's European integration policy, 1947–1972", *Journal of European Integration History* 7 (2001), pp. 25–35.

ume. The scope of the analysis of the "Europeanization effect" in all contributions is clearly on post-1974 Portugal.

Second, of the years since 1974 era, most have been spent as member of the EEC and its successor, the European Union (EU). This means that most of Portugal's modern democratic history is simultaneously a European story. Third, and more important, connecting with the community of modern European societies with liberal democracies and market-based economies was an essential part of the consolidation strategy in the nascent Portuguese democracy. As Teixeira argues, "democratic consolidation and Portugal's integration in the European economic space were... inseparable".[3] Moreira et al make a similar observation: "the European option was an important factor in the break from a dictatorial, isolationist and colonialist past".[4]

I call this view, in which democratization and Europeanization are seen as two processes that simultaneously contribute to the development and modernization of Portugal, the "brothers-in-arms" view. It is safe to say this view captures the common opinion (*communis opinion*) as to why Portuguese governments in the early years of post-revolution democracy recognized the importance of seeking a place in the European sun: EEC/EU membership was seen as offering political stability, economic growth and social modernization. Portuguese public support for European integration, strong since accession, certainly from a comparative European perspective, tends to be viewed in line with such an instrumentalist view of European integration: while there may be costs in terms of the loss of national autonomy, these are greatly outweighed by the benefits of political stability and economic growth.

3   Teixeira (note 2).

4   Ruivo, Moreira, Pinto and Almeida, chapter 2.

In contrast with the perhaps overly optimistic brothers-in-arms view, however, there is also a more sceptical take on the relation between European integration and national democracy. I call this the *frères ennemis* (sibling rivals) view.[5] This perspective tends to get less attention in the Portuguese public discourse, and is touched upon only sporadically in some of the contributions to this volume. Yet, for a balanced discussion of the effects of European integration on national democracy, I believe it should be taken into account. From this perspective, Europeanization and democratization are seen as simultaneous, but rival processes that push member states in different directions. Rather than fighting hand-in-hand, sibling rivalry drives them apart. The underlying rationale for such a view is that the integration process has always been driven more by liberal than by democratic concerns; it is more about output legitimacy than about input legitimacy.[6] Europeanization thus potentially strengthens national democracy by increasing the effectiveness of public policies, and in more general terms empowers national executives.[7] Yet at the same time it also potentially affects the quality of national democracy by subjecting the domestic political and legal order to a supranational European order and, thus, takes decision-making capacity away from core domestic democratic institutions, such as national parliaments.

These two perspectives present fundamentally different takes on the impact of European integration on national democracy and signal a tension between the two concepts of

5   I draw here on an analogy with Wallerstein's inspiring account of liberalism and democracy. See I. Wallerstein, "Liberalism and Democracy: *Frères Ennemis?*" *Fourth Daalder Lecture* (Leiden: Leiden University, 1997).

6   F. Scharpf, *Governing in Europe: Effective and democratic?* (Oxford: Oxford University Press, 1997).

7   A. Moravcsik, "Why the European Community strengthens the state: Domestic politics and international cooperation", *Center for European Studies Working Paper* 52 (Cambridge, MA: Harvard University, 1994).

Europeanization and democratization. This is not just an abstract issue that plays out at the conceptual level, but is ultimately a matter of political choice. After all, while the underlying rationales of either perspective are seemingly not so different, they represent fundamentally different ideas about the relation between European and domestic institutions. In the "brothers-in-arms" perspective, the central idea is that of a vincolo esterno (external constraint), in which the notion of subjecting the national to the European is viewed positively as a way to "lock" domestic reform processes in a strong European context. Hence, the antidemocratic aspect of the integration process is recognized, but valued positively from the perspective of relatively weak domestic political institutions. In the *frères ennemis* perspective, by contrast, subjecting the national to the European is viewed negatively, as a process that ultimately curtails national democracy. It thus considers that while the process of European integration may have a solid foundation in terms of contributing to prosperity and peace across the European continent, it is also a process that needs to be kept in check by strong domestic institutions.[8]

Domesticating Europe

When it comes to Portugal the first perspective has clearly been dominant. Europeanization has been viewed almost entirely as an external link supporting democratic consolidation.[9] The chapters

8   See R. M. Fishman, "Shaping, not making, democracy: The European Union and the post-authoritarian political transformations of Spain and Portugal", *South European Society and Politics* 8 (2003), pp.1–2, 31–46.

9   K. Dyson and K. Featherstone, "Italy and EMU as a 'vincolo esterno': Empowering the technocrats, transforming the state", *South European Society and Politics* 1, 2 (1996): pp. 272–99; J. Magone, "The difficult transformation of state and public administration in Portugal: Europeanization and the persistence of neo-patrimonialism", *Public Administration* 89, 3 (2011), pp. 756–82.

in this volume largely agree on this positive perspective of the relation between European integration and national democracy. Yet, the different analyses of institutional and behavioural adaptation within Portugal to European integration also signal—sometimes explicitly and sometimes implicitly—that the relationship between European integration and national democracy is less straightforward than might be assumed from the somewhat naïve brothers-in-arms perspective.

The clearest signal of an increasingly troubled relationship comes from Magalhães who observes that while instrumental support for European integration might have been very strong in the early years of EEC/EU membership, "saying there is a consensus in Portugal on the benefits of integration may have become excessively optimistic".[10] Magalhães stresses that this is not necessarily problematic, because while instrumental support for European integration is decreasing, what he calls "political support" for integration has increased. This means support of the EU is based more on the acceptance of the EU as a political community, than in the perception of specific benefits deriving from Europe. This trend from instrumental to political support for integration may perhaps be viewed as a maturation of support for European integration. However, Magalhães warns us to be careful with over-interpreting these findings, as trends of support in the past have also turned around. Given that instrumental support for European integration is very much a correlate of the satisfaction with national democratic institutions, these findings may well say more about domestic changes than about a changing relation with Europe.

Another signal comes from Freire, who criticizes the second-order nature of European Parliament elections and argues that, at

10 Magalhães, chapter 8.

least in the Portuguese case, what is striking is not the influence of Europe on national party systems, but rather the absence of this influence.[11] Friere seems to argue that rather than the Europeanization of national party systems, we are witnessing the domestication of European elections.

Domestication is a term used by Helen Wallace to indicate "the ways in which domestic factors frame and influence the incoming impacts of Europeanization".[12] It is an important notion because it highlights the fact that Europeanization is not just passively encountered. Rather, it is a process shaped by domestic actors and mediating institutions. With regard to the influence of European elections on national party systems, Freire argues the fact that Portugal already had a "nearly fully-established party system" meant European elections had relatively little effect on disloyal voting behaviour. Portuguese voters largely vote for similar parties at the national and the European level, and when they switch at one level this is often a sign that they are about to switch at the other. What matters most is domestic political matters.

Moving to the institutional level, Jalali argues that the process of adapting Portuguese central government to European integration has been noticeable, albeit rather limited.[13] There has been administrative change, for example, in terms of the creation of a Secretary of State for European Affairs and a support General-Directorate of European Affairs (DGAE), as well as European offices in individual ministries, such as education and finance. However, Jalali doubts whether this has truly transformed the Portuguese core executive and national bureaucracy. It is more a

11 Freire, chapter 7.

12 H. Wallace, "Europeanization and globalization: Complementary or contradictory trends?", *New Political Economy* 5, 3 (2000), pp. 369–82.

13 Jalali, chapter 3.

pattern of absorption than of transformation, he concludes. Jalali argues that the same goes for domestic interest groups: they play along at the European level, but a lack of resources keeps them focused strongly on the national government. This also confirms the impression from Royo's chapter on trade unions and employers, which concludes that the role of the government vis-à-vis the social partners remains very strong and focused on centralized national concertation schemes.[14] Europeanization, he argues, has opened the Portuguese economy, but has done little to affect the main features of the Portuguese industrial relations framework, which is still determined strongly by the legacies of authoritarianism and revolutionary experiences.

Jalali also points to another side of Europeanization, namely that European integration not only constrains domestic policy-making, but also offers strategic opportunities—in particular to core executives.[15] In Portugal, European integration thus exacerbated a situation in which the domestic legislature already has a traditionally weak control over government. This is reflected, according to Resende and Paulo, by the very late institutionalization of domestic scrutiny procedures for EU affairs. Only in 2006, with the so-called European Scrutiny Law, did the Portuguese legislature institute a European Affairs Committee and begin the systematic scrutiny of matters that fall within parliament's legislative remit. Resende and Paulo acknowledge that the new Portuguese system falls short of a mandate procedure as used in countries such as Austria and Denmark. Yet, based on the high number of parliamentary opinions sent to the European institutions they argue that "[f]rom 2006 the parliament became one of the most effective scrutinizers of European legislation in the

14 Royo, chapter 6.

15 Jalali (note 13).

EU".[16] One could of course argue against using opinions sent to Brussels as benchmark for effective scrutiny, which is after all much more about holding national rather than European executives accountable, as Resende and Paulo also point out. Hence, the main question is about the extent to which newly-acquired European scrutiny powers might spill over into more general executive-legislative relations in Portuguese politics. Here it seems the jury is still out, although there is some ground for modest optimism about a more balanced relationship.

One final and fascinating aspect of Europeanization is the application of European law by the Portuguese courts. The first observation is that Portuguese courts, on the whole, make very little use of the so-called preliminary reference procedure that allows national judges to clarify questions about the interpretation by sending a question to the Court of Justice of the European Union (CJEU) in Luxembourg. This is striking because in line with the monist legal culture the principles of supremacy and direct effect of European law has been quickly accepted. In contrast to the position in some other states, the Portuguese legal system has been quite receptive to European law. Yet, it would be naive to interpret the relatively low number of questions sent to Luxembourg as the absence of any issues related to the transposition of European law.

Piçarra and Coutinho make two important observations: first, there is "a certain lack of understanding on the part of some Portuguese courts as to how the preliminary rulings procedure works" and, second, with regards the interpretation of European law there seems to be a certain confidence on the side of Portuguese courts that leads judges to resolve any doubts without recourse to the CJEU.[17] Piçarra and Coutinho are ambivalent about whether this

16 Resende and Paulo, chapter 4.

17 Piçarra and Pereira Coutinho, chapter 5.

proactive attitude based on the constitutional autonomy granted
to lower courts in Portugal should be appreciated for its proactive
attitude or, perhaps, problematized as a form of slight arrogance.
To establish to what extent European integration has been "do-
mesticated" in Portugal, that would be a crucial question.

On Balance?

What can we conclude about the effect of European integration
on national democracy in Portugal? On balance, the contributions
from this volume point to an optimistic scenario. Europeanization has strengthened the process of democratic consolidation
in Portugal and both national institutions and attitudes and behaviour of population and elites have adapted to the demands of
EU membership. The dominant view is that Europeanization and
democratization are more brothers-in-arms than sibling rivals.
Yet readers would be mistaken should they take it for granted
that Portugal has fully adapted to European integration and to
conclude that the relationship between European integration
and national democracy is unproblematic. Instrumental support
for European integration is on decline, European elections are
not really about Europe and the outcomes are quite in line with
those of national elections, the system of interest representation is
strongly determined by historical legacies, parliament is only just
beginning to fight back and regain some political territory lost to
the executive, judges are accepting the primacy of European law
but reluctant to demonstrate any doubts about the interpretation
of the treaty that have been resolved by the Europe court. These
observations show that European integration goes to the heart of
the functioning of national democratic institutions and that the

way in which Portugal adapts to Europe is determined strongly by its idiosyncratic social and political context.

Contributors

ANDRÉ FREIRE is assistant professor with *agrégation* at the Instituto Universitário de Lisboa—ISCTE-IUL, head of the bachelor degree in political science at that institute and a senior researcher at CIES-IUL. He has published several books, book chapters and articles in peer reviewed journals about electoral behaviour, political attitudes, political institutions and political elites.

ANTÓNIO COSTA PINTO is a research professor at the Institute of Social Sciences at the University of Lisbon (ICS-UL). He received his doctorate from the European University Institute, Florence. He has been a visiting professor at Stanford University (1993), Georgetown (2004) and a senior visiting fellow at Princeton University (1996) and the University of California, Berkeley (2000). He was also president of the Portuguese Political Science Association. His research interests include fascism and authoritarianism, democratization, the European Union and the comparative study of political change in Southern Europe. His publications include *Southern Europe and the making of the European Union* (2002), *Who Governs Southern Europe* (2003) and *Dealing with the Legacy of Authoritarianism: The 'Politics of the Past' in Southern European Democracies* (2011).

CARLOS JALALI is a professor at the University of Aveiro and vice-chairman of the University of Aveiro's Department of Social, Political and Legal Sciences' scientific committee. His research concentrates on Portuguese political institutions, party systems and electoral behaviour in comparative perspective. His doctoral thesis considered the evolution of the Portuguese party system since 1974 in a comparative perspective. His recent publications include *Partidos e democracia em Portugal 1974–2005* (2007).

DIOGO MOREIRA is a doctoral candidate in comparative politics at the Institute of Social Sciences of the University of Lisbon (ICS-UL). His research interests include the study of political elites, democratic transitions and electoral systems. He has recently co-authored (with André Freire and Manuel Meirinho) *Para a melhoria da representação política: A reforma do sistema eleitoral* (2009).

FRANCISCO PEREIRA COUTINHO has a doctorate in law from the New University of Lisbon. He is a professor at the Instituto Superior de Ciências Sociais e Políticas (ISCSP) and since 2005 has been involved with the Diplomatic Institute of the Portuguese ministry for foreign affairs.

JOÃO PEDRO RUIVO has a masters degree in comparative and European politics from the Università degli Studi di Siena and is currently conducting doctoral research in political science at the Universidade Nova de Lisboa. He has been a research assistant working on projects on political elites and regional integration within the European Union and has worked at the Portuguese ministries of science and of education.

MARIA TERESA PAULO is a graduate in international relations studies and started her professional life as a university assistant, teaching political science at the Instituto Superior de Ciências Sociais e Políticas from 1997 to 2006. As an adviser to the Portuguese parliament's European affairs committee from 2000 to 2011, she had responsibilities related to the parliamentary scrutiny system and the organisation of the EU presidencies (2000 and 2007). From 2008 to 2010 she was the permanent representative of the Portuguese parliament to the EU, with special responsibilities for promoting cooperation between it and the parliaments of other EU member states, mainly on EU parliamentary scrutiny activities. She has been writing and presenting papers and lectures on the role of national parliaments at the EU level. Currently she works at the research department of the Portuguese parliament (legislative and parliamentary information division), while working towards finishing her masters.

MAARTEN PETER VINK is an associate professor at the Department of Political Science, Maastricht University, in the Netherlands. He holds a doctorate in political science from Leiden University (2003). He was Jean Monnet Fellow at the Robert Schuman Centre for Advanced Studies at the European University Institute in Florence, Italy (2003–2004), and a post-doctoral research fellow at the Institute of Social Sciences at the University of Lisbon (ICS-UL) from 2007 to 2010. He has also held visiting scholarships at the Center for European Studies, New York University (2004) and at the Department of Philosophy and Culture at the University of Minho, Braga (2005). He is co-editor of *Europeanization: New Research Agendas* (2007) and author of *Limits of European Citizenship* (2005). He has published papers in several peer-reviewed journals.

NUNO PIÇARRA is a professor of community law at the New University of Lisbon, having previously taught at the European Institute of the Saarland University, Germany. Amongst other things, he teaches the European law of area of freedom, security and justice. From 1990 to 1995 he was legal secretary in the European Communities' Court of the First Instance. From 1996 to 2000 he was national coordinator for matters related to the free movement of persons in the European Union and Portugal's representative on Committee K4 and the Schengen central working group. Since 2005 he has been Portugal's representative on the network on free movement of persons within the EU: a body funded by the European Commission and coordinated by Neijmegen University in the Netherlands.

Nuno Severiano Teixeira holds a doctorate in history and civilization from the European University Institute, Florence. He is a professor of international relations at the New University of Lisbon and former director of the Portuguese Institute of International Relations at the same University (2003–2006). He has been visiting professor at Georgetown University (2000) and visiting scholar at the Institute for European Studies, Berkeley, University of California (2004). He was director of the National Defence Institute, Lisbon (1996–2000), interior minister in the Portuguese government (2000–2002) and minister of defence (2006–2009). He has published extensively on Portuguese foreign policy, including *L'Entrée du Portugal dans la grande Guerre: Objectifs Nationaux et Stratégies Politiques* (1998), *Southern Europe and the making of the European Union* (2002) and *The International Dimension of Democratizations* (2009).

Pedro Magalhães received his doctorate in political science from Ohio State University and received that university's Henry R. Spenser Prize for the best doctoral thesis presented in 2002–3. He is also the recipient of the Democracy and Liberty Institute's

Adelino Amaro da Costa Prize. He is currently a researcher at ICS-UL and a board member of the Portuguese Catholic University's Centre for Opinion Poll Studies. His research interests focus on public opinion, political attitudes and political behaviour, and political institutions.

PEDRO TAVARES DE ALMEIDA is professor of political science at the Department of Political Studies, Faculty of Social Sciences and Humanities, New University of Lisbon. He has written extensively on state-building, elections and elite recruitment in contemporary Portugal. He co-edited (with A. C. Pinto and N. Bermeo) *Who governs southern Europe? Regime Change and Ministerial Recruitment, 1850–2000* (2003) and (with F. Catroga) *Res Publica: Citizenship and Political Representation in Portugal 1820–1926* (2011).

SEBASTIÁN ROYO is a professor at the Department of Government at Suffolk University, Boston, and director of its Madrid campus. His articles and reviews on comparative politics have appeared in several leading peer-reviewed journals. His books include *From Social Democracy to Neoliberalism: The Consequences of Party Hegemony in Spain, 1982–1996* (2000), *A New Century of Corporatism? Corporatism in Southern Europe: Spain and Portugal in Comparative Perspective* (2002), *Spain and Portugal in the European Union: The First 15 Years* (with P. Manuel, 2003) and *Portugal, Espanha e a Integração Europeia: Um Balanço* (2005). His research interests include southern European and Latin American politics and economic institutions. He is co-chairman of the Iberian study group at Harvard University.

Index

WITHDRAWN
FROM STOCK
QMUL LIBRARY